Economics for builders and surveyors

Economics for builders and surveyors —

Principles and applications of economic decision making in developing the built environment

STEPHEN D. LAVENDER

Longman
Scientific &
Technical

Copublished in the United States with
John Wiley & Sons, Inc., New York

Longman Scientific & Technical,
Longman Group UK Limited,
Longman House, Burnt Mill, Harlow,
Essex CM20 2JE, England
and Associated Companies throughout the world.

© Longman Group UK Limited 1990

First published 1990

British Library Cataloguing in Publication Data

Lavender, Stephen D.
  Economics for builders and surveyors
  1. Environment. Economic aspects
  I. Title
  304.2
  ISBN 0-582-04295-X

Set in 10/12 pt Garamond

Produced by Longman Group (FE) Limited
Printed in Hong Kong

This book is dedicated to the memory of my father
Samuel Lavender

Contents

List of figures   *xiii*
Preface   *xv*
Acknowledgements   *xvii*

Part 1   Developing the built environment and economic problems   **1**

Introduction   3
Economic problems   5
Developing the built environment — a general framework for analysis   6
A case study — Carbury   7
Stage 1 — Identification of urban and building need   11
Stage 2 — Decision to build   13
Stage 3 — Design of buildings   17
Stage 4 — Construction of buildings   19
Stage 5 — Occupation and use of buildings   20
Summary   22
Tutorial questions   24

Part 2   Principles of economics   **25**

Introduction to Part 2   27

1   The nature of economics   29
    Introduction   29
    Definitions and questions   29
    Methods for studying economics   39
    The status of economics   41
    Summary   44
    Tutorial questions   44

2   The microeconomic process   45
    Introduction   45
    Economic systems   46
    The microeconomic process in the market economy   48
    Performance of the microeconomic process   49
    The microeconomic process in context   52

Summary 54
Tutorial questions 55

3 The market system   56
Introduction 56
Basic market theory 56
Assumptions of market theory 60
The market system in practice 67
Classification of market conditions 74
Markets and the built environment 77
Summary 79
Tutorial questions 80

4 The firm   81
Introduction 81
Objectives of the firm 82
The nature of profit 84
Measuring performance 86
Determinants of the firm's performance 88
Summary 102
Tutorial questions 102

5 Industry and industrial structure   103
Introduction — the microeconomic process in context 103
Definition of an industry 104
Industrial structure 106
Market structure 108
Firms' objectives and changing market structure 111
Public policy and changing market structure 112
Summary 113
Tutorial questions 114

6 The national economy   115
Introduction 115
Problems of macroeconomics 116
Modelling the economy 119
The national accounts 123
Macroeconomic analysis 125
Summary 135
Tutorial questions 136

7 Policy issues   137
Introduction 137
Objectives of macroeconomic policy 138
Post-war economic policy 139
Problems of demand management 141
The UK economy and policy into the 1990s 146
Short-term policy measures 147
Long-term policy measures 155
Summary 161
Tutorial questions 162

Part 3 Applications of economic principles to the development of the built environment 163

Introduction to Part 3   165

Application A — Markets for land uses   168
Introduction   168
The market in theory and practice   168
The practical problem of land allocation   169
Problems of a market for land uses   170
Solutions to the land allocation problem   174
Summary   177
Tutorial questions   177

Application B — Special features of land   178
Introduction   178
The traditional view of the economic purpose of land   178
An alternative view   179
The power of landownership   180
Publicly created land values   182
Summary   184
Tutorial questions   185

Application C — The inner cities   186
Introduction   186
The nature of the inner-city problem   187
Imperfections in the land market affecting inner-city revival   188
Solutions to the inner-city problem   189
Summary   191
Tutorial questions   192

Application D — The housing market   193
Introduction   193
Characteristics of the housing market   193
General factors influencing demand and supply   195
Changing attitudes to the housing market   196
Changes in housing-market participants   197
Imbalances in the housing market   199
Interaction between the housing and other markets   202
Summary   203
Tutorial questions   203

Application E — Transportation   204
Introduction   204
Purposes of transport   204
Means of transport   205
The economic problem of transport   206
Solutions to the transport problem   207
Summary   209
Tutorial questions   210

Application F — Construction clients 211

Introduction 211
The role of clients 211
The functional purposes of construction projects 213
Why clients build 214
Changes in patterns of client behaviour 215
The nature of investment 217
Construction projects as investments 218
Summary 219
Tutorial questions 219

Application G — Fulfilling the client's objectives 220

Introduction 220
Traditional tendering systems 220
Problems of the traditional system 222
Alternative systems 225
Summary 230
Tutorial questions 231

Application H — Feasibility of projects 232

Introduction 232
Investment appraisal 233
Methods of investment appraisal 234
Investment appraisal and social projects 237
Developers' budgets 238
Approximate estimating 240
Summary 241
Tutorial questions 241

Application I — Cost control during design 243

Introduction 243
The nature of cost control 244
Approaches to estimating 244
Methods of approximate estimating 247
Cost planning 248
Cost checking 249
Summary 250
Tutorial questions 251

Application J — The construction industry as a whole 252

Introduction 252
The construction industry and the economy 253
Construction workload 255
Market structure in construction 256
Competition in the construction industry 258
Construction resources 259
Summary 262
Tutorial questions 263

Application K — Post-tender cost control   264

Introduction   264
The stages of post-tender cost control   265
Liquidity and the client   268
Liquidity and the contractor   270
Summary   275
Tutorial questions   275

Application L — Market strategy of construction firms   276

Introduction   276
Markets and the firm   276
The construction firm and control over revenue   278
Pricing   279
Protecting and improving market position   282
Summary   285
Tutorial questions   286

Application M — Production methods in construction   287

Introduction   287
Production methods   288
Management approaches to production   288
Approaches to production in construction   291
Impact of changes in production methods   296
Summary   299
Tutorial questions   299

Application N — The life of buildings   301

Introduction   301
Long-term finance   301
Management of buildings   303
Cost control during the life of a building   305
Replacement of buildings   307
Summary   308
Tutorial questions   309

Index   310

List of figures

Fig. 1.1   Land uses in Carbury   7
Fig. 2.1   Simple microeconomic process   45
Fig. 2.2   Economic systems   48
Fig. 2.3   Micro economic process, including economic roles   49
Fig. 2.4   Micro economic process as a building block of economic analysis   53
Fig. 2.5   Relationship between two microeconomic processes   53
Fig. 3.1   Market forces   57
Fig. 3.2   Behaviour of buyers in the market   58
Fig. 3.3   Behaviour of sellers in the market   58
Fig. 3.4   The market model   59
Fig. 3.5   (a) Shifts in demand curve   (b) Shifts in supply curve   62
Fig. 3.6   Change in market equilibrium   63
Fig. 3.7   (a) Inelastic demand   (b) Elastic demand   64
Fig. 3.8   Market model appropriate to development of the built environment   78
Fig. 3.9   Effect of increase in demand for housing   79
Fig. 4.1   Profit making and the microeconomic process   84
Fig. 4.2   Analysis of profit   85
Fig. 4.3   Simple labour market model   93
Fig. 4.4   Traditional structure of the firm   95
Fig. 4.5   Multi-divisional structure of the firm   96
Fig. 5.1   Simplified structure of the construction industry   105

Fig. 6.1   Buyers and sellers in the national
            economy   120
Fig. 6.2   The private sector of a market
            economy   121
Fig. 6.3   The national economy with private,
            public, and international trade
            sectors   122
Fig. 6.4   Circular flow of income   123
Fig. 6.5   Measuring the size of the economy   124
Fig. 6.6   Full employment equilibrium   127
Fig. 6.7   De-stabilising effect of savings   127
Fig. 6.8   Stabilising effect of investment   127
Fig. 6.9   Neo-classical view of the money
            market   129
Fig. 6.10   Neo-classical view of the labour
            market   130
Fig. A.1   Externalities and a chemical plant   172
Fig. K.1   Cash outflow   271
Fig. K.2   Cash inflow   272
Fig. K.3   Whole project cash flow   273
Fig. K.4   Expanded detail of whole project cash
            flow   273

Preface

This book is intended for students, lecturers and practitioners in a wide range of built environment disciplines including building, quantity surveying, estate management, and town planning. In particular the book is designed for use on degree, professional and technician courses in these disciplines. In addition to being suitable for teachers of economics, the book should assist lecturers in subjects such as building management, cost planning, property market studies and land use planning, to integrate aspects of economic analysis into their teaching. Consequently the book should be of use not only in the subject of economics, but throughout the above courses. It should also be of interest to practising builders and surveyors who wish to gain a wider understanding of the economic forces which influence their work.

The book, which is in three parts, seeks to emphasise the importance of economic decision making in developing the built environment. No prior knowledge of economics is assumed. Part 1 shows, with the aid of a case study and an illustrative framework of the development process, how economic problems can be understood and solved partly by a 'common sense' approach. Part 2 deals with the principles of economics. Emphasis is placed on economic decision making rather than on economics as an academic discipline. Whilst the latter provides a sound logical framework on which initially to base the analysis of economic problems, the real world requires a broader approach to take account of social and political as well as economic criteria. The economic theory in Part 2 is therefore reduced to its essentials whilst ideas from related disciplines such as management are assimilated. The result is a simpler, more manageable and relevant set of principles which are used in a variety of applications in

Part 3 to help explain economic decision making in developing the built environment.

It should be emphasised that economics is a living, constantly changing subject. It is therefore essential that the reader keeps up to date with the current situation. For general economic matters the financial pages of good daily newspapers provide a valuable source of information. For built environment issues reference should be made to professional periodicals.

It is hoped that all those who read this book will gain an insight into the economic forces which shape the development of our built environment, and that they will discuss the issues with their colleagues and pursue their interest in the subject into the future.

Acknowledgements

I wish to thank all those who have contributed to my knowledge and understanding of the material necessary to write this book. In this connection I would like to thank staff and fellow students at the colleges where I undertook professional, degree and post graduate studies — Chelmer Institute of Higher Education, The Polytechnic of Central London, and The University of Warwick. I would also like to thank those with whom I have worked in industry and education, particularly my former colleagues and students at Essex Institute of Higher Education.

Above all, I gratefully acknowledge the encouragement, support and assistance of Kathy Tremain, who spent many hours acting as a model user by carefully reading the material and offering numerous suggestions for improving content, presentation and style. In addition I thank her for undertaking all the necessary typing.

Part 1

Developing the built environment and economic problems

Developing the built environment and economic problems

Introduction

Everybody makes use of buildings — to live, work, and be entertained in, to derive visual pleasure from, and so on. A collection of buildings which functions as an urban area needs a range of supporting services, or infrastructure, such as roads, railways, telecommunications, water, electricity, gas, and sewerage.

Thus the built environment evolves by the adaptation of the natural environment to fulfil human needs.

Any study of the built environment must ask some basic questions, including:

1. *Why* does development of the built environment take place? For example, who instigates it?
2. *How* does this development take place? For example, by which mechanisms?
3. *Who* benefits from this development? For example, how are the benefits distributed?

None of these questions has a simple answer. By asking why development takes place, the following criteria can be identified:

1. economic
2. social
3. political

It is also important to consider how these criteria may be applied to, and whether there is a conflict between:

1. the **public** interest as a whole
2. the **private** interest of individuals and organisations.

The classification of economic, social and political criteria is

3

rather artificial as in reality all decisions made have to take a broad view. However the subject of economics does attempt to define a framework of thought based on economic criteria. It is important that this framework is used only as a starting point and that broader social and political criteria are incorporated.

There are many instances in the analysis of the built environment where the term economic should be examined very carefully. For example if a new transport system for an urban area is being contemplated, it is possible that the income generated by charges for using the system may be less than the construction and running costs. In financial terms this represents a loss, but it may not mean that the project is uneconomic. To explain this, reference can be made to question 2 above where it is implied that there are various mechanisms through which development takes place, the two major ones being market forces and public provision. In terms of market forces, financial loss usually means that a project is uneconomic. However with public provision, the wider benefits of an efficient transport system (for example, less congestion, faster movement of goods, people getting to work more quickly and in a better frame of mind) may outweigh the costs. Therefore the project could be economic in social terms. In the context of question 3 above, public provision of a transport system may also enable fares to be set at a level which allows a wider range of people to travel than might have been possible otherwise. Of course, these wider social benefits are harder to measure, and so decisions of this kind will often be based on social and politicial criteria as well as economic.

This example also helps to highlight the important philosophical question of whether the use of market forces is generally the best basis on which to organise economic activity. This question arises because the market involves individuals and organisations acting out of self interest, and there is some dispute, stretching back more than 200 years, about whether this results in the best outcome for society as a whole. Whatever economic topic is studied, it is extremely difficult to get away from this fundamental question. Many people strongly support the more widespread use of market forces, whereas others think the market has serious deficiencies and should not be relied upon. Transport provision is an example of a topic where the market/non market debate is strongly contested.

The aim of this book is to explore the relationship between economic decision making and the built environment. As already emphasised narrow economic factors cannot be treated in isolation, so a broad view will be taken. However the framework of economic thought previously mentioned is very helpful as a starting point for the broader analysis. Therefore aspects of this framework, known as economic theory, will be discussed. However it must be emphasised at the outset that there is not just one set of theories to explore economic problems of the built environment. As previously mentioned, economists may vary as to their perspectives on fundamental issues such as how effective market forces are in organising economic activity. This means that problems may be defined in different ways, and so the reader must accept that there may not be a single clear cut answer to all problems. Indeed there are few problem areas where there *is* general agreement on the correct solution.

Although the main focus is on the application of economic principles to the built environment, it must be recognised that these principles have general applicability to a wider range of issues and situations. Therefore great stress will be laid on the importance of economic principles even where there is no obvious and direct application to the built environment.

This part of the book is designed to introduce the many aspects of economic decision making in developing the built environment. First, it is necessary to define what is meant by economics and economic problems. This will be brief to allow for a study of greater detail in Chapter 1, the nature of economics. Then a general five stage framework for analysing the development of the built environment will be introduced. Before examining each stage in detail and as a pre-requisite for it, a case study based on the imaginary town of Carbury will be introduced. The aim is to introduce informally some of the problems associated with the growth of an urban area and in particular to introduce some of the economic principles and issues involved without using formal economic models. It will be shown how economic problems can be understood and solved partly by a common sense approach in a broad context. The material introduced here should then enhance the understanding of more formal economic principles studied in Part 2.

Economic problems

Some indication was previously given that the term economic can be interpreted with varying degrees of breadth. The narrowist interpretation is that an economic question is something to do with finance (see the transport system example previously mentioned). However it is not finance or money *per se* which is of interest to people but what can be done with it. Therefore money is the means to an end, this being the enjoyment of a range of goods, services and conditions which are collectively called **wealth**. This means that the creation of wealth is central to economics. However the reason why a problem arises is that wealth cannot be created in unlimited quantities. There are limits imposed by the amount of resources which are available. Therefore two attendant problems to the actual creation of wealth are how to decide the manner in which:

1. the available resources are allocated to different forms of wealth creation, and
2. the wealth created is to be distributed among all the possible recipients.

Thus a short definition of economics is:

> '**Economics is a study of the use of limited resources to create wealth, and of the subsequent distribution of that wealth.**'

This will be analysed in greater detail in Chapter 1 where various interpretations on aspects of this definition will be considered.

Developing the built environment — a general framework for analysis

There are **five** stages or sub-processes which have to occur before a building or group of buildings is established and in use.

1. Identification of urban and building need, that is deciding on the kind and quantity of buildings required and how the available land should be used.
2. Decision to build, that is whether particular buildings or groups of buildings should be built on particular sites.
3. Design of building(s).
4. Construction of building(s).
5. Occupation and use of building(s).

Before examining each of these in detail the Carbury case study will be introduced. Examples from the case study will be used in subsequent analyses.

A case study — Carbury

Carbury is an imaginary town. Figure 1.1 shows a sketch map and notes on land uses in Carbury.

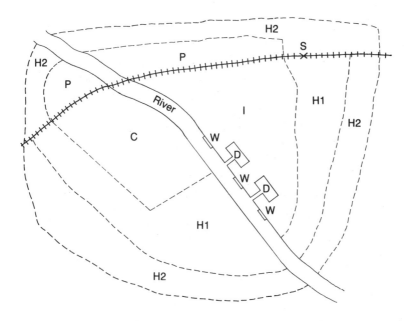

```
------  Approximate boundary of land uses
  D     Docks (disused)
  W     Wharfs (disused)
  I     Industrial area
  C     Commercial and civic centres
  H1    Pre-war housing
  H2    Post-war housing
++++++  Railway line
  S     Station
  P     Parkland
```

Fig. 1.1   Land uses in Carbury

Introduction

The town of Carbury has expanded in recent years, and currently has a population of about 60,000. Pressure for further expansion is now envisaged and it is hoped that by thinking about it at an early stage, the expansion will occur in a manner consistent with the public interest.

Recent history

Carbury has an industrial background but many of the buildings associated with this together with the docks and wharfs which served it are falling into disuse and disrepair. However, the town has remained prosperous for a number of reasons:

1. The remaining industry has been successful.
2. A considerable amount of development has taken place in the town centre due to the building of a new shopping centre. This co-exists with older commercial and civic buildings.
3. A great deal of residential development has taken place due to the growth of the commuter population. Carbury is forty miles from the metropolis and increasing numbers of people have moved out searching for more reasonably priced housing. This trend has been accentuated by infrastructure improvements such as the building of a new by-pass to the north of the town, and a better railway service.

These factors have ensured the prosperity of the town but have been criticised on the following grounds.

1. The building development which has taken place in the post-war period has mainly been to a poor standard undertaken too quickly with only profit in mind and with no overall conception or plan. In other words Carbury has suffered urban sprawl.
2. The result of the expansion is that Carbury is in danger of becoming a predominantly 'dormitory' town.
3. The development has done little to improve the older run-down parts of Carbury, that is, the 'inner city' area.

Requirements for expansion

The local authority is determined that future expansion and development will be more balanced, and in the interests of the town as a whole. Instead of simply having to respond to the pressures of private developers, the authority wishes to influence them. The council is balanced politically and is quite keen to work with the private sector to get the best results. In particular the council is prepared to use its powers of compulsory purchase to assist the process of development. In short, the council is looking

8

for well-balanced development which provides:

1. Sufficient new housing of an appropriate standard which is within the price range of local people and their children and not just those earning the high salaries in the metropolis.
2. New employment opportunities in commercial and industrial activities. This could be office development in the centre, or new light industry either in existing industrial areas or on new industrial sites. It is hoped that the recent infrastructure improvements which have so far attracted commuters might also attract firms relocating from the metropolis.
3. A better environment particularly in the run-down parts of the town.

Possible solutions

To achieve the above aims the **development** and **redevelopment** which takes place must be suitable.

Development
This involves building on sites not previously developed, that is, 'green field' sites. This may be:

1. In-fill sites in an otherwise built-up area which for some reason have not been previously built on.
2. Sites which extend the boundaries of the urban area. This includes the extension of existing housing estates further into the countryside. This is the type of development which has occurred in Carbury in recent years.
3. Completely new sites which are in the vicinity of, but differentiated from, existing built-up areas. These may be new industrial estates or new residential 'villages' each with their own infrastructure and basic facilities.

Redevelopment
This involves building on sites which have previously been developed. This may apply to small areas (for example, a single site), or to more extensive areas. Many cases of the latter are often referred to as inner city regeneration. This redevelopment might be:

9

1. demolition of existing buildings and replacement with new,
2. refurbishment of existing buildings for re-use in previous function,
3. adaptation of existing buildings for re-use in new function, for example, old warehouses converted into flats.

Implementation

In the introduction to Part 1 it was seen that important questions arise about who instigates development, by which mechanism, and for whose benefit. The possible solutions to the problem of expanding Carbury were outlined above, and the two main mechanisms for implementing change are through the action of:

1. Individuals or organisations who undertake development for their own benefit. These private actions are stimulated by market forces, the aim being the achievement of profit for the developer.
2. Public bodies who undertake development for the benefit of the community as a whole. The object is to generate maximum social benefits. This of course is a much more difficult concept than profit to define and measure.

The question arises about which of these two mechanisms should predominate. In Britain market forces are usually given priority but with some degree of public intervention. This is based on the belief, to be considered at length later in the book, that allowing the play of market forces may also give a satisfactory result for society as a whole. In developing the built environment market forces are usually amended by town planning, although different authorities feel that varying levels of intervention are appropriate. The previous expansion of Carbury occurred through market forces, with high demand for new housing met through developers putting forward schemes. At the time, the local authority saw these schemes as likely to give a satisfactory result and therefore accepted them. However, as previously mentioned, the resulting urban sprawl has since been heavily criticised.

This time the local authority is anxious to establish criteria for development at the outset so that the right balance between market forces and public intervention is achieved for the maximum benefit of the town.

For the remainder of Part 1 the five stage framework for studying the development of the built environment will be examined stage by stage, with reference made to the specific case of Carbury. The ideas identified here will be used to illustrate the economic principles studied in Part 2. These ideas will be reconsidered in Part 3 in the light of the economic principles studied. The reader is encouraged to refer to the case study of Carbury whenever appropriate throughout the book.

Stage 1 — Identification of urban and building need

It must be decided what kind and quantity of buildings are required and how the available land should be used. For example, how much land should be allocated to uses such as residential, industrial, commercial, open space and agricultural. It is generally thought that if this were left to market forces alone, then there may not be the balanced development an urban area requires. For example, the whole central area may be lucrative commercial development with no public open space, housing or entertainment. For reasons of this kind, the town planning system has evolved in Britain to try to ensure that land use in urban areas serves the population as a whole.

The planning authority will usually zone the available land into particular uses such as residential, industrial, commercial or agricultural. This designation is extremely important as it can greatly affect land values. Thus a piece of land whose designation is changed from agricultural to residential will dramatically increase in value giving a windfall gain to the landowner. This is in effect a **publicly created land value**, and it is a matter of strong debate whether landowners should be allowed to retain this windfall gain or whether it should be extracted (for example by taxation) for public benefit. Another way of generating publicly created land values is by infrastructure provision. For example, good roads will make particular sites more attractive and hence more valuable.

Beyond the basic zoning of urban land, different planning authorities will be involved with the development process to varying degrees. Sometimes the policy may be simply to approve or reject the proposals of private developers, whereas other authorities may take an active role in development, either alone or in partnership with a private sector developer. This is in addition to the authorities' responsibility with regard to the building and maintenance of infrastructure.

11

In the case of Carbury, the planning authority is the local council. Here some clear indication has been given by the authority about the criteria for expansion. These guidelines are political in that the council has decided the objectives of proposed development from the point of view of the town as a whole. In some cases, social and economic factors, over which there is little control, will help determine what is possible. For example, if there is a growing younger population then this will influence the type of amenities to be created. In other cases, the council may have greater control and influence. For example, the provision of infrastructure can make sites more attractive and valuable as mentioned above. If there is extensive infrastructure provision of roads, communications and training facilities, then this can make the town as a whole attractive and can act as a strong incentive to firms to locate in the area, be it for the provision of employment and/or shopping and leisure facilities.

The options for expansion in Carbury are detailed in the case study and may be summarised as:

1. development of green-field sites
2. redevelopment of sites previously built on.

Each of these options may have its own problems, and it is worth mentioning some of them at this stage.

1. What are the financial costs of each option? For example, demolition, building and infrastructure costs.
2. What is the effect of the demolition of old inner city sites? For example, loss of heritage and character.
3. What is the consequence of the loss of green field land? For example, loss of open space and leisure amenities.
4. Which option is more likely to attract new industry and employment?
5. Which option is more likely to attract private capital to finance the development? This assumes that the council would be unable or unwilling to do this alone.

As previously stated strategic decisions of this kind are not left to market forces. However the options adopted will depend on how much involvement from the market the council requires in the later stages of expansion.

In choosing between alternatives, the council must base its decisions on the *public interest*, a concept which is not clear and which includes a mixture of social, political and economic criteria. From the economic point of view the council must take account of:

1. How *efficient* will the various options be at meeting the overall needs of Carbury?
2. What effect will the various options have on the *distribution* of benefits?

These two criteria of efficiency and distributional effects are usually considered by policy makers when intervening in the economic process to modify or replace market forces. As has been seen, the strategic guidelines laid down for the expansion of Carbury amount to replacing market forces at this early stage of developing the built environment. However, deciding the kind and quantity of buildings required, and how the land should be used, is only the first part of the process.

Stage 2 — Decision to build

Deciding on the strategic guidelines under which the built environment may develop is the first stage of the process. The next stage is to decide whether particular buildings or groups of buildings should be constructed on particular sites. This is often referred to as deciding on the **feasibility** of the project.

Whereas the role of market forces may be limited in the previous stage, it almost certainly will not be here, because this stage is about the decision to build made by construction clients. It has already been mentioned that the council would not commission all or even much of the building work itself. Therefore it is expected that private sector clients would play a role, and indeed the decisions previously made should take account of what would encourage private housebuilders and developers to participate.

The question now becomes then, why do people and organisations decide to build? The obvious answer is that building is for some benefit, which may be defined and measured in a variety of ways. Before this is examined more closely a list will be made of the various types of client who may wish to build in Carbury. (It should be realised at the outset that not all clients build for their own occupation and use. Many clients are in the business of providing for others, and the implications of this will be explained later).

Possible clients (defined as persons or organisations who initiate a construction project) include the following:

1. families building their own homes
2. speculative housebuilding firms building houses individually or on estates for sale
3. industrial or commercial firms requiring factories, warehouses, shops and offices for the purpose of carrying on their businesses
4. property development companies and insurance companies building commercial and industrial property for sale or rent
5. government departments or nationalised industries building offices or other installations
6. the river authority undertaking construction in relation to waterway maintenance and flood protection
7. the council building new houses and maintaining existing ones. The council will also have some responsibilities for infrastructure, shared with the county council.
8. the county council itself will be responsible for educational buildings and will have its share of infrastructure to construct and maintain.

How is sense to be made of this by no means exhaustive list of potential construction clients? It is necessary to return to the basic question of why people and organisations decide to build. It was previously mentioned that building takes place for benefit. However looking down the long list of clients it may be hard to discern a common motivation beyond the vague notion of 'benefit'. However, there is some commonality because of the very nature of buildings — they are large, expensive, durable and often re-saleable. They usually require a long term financial commitment, which means that the benefits may be spread out over a period of time. This introduces the concept of **investment** which means that income and spending is being given up now in exchange for greater benefits in the future. This is even true to some extent of clients who dispose of the building immediately, such as speculative housebuilders, since they have to invest in stocks of resources such as land, and maintain their organisation to continue a building programme.

Beyond the idea that benefits are spread out and therefore of an investment nature, what form do these benefits actually take? Examining the list of clients, four different forms of benefit can be identified. They can be described as follows:

14

Consumption

These are benefits of a personal enjoyment rather than a financial nature. They are often called consumption benefits, and are difficult to measure being largely subjective. An example of consumption benefits in building relates to residential occupation where shelter, comfort and pleasure is obtained over a number of years.

However it is important to note that even residential building is not for consumption benefit alone because many people see their home as an investment for financial gain as well, and as such it more closely resembles direct financial benefits described below. In any case it is unusual for a family to commission their own house. They usually buy a new house from a builder, or buy an existing property.

Direct financial

These benefits occur where an individual or organisation commissions a building for direct financial gains, which could take the form of:

1. profit on the sale of the building after completion, for example speculative housebuilding
2. profit from rents received over time, for example commercial developments of property companies or insurance companies.

This type of benefit, being strictly financial, is much easier to measure. For housing, the builder is in a similar position to a manufacturer, that is, in deciding how many units to build at what price. For commercial developments the skills of the general practice or valuation surveyor may be utilised to assess the viability of a proposed project. Some kind of balance sheet would need to be drawn up to include various incomes and expenditures. A simplified form is as follows:

INCOME	EXPENDITURE
Forecast rents or sales	Land costs
	Building costs
	Financing costs
	Developer's profit
	Management costs

These calculations are often undertaken to isolate how much will be available for building costs and provide the basis on which the design team works (see next stage). The pattern of expenditure and income will vary between the different Carbury options. For example, commercial property may command a higher rent in the inner areas, but demolition and building costs will be higher, and land prices may be higher. For housebuilding, refurbishment of older properties may be cheaper but again sites may be more expensive than on green-field land.

Indirect financial

These occur where the building is not required to make money in itself but where it is required to make something else which in turn makes money. The best examples are factories, offices and shops, these being the buildings which house the productive activities which make money for the client. In this sense the building is just like a machine, that is it will be 'bought' if it improves the performance and profitability of the firm.

Because of the indirect nature of the financial gain, it is less easy to measure than direct financial gains. Investment appraisal techniques are used to assess the contribution which the building (or machine) would make to efficiency (or productivity) of the firm.

The type of client who would obtain these types of benefits are private sector industrial and commercial firms, plus nationalised industries or other public sector organisations who operate under market forces criteria. However it should be noted that there has been a trend amongst such organisations away from building for themselves towards leasing suitable units built by a developer.

Social

These refer to public sector or charitable projects which are not judged purely on financial grounds. In other words there is less emphasis on market forces as would be the case with direct and indirect financial benefits as described above.

Sometimes these social benefits are completely intangible and cannot be measured at all, but there are cases where attempts can be made to measure the costs and benefits of public sector construction. For example, education can be regarded as an investment in the future skills of the workforce. Investment in infrastructure and transportation can be seen as ways of making the town run more smoothly and hence lead to more efficient wealth creation.

Let us take a possible scenario. If Carbury Council were to invest in an efficient transportation system then the speed of communication would be increased and efficiency would rise. In the long term the reduction in private transport, if such a pattern is established, could lead to reduced space being required for roads and car parking thus releasing land for other uses.

This whole idea of building for social benefits is yet another example of how market forces are modified or replaced in certain circumstances. Having said that, it should be emphasised that the market plays a much larger role at this second stage of the process of developing the built environment, that is, where decisions are made about whether to build a particular building or group of buildings.

Stage 3 — Design of buildings

Once the decision to build has been taken then the next stage is for more detailed design of the building project. The previous stage was about assessing the feasibility or viability of a particular size and quality of a project, while this stage is about translating those broad criteria into detailed proposals.

This stage has tended to be seen very much as a separate technical operation and dependent on the professional expertise of the building design team, normally headed by the architect under the traditional tendering system. Thus it has not been seen as a market or commercial process. However in recent years a number of changes have occurred which have altered this position in many cases:

1. Building design has become more complicated in terms of structure and accommodation of services. This has meant an increase in the number of specialists involved to include structural and services engineers. This has made it more difficult for the architect to head the team effectively.
2. Increasing numbers of building firms have become involved in building design, either:
    (*a*) as adviser to the client through package deals and management contracting, or

(*b*) as clients in their own right, whereby they initiate and develop building projects themselves. The most obvious example is speculative housebuilding, but in addition many building firms have property development divisions concerned with industrial and commercial property.

The effect of builder involvement has been that building design has become more obviously subject to commercial and market pressures.

3. The typical client today is knowledgeable and commercialy minded, seeking a profit from the investment made in the building.

However, if building design is treated as an entity, then the objective of this stage is to get the best possible value for money in design. An important role here is played by the quantity surveyor, who is sometimes referred to as the building economist. The usual method is to work within a cost limit laid down by the client's brief, which will also include details of the client's requirements about size and quality of the accommodation to be provided. This cost limit would have been established during the previous stage. In the case of public sector projects the cost limit may be in accordance with standard rates per unit of accommodation.

As previously mentioned, building design is a highly technical process where alternative solutions to problems need to be considered. In some cases the cost may not be a particular constraint but this would only apply to a few prestige buildings. Normally it is, so the design team must attempt to meet the client's functional and aesthetic requirements within the cost limit.

Comparisons have to be made between different materials and structural solutions, for example, brickwork or timber-framed houses; steel or reinforced concrete framed offices. One of the major uncertainties is usually in the groundworks, where different foundation types are suitable for different soil conditions. Where there are difficult soils then groundworks can take a disproportionate part of the building costs.

Another important design consideration may be guidelines laid down by the planning authorities. For example there may be regulations regarding number of storeys or facing materials. This is particularly true in an established area where there may be a requirement to fit into the existing environment. This is certainly a factor to be borne in mind in Carbury if use is made of the option to expand the town by demolition and rebuilding in the inner city. As well as localised forms of public intervention into the design process as described above, there are also a variety of more generally applicable influences on design, notably the Building Regulations.

Stage 4 — Construction of buildings

After design, the next stage is the construction of the buildings. In the traditional tendering system this consists of two parts:

1. A building contractor must be engaged to undertake the work. This is achieved by inviting a number of contractors to tender for the work based on a bill of quantities. The lowest tenderer is usually offered the contract.
2. The site process is then carried out, involving the construction of the building in accordance with the drawings and bill of quantities.

In the case of builder-initiated work such as speculative housing then these two parts are unified. But in any event the commercial decisions of the building firm are of fundamental importance. For example in 1 the builder has to assess the **price** which the market will bear, and in 2 the **costs** of construction are incurred. Clearly the builder has to expect the price in 1 to exceed the costs in 2 in order to make a profit, this being an essential requirement for the firm to stay in business. (Chapter 4 examines this in detail.)

So, whether there is contracting or speculative work, market forces play an important role in the construction process in that:

1. The building firm must set a *price* in accordance with market demand conditions.
2. Certain *costs* are incurred in producing the building, and these are largely determined by firstly the market conditions which determine the prices of materials, labour, plant, and so on; and secondly the way in which the work on site is managed, that is, the efficiency with which materials, labour and plant are used.

It is important over a period of time that the firm can raise enough revenue through selling at a high enough price to cover

19

the costs of production and leave enough surplus (or profit) to keep the business intact by replacing worn out plant and replenishing stocks of materials.

Although market forces play the major role in the construction process there are ways in which they are modified. From the price point of view, public policy has for many years been one of encouraging price competition by ensuring that firms do not achieve monopoly powers. This problem is not normally associated with the construction industry where firms are usually thought of as small and in strong competition with each other. This may often be the case, but for certain types of work in certain areas there may only be a small number of firms able to carry out the work. For example, in a town the size of Carbury there may be enough housebuilders to give competition, whereas major infrastructure improvements may only be within the scope of a few firms, thus reducing the level of competition and leading possibly to higher prices. Market forces may also be modified to affect the costs of production, for example through employment legislation, building regulations and health and safety requirements.

Stage 5 — Occupation and use of buildings

After construction is completed the building or group of buildings is ready for occupation and use. The problems which arise during this stage are:

1. maintenance
2. management
3. replacement

Maintenance

This includes a range of items such as:

1. running costs — heating, lighting and cleaning.
2. refurbishment — replacement of worn out items, redecoration and adaptation of use.

The maintenance requirements are heavily dependent on what happened at the building design stage. Some extra money spent on better components or on thermal insulation could save considerable amounts on maintenance at a later stage. It would be for the client to decide on whether to spend more at design stage, with the decision resting on matters such as:

1. the client's financial situation — for example, whether it was possible to obtain enough finance for a better quality job;
2. whether the client sells the building or not on completion — for example, the market for housing may be such that the builder has to produce as cheaply as possible to sell at a lower price;
3. who is responsible for maintenance — for example, even where the client retains ownership of the building, it may be let out to another occupier who will have to maintain the building under the terms of the lease. This is common with commercial property where the occupier may wish to retain the freedom to alter the property internally;
4. whether the client has a maintenance organisation — for example, large firms or local authorities may have their own building departments who would engage in planned maintenance and emergency repairs.

Management

Management of property is necessary where the client retains ownership even though some other group or organisation is the occupier. This is true of commercial property as previously mentioned, and also of local authority housing.

The management function is important to the client from the same points of view of *price* and *cost* that were mentioned when considering the construction stage.

To maximise the client's income, as much of the property as possible must be let at the best market price. Thus the management function includes assessing rents achievable, finding tenants and negotiating leases.

To minimise costs to the client, any repairs or maintenance for which the client is responsible must be planned for carefully. This would include having a programme of work which minimises disruption to the normal work of the building and employing suitable firms or labour to carry out the work.

From this illustration it is clear that the client must always be aware of how much costs are going out against the income coming in, since this will determine profit and hence the inclination of the client to retain the building. This is certainly true of the private sector client. The public sector client may modify the objective in that social benefit is important. Hence prices or rents charged to local authority tenants may be less than the market rate since public housing has the function of redistributing income and putting better housing within the reach of more people. Having said that, it seems that public sector housing is much less of a force since the beginning of the 1980s because new building has virtually ceased, and the existing stock has been depleted by sales. Furthermore the rents charged are closer to the economic rate. Arguably there is little to choose between the behaviour of the private sector and public sector client.

Replacement

The replacement of the building will probably have entered into the calculations from the outset. This should be so because buildings are long term assets, yielding a return to the client over a number of years. Therefore a certain **economic life** would have been planned for, at the end of which the building has served its function whatever physical condition it may be in. It may be more profitable to replace a building with a more modern design even though the existing building is in good physical condition.

This process may work in reverse in that buildings may be retained in use even though they are in poor physical shape. In other words there is still economic if not **physical life** left in the building. This situation may occur in inner city areas where landlords may find it worthwhile to let out such properties at high rents rather than replace them. There may be some examples of this in the inner city areas of Carbury.

This raises the question of whether the option of demolition and rehabilitation for expanding Carbury can be achieved through market forces. It would appear on the face of it that where economic life exceeds physical life then the market alone will not encourage redevelopment without public intervention.

On the other hand, the prevention of the demolition of a sound building in favour of a more modern and profitable one may be difficult within the scope of town planning.

Summary

This chapter has been a broadly based introduction to economic

22

decision making in the built environment. Main emphasis has been placed on developing the built environment itself rather than on economic analysis. However a definition of economics was discussed, that is 'Economics is a study of the use of limited resources to create wealth, and of the subsequent distribution of that wealth'. Also certain economic issues were identified, particularly the question of the extent to which the use of market forces is the best way of developing the built environment.

These brief excursions into the economics discipline were necessary in order to proceed to the main section of Part 1 which was a general framework for analysing the development of the built environment. The study used examples from the proposed expansion of the imaginary town of Carbury, and was given as a five stage process:

1. Identification of urban and building need — deciding on the kind and quantity of buildings required and how the available land should be used.
2. Decision to build — identifying why clients build and how they assess the feasibility of a particular project.
3. Design of buildings — the technical process of designing the proposed building in detail within the cost limits and other criteria laid down as a result of decisions in Stage 2.
4. Construction of buildings — carried out by the building firm in the context of its commercial objectives of making a profit. This depends on the price obtained for building, set against the costs of construction.
5. Occupation and use of buildings — which includes consideration of maintenance, management and replacement of buildings.

In each of these five stages consideration was given to the kinds of problems encountered and issues at stake. Economic influences were particularly discussed but in their broader social and political context, and with the minimum of formal economic analysis.

In the first chapter of Part 2 the economics discipline will be examined in a more formal manner. In that and subsequent chapters the principles of economics will be examined. The material relating to developing the built environment discussed in this chapter will be used where appropriate to show the importance of economics in understanding the built environment. In Part 3 many of the issues raised in this part will be re-examined in the light of the principles studied in Part 2.

Tutorial questions

1. What factors might influence the local council in Carbury to invest in improved transport facilities?
2. Is the proposed expansion of Carbury likely to be affected by limited availability of resources?
3. What planning decisions taken by the council could lead to changes in the price of the pre-war housing in Carbury?
4. What would be the most effective way of attracting new industry and employment to Carbury?

Part 2

Principles of economics

Introduction to Part 2

This part of the book introduces the logical principles of economic analysis so that they can be used to explain economic decision making in developing the built environment. Reference will be made both to Part 1, and to the more extensive built environment applications in Part 3.

Emphasis will be placed on economic decision making rather than on the economics discipline itself. Economic theory will be reduced to its essentials whilst concepts from related disciplines such as management will be incorporated. The aim is to produce a manageable and relevant set of principles which can readily be used to explain economic decision making in developing the built environment.

While Part 2 will mainly concentrate on a framework of economic principles, reference will be made to built environment applications where this can be done without interrupting the logical flow of the argument.

Part 2 will be divided into seven chapters as follows:

Chapter 1 formally introduces the economics discipline by considering definitions and problems, methodology and the status of the subject.

Chapter 2 introduces a simple model of the basic economic activity of wealth creation which will be used throughout the book. A study of various economic systems is also undertaken.

Chapter 3 considers in detail the theory and practice of the market system, as predominantly used in the UK economy.

Chapter 4 considers the firm, one of the major actors in the economic process. The firm is not regarded as being passive to the market, but as having a significant influence on the economic activity that takes place. A managerial approach is adopted in that the objectives, performance and internal organisation and operation of the firm are given full consideration.

Chapter 5 broadens the study to consider aspects of industry, industrial and market structures and the way in which they change over time.

Chapter 6 studies the economy as a whole, and involves consideration of markets and firms at a broader more aggregate, or macro level. The problems of macroeconomics, models of the economy and different views of the way in which the economy operates are considered.

Chapter 7 studies more systematically the issue of public intervention into the market economy. Many of these aspects of public policy appeared in earlier chapters.

1

The nature of economics

Introduction

Part 1 was mainly concerned with describing the process of developing the built environment, using examples from the imaginary town of Carbury. Although connected economic issues were identified, particularly the fundamental question regarding the effectiveness or otherwise of market forces, no formal economic analysis was undertaken. However a definition of economics was proposed which now forms the starting point for the formal analysis required to understand economic principles and applications to the built environment. With this definition in mind, a number of questions arising from it will be examined. Following this, the methods by which economics is studied will be considered. Finally, the status of the subject will be discussed, particularly the claim that it is a science. This will involve introducing various approaches to studying economic problems.

Definitions and questions

The definition of economics proposed in Part 1 was:

> 'Economics is a study of the use of limited resources to create wealth, and of the subsequent distribution of that wealth.'

As mentioned in Part 1 the *creation of wealth* is central to economics, but because *resources are limited* decisions have to be made regarding:

1. how the available resources will be used
2. how the created wealth will be distributed and who will benefit.

It has already been seen that 'the market' or market forces play an important role in making these decisions in the UK economy, supplemented or replaced by public intervention where appropriate.

Any study of economics, even in its narrowest form, would need to ask how these decisions are made. In this book a broader view will be taken and therefore a broader range of questions based on the definition will be posed.

These questions are:

1. What are economic resources?
2. By which criteria are resources allocated to different uses?
3. How is 'wealth' defined and measured?
4. Which methods are used to create or produce wealth?
5. What happens to wealth after creation? That is, how is it distributed?

These are all broadly-based questions, which have to be fully appreciated to understand the subject of economics. A preliminary discussion on each will follow immediately, but greater understanding will develop in subsequent chapters.

Economic resources

These are the various requirements which, when combined, create wealth. This makes for a very long and varied list. For example the production of a building would require resources such as:

1. building land
2. materials such as bricks, cement, and timber
3. components such as windows, doors, and heating units
4. manual labour skills
5. management skills
6. plant on site
7. vehicles.

Since a list of this kind is unwieldy, a method is required to classify resources. The most common approach is to describe resources as **Factors of Production** and to classify them as:

1. **Land**, which includes the land itself, plus natural resources such as minerals and fossil fuels
2. **Labour**, which includes the physical and mental skills of people
3. **Capital**, which includes factory buildings, plant,

30

machinery, vehicles and other manufactured items which aid production.

This three-way classification is the most commonly used today although there is some recognition of a fourth factor called 'enterprise', which is partly labour (that is, the human entrepreneurial skill element) and partly 'capital' (that is, the provision of risk money needed to set up the venture).

Alternatively it is possible to argue, as the early economists did, that there are only two factors of production — land and labour, because capital is simply an amalgamation of the two in some past economic process. Thus an item of capital such as a machine, if analysed into its constituent parts, was once raw materials such as iron ore, which had to be acted on by labour to form the steel which eventually became a machine. In this analysis, labour is seen as the active factor, and indeed capital is sometimes referred to as 'past labour' or 'dead labour'. There are many cases in economic analysis where the quantity and performance of labour is particularly significant, as will be seen. The two-way classification of factors of production was relevant in the nineteenth century, but in a modern industrial economy where the capital base is well developed, capital is seen as a separate factor of production.

Although the three-way standard classification has some conceptual benefit, it is less useful in practice because the resources used in production are not land, labour or capital in their pure states. Any single resource will have elements of two or more factors. For example, building materials consist of raw materials (land), processed by labour, usually with the help of machines (capital). Even labour resources such as bricklayers, carpenters and site managers will not be pure labour inasmuch that their skills are derived from capital investment in their education and training. For this reason expenditure on the education system is often described as investment in **human capital**.

Further reference is made to factors of production in Chapter 2.

The allocation of resources

The allocation of scarce resources between competing uses is sometimes regarded as the principal economic problem. This raises the fundamental question of the effectiveness or otherwise of market forces.

In essence the two methods of allocating resources are:

1. through the market, and/or
2. through public intervention or planning.

The UK economy is primarily based on the market for allocating resources, with public intervention amending market forces in certain spheres and replacing them in others. The material in Part 1 gave some examples, in the context of Carbury, of these two methods. The balance between the use of these two methods varies over time. For example, in the post-war period increasing levels of intervention were used until the end of the 1970s, a trend which has been reversed in the 1980s.

Obviously a study of the market, and its alternatives, forms an important part of economics and needs to be examined carefully. In simple terms, market forces are supply (sellers) and demand (buyers) which many believe interact to give an outcome which results in the most efficient allocation of resources. Whether this is an accurate description of what the market system can actually do is one of the fundamental debates of economics. This will be discussed in Chapter 3.

The five-stage framework discussed in Part 1 showed which aspects of developing the built environment are more likely to be subject to market forces, and which aspects have a degree of public intervention.

Definition and measurement of wealth

The notion of wealth has been taken as fairly self evident up to now, but this needs to be further examined. Specifically consideration needs to be given to:

1. What is meant by wealth?
2. How should it be measured or valued?

The narrowest definition of wealth is that it is the amount of money held. This is not really accurate because *money wealth* merely gives to those who have it the power to obtain *real wealth*. It is this real wealth which actually gives people pleasure, or utility. The amount of money an individual or group has measures the amount of real wealth *relative to others* which is obtainable. If one family receives ten percent more money, then this increases their power to obtain real wealth. But if everybody receives ten percent more money, then nobody is better off in terms of the real wealth obtainable.

None of this defines what real wealth is, beyond that it gives pleasure, or utility. It is mainly thought of as tangible and material goods, but should certainly be extended to include services, those which are bought directly, and those provided publicly. However it should not be forgotten that much of society's wealth may be non-material, such as clean air, a pleasant environment, an educated workforce and so on. This is the sort of wealth which is often taken for granted but would certainly be missed if it were diminished.

Some economic activity has side effects which diminish wealth. Important examples include pollution, and the overworking of people or machines so that they break down. This can be thought of as negative wealth in that activities of this kind require the use of resources to put them right.

To sum up what is meant by wealth — it is those things which give pleasure or utility to people. It may be goods and services bought through the market, or provided publicly, or it may be intangible items which are taken for granted. Finally, some economic activities generate 'bads' or negative wealth such as pollution, and economic resources must be expended to 'clear up the mess'.

Defining wealth is one thing, but measuring it or putting a value on it is something else. Probably the method most people would adopt to value wealth is to take its **price**, since this determines how much spending power has to be given up in order to acquire it. The price of something is determined through the market forces of demand and supply (Chapter 3 examines this in detail), hence the term **market price** is derived.

However it cannot necessarily be accepted without question that market price is an accurate value of wealth. Some of the reasons for this will be considered.

Subjectivity

Market price does not take account of subjective measures of wealth or intrinsic values which individuals may hold. Obviously it is difficult to measure subjectivity, but an economic concept which is useful is one of **opportunity cost**. This measures the value of something in terms, not of price or money, but of the best alternative foregone.

Thus, an individual may value a car in terms of the holiday which could have been taken instead; or a firm may value an

33

investment opportunity in terms of the best alternative; or a nation may value a new defence system in terms of the school building programme which was an alternative.

Opportunity cost is a useful concept for comparing alternative courses of action, but suffers from the limitation that it gives no absolute value of wealth.

Long term considerations
Market price does not take account of long term considerations. Price is set by short term changes in market conditions, which may not be the best basis on which to make long term decisions on matters such as investment or energy production and usage.

Investment This was originally described in Part 1, and can be defined as giving up spending power now in exchange for some greater benefits in the future. Many individuals and organisations invest. Consumers give up the chance to spend on a range of items in order to purchase a house; firms raise capital or plough back profits into new plant and machines instead of paying more income to shareholders. In all cases there is a price to be paid. This might be the cost of borrowing, or if using one's own money, it will be the income given up by not lending the money to someone else. This cost is measured by the **rate of interest**, which can be thought of as the market price of money or capital. The rate of interest changes with short term changes in market conditions, but because investment is a long term decision, only limited notice can be taken of it. This will be further considered in Chapters 6 and 7. A firm's decision to invest will principally be determined by long term factors such as business expectations, rather than short term interest rates. So if a firm feels that there is going to be a rising demand for its products in the coming years, it will want to invest even if the interest rate (that is, the market price of money) is currently high.

Energy Energy resources are exploited and used over a long period of time and therefore represent long term wealth. In considering whether a particular form of energy is economic, reference to current market prices could be misleading. Controversies have arisen in recent years related to the coal and nuclear power industries. In the case of coal, falling world prices due to say a glut of oil could mean that costs of production in some pits might exceed price, making those pits loss makers. On

34

market criteria such pits should be closed. However if the world price of coal later increases, as it did in the 1970s following an oil shortage, then the pits could become economic. But this may not be a possibility because once closed a pit cannot easily be reopened. So there are definite problems of valuing the wealth embodied in unmined coal reserves on the basis of current market price. This is without considering any of the social or political implications of pit closures. In the case of nuclear power there have been similar arguments related to whether a new generation of power stations should be built. Account has to be taken of building costs, future prices of electricity, safety considerations, and eventual decommissioning costs. It is obviously difficult to look too far into the future on these matters. Current market prices may be a very poor guide indeed.

So if wealth is regarded as having a long term component, there are deficiencies in using short term market price as a measure of value.

Resource usage

Market price may not reflect the amount of resources used. If it is assumed that 'true' value is measured by the amount of resources which are used to produce an item of wealth, then market price does not measure this except in very limited circumstances (that is, perfectly competitive conditions, which will be explained in Chapter 3).

Attempts have been made in the past, particularly by the early economists, to derive a measure of value based on the **quantity of labour time** used to produce an item. This is another example of how the quantity and performance of labour plays an important role in economic analysis. This concept of the quantity of labour is very important but unfortunately is difficult to apply in the modern industrial world where use is made of components and plant. To divide, say, every component into its various labour contents would be an impossible task.

Social costs

Market price does not take account of all social costs, that is costs to society which occur as a by-product of some economic activities conducted through the market. These are costs external to market forces and are usually referred to as **externalities**. A common example is pollution. This inflicts costs on society which the participants in a market transaction have no incentive to take account of because it does not affect their own costs (that is, private costs). For example, in a free market without public controls, a chemical plant may discharge waste into the river because it is the cheapest method of disposal. Social costs arise because someone, be it other firms affected or a public authority, will have to pay to clear up the pollution caused. If nobody clears it up, then society 'pays' through a degraded environment.

There will be more on externalities in Part 3, particularly in Applications A and E.

Production of wealth

This is the core economic activity and consists of converting resources (that is, the factors of production — land, labour and capital) into an item of wealth. Production adds value to the resources in that the output produced is greater in value than the sum of the resource inputs in their previous state.

To understand and analyse the **production process** it is necessary to examine the influences on its performance. These influences are many and varied but can be classified under two categories:

Technological

The technological aspect of production is relatively straightforward. By combining factors of production in certain proportions, a certain output can be expected. This is a mechanistic approach and is usually expressed in the form of a **production function**, a very simple example of which is:

$$\text{Output} = f \text{ (land; labour; capital)}$$

This shows that a change in any of the independent variables on the right hand side of the equation affects the dependent variable of output.

Of course these factors of production cannot be interchanged at will, and indeed in what is known as the *short run* one or more factors will be fixed. In manufacturing industry the amount of capital, and in agriculture the amount of land, tends to be fixed in the short run. Usually labour is regarded as the most variable factor, and certain theories attempt to explain the behaviour of the production process in terms of variable labour acting on fixed capital or land. These are known as the theories of Diminishing Returns or Diminishing Marginal Productivity, and basically argue that up to a point efficiency of production can be improved by dividing up the work into smaller tasks through the 'division of labour'.

If technological influences could completely define the production process, then management decisions would be relatively easy and could be made by the use of computers. Unfortunately life isn't as simple as that, the reason being that one of the factors in the production function is labour, that is, people.

Social

The social influences on production can substantially alter the production function. As previously indicated the variable quantity and performance of labour has a strong effect on the economic process. People can be unpredictable and may not conform to neat technological equations. If they did, then it could be argued that there would be no need for management.

Social elements of production include topics such as managerial organisation of work; trade union and worker behaviour; and industrial relations. These all have great influence on the performance of the production process, and one need look no further than to industrial disputes which occur over issues such as the introduction of new technology, manning levels, overtime, and shift flexibility. In fact, the 'division of labour' mentioned above may not always be easy to implement.

The performance of the production process is measured by **productivity**, which will be examined in Chapter 2. Also the production process will be examined in greater detail when the firm is considered in Chapter 4. Many of the points briefly introduced here will be examined further.

Distribution of wealth

This is the question of what happens to wealth after production. There are two things to consider: transfer mechanisms and the division of spending power.

Transfer mechanisms

The mechanisms for transferring wealth from the producer to the recipient are very similar to those used for initially allocating resources to producers, that is, through the market, and/or through public intervention or planning.

The allocation of resources before production, and the transfer of wealth after production are really the same process. This may seem surprising but it will be fully explained in Chapter 2.

Before leaving this point it must be emphasised that the market is the major mechanism used in the UK economy for the transfer of wealth (as it is for the allocation of resources). However there are substantial areas where public intervention alters or replaces the market, from tax relief on mortgage payments through to provision of health and education services.

Division of spending power

The division of spending power between each individual or household is of course a highly contentious issue. This division is normally called the distribution of income. It consists of a number of components, the chief of which is the distribution of earnings. This is determined through forces in the **labour market** which distribute different incomes to different occupations, industries and regions. The performance of the labour market has very important implications for the economy.

Apart from the distribution of earnings, income is also derived from non-earned sources such as investments.

In addition to the spending power of individuals and households, much spending in the economy is carried out by firms or producers which has important implications for the economy (see particularly Chapter 6).

As has been seen, the distribution of spending power or income is mainly determined through market forces, that is, through the labour market. However there is a degree of public intervention, mainly through the tax system, and public spending. Possible forms of intervention include:

1. progressive income tax
2. tax relief
3. benefits (for example, unemployment and sickness)
4. public services (for example, health and education).

The subject of economics has now been defined and some important questions regarding its scope have been posed. The answers given to these questions should be regarded as preliminary, with a study of economic principles in subsequent chapters necessary to increase understanding. The next task is to outline the methods by which economic questions are studied.

38

Methods for studying economics

With any subject or discipline there have to be methods or approaches to facilitate its study. In economics there are two methods adopted, known as **micro**economics and **macro**economics. Although these are sometimes treated as two branches of the subject, indeed almost as two separate subjects, it is more helpful to treat them as two methods since the same economic problem may often be approached using either of the methods.

For example, unemployment may be explained by analysing the structure of the labour market which is a microeconomic approach, or by examining overall wage or demand levels which are macroeconomic approaches.

Let us consider each of the methods in turn:

Microeconomics

Using this method the individual parts of economic processes are examined and built up into a larger picture. This can be thought of as an approach from the 'bottom up'. Thus by returning to the basic definition, it can be seen that economics is about studying wealth creation. A microeconomic approach would be to study an individual wealth-creating process, including the stages of, and the participants in, the process. This will be studied in detail in Chapter 2, and will include matters such as how production takes place, by whom and for what purpose. It will include questions such as those posed earlier in the chapter about resources and their allocation, and the distribution of wealth.

In the context of an urban area such as Carbury a microeconomic approach would include studies of patterns of land use, operation of firms, and the structure of the workforce.

It is possible to take the basic microeconomic process and build it up into a larger picture to include industrial structure. However there comes a point when the addition of more and more detail causes confusion, and so an alternative method is helpful.

Macroeconomics

This method, rather than building up a mass of detail from the bottom, takes a bird's eye or 'top downwards' view. Thus it is a way of looking at an economic unit as a whole without becoming too involved with the individual parts.

In the context of Carbury this would include studying overall levels of income, demand, population, and employment.

Use of the two methods

As previously mentioned microeconomics and macroeconomics represent alternative methods of tackling economic problems. However, conventionally, the two tend each to be used for particular purposes, thus:

1. Microeconomics is used to study topics such as resource use, production, firms, markets, industry, land use, and distribution of income
2. Macroeconomics is used for studying the national economy, or the economy as a whole, including topics such as overall levels of employment, wealth, and inflation.

However it must be stressed again that these are two methods and it may sometimes be useful to use either or both to try to understand economic principles and their applications. Certainly in studying the UK economy, the performance of the market or the operation of market forces can never be far from the analysis. This applies whether considering the built environment or any other form of economic activity.

In this book the microeconomic method is more widely used, starting with a detailed examination of the microeconomic process in Chapter 2. Then follow two chapters on important aspects of the process: firstly, the market system, which is the main mechanism used in the economy for allocating resources and distributing wealth, and secondly, the firm, which is a major participant in the microeconomic process. Chapter 5 broadens out the microeconomic process into a context which includes details of collections of such processes known as industries. Chapter 6 adopts the macroeconomic method to study the national economy, while Chapter 7 considers policy issues. Policy is about how and why the operation of market forces is amended or replaced by public intervention in accordance with the objectives of society. This will start with macroeconomic problems such as unemployment, but will include use of micro methods where appropriate. Apart from this chapter on economic policy, aspects of public intervention will be illustrated at other points in the book and indeed examples of this have already been seen in Part 1.

The status of economics

It was indicated in the introduction to Part 1 that studying the development of the built environment (or any other form of economic activity) requires the application of social and political criteria as well as economic. It was also said that there is a framework of economic criteria, which has since been introduced. Before leaving this chapter on the nature of economics it is necessary to discuss just how watertight this framework of economic theory is as a separate discipline or science.

A discipline is a field of study which has its own set of rules or method. For a discipline to be a science it needs to have an agreed set of principles which can be tested against the real world. Thus in the natural sciences such as chemistry and physics there are great areas of knowledge agreed to be 'true' by everybody. Those disciplines which study aspects of human behaviour such as psychology, sociology and economics have become known as **social sciences** on the grounds that they use scientific criteria to study human behaviour. This raises the important question of whether it is possible to agree sufficiently on economic relationships to be able to use scientific criteria. In other words can economics be regarded as an objective study free of political controversy or is the whole thing just a matter of opinion which anybody can argue about in the pub. To answer this, consideration will be given to how the economy and the subject of economics have developed in recent years.

The post-war period, until the middle to late 1970s, was seen as one of relative economic prosperity with growth, full employment and rising standards of living the norm. It was particularly felt that the evil of mass unemployment, which had periodically reared its head before, was now banished. This belief was based on a **new consensus** regarding how the economy should be organised. This consensus had a number of features, the chief of which was that there should be a **mixed economy** which was basically market orientated, but with substantial areas of public intervention where market forces do not achieve the desired result for society. An important associated feature was

41

that industry should be based on partnership between firms, workers, and the government. This led to extensive collective bargaining in the economy and hence an important role for trade unions, plus a third-party role for the state in ensuring fair play.

With the growth in this consensus a parallel development occurred in the subject of economics where a great deal of knowledge came to be seen as 'fact'. This was particularly the case in macroeconomics where it became common to depict the economy as being kept in order by high levels of government activity. With this development economics began to be categorised as **positive** or **normative**, with a clear separation between what was objective and scientific (positive) and what was subject to political influences (normative).

The point is that the scope of positive economics grew substantially and led to a growth in scientific theoretical and statistical analysis. After a while it seemed as if the assumptions of basic economic theory, including such fundamental matters as how markets worked, were no longer questioned but instead used as a basis for ever more complicated analysis.

The economic crisis which commenced in the mid 1970s has changed the situation considerably. The post-war consensus has broken down and there is consequently much more to argue about. The assumptions of positive economics are much more likely to be questioned and consequently much less can now be considered as 'fact'. This was originally mentioned in the introduction to Part 1 where it was argued that few economic decisions are based on objective criteria and are normally subject to a range of social and political influences as well. It was stated that economic analysis can only be a starting point to help understanding of economic problems and that the perspective of the economist influences the way in which problems are tackled.

It was mentioned in Part 1 that the focus of debate has tended to be on how effective are market forces in achieving the economic objectives of society. The post-war consensus was based on the view that market forces are quite effective but need to be modified or replaced in certain circumstances. The breakdown of the consensus has led to a diffusion of views which can be categorised under three broad headings or *schools of thought*.

In very brief summary, these are as follows.

42

Monetarism

Monetarists believe that the market is by far the best method of organising economic activity because it achieves economic and political freedom and offers the maximum choice to consumers. Problems occur when the government intervenes to try and run the economy. This can only have a detrimental effect and so everything should be done to eliminate intervention and ensure free market forces throughout the economy.

This school of thought has been adopted by the government since 1979.

Keynesian

Keynesians believe that the market is generally a good method of organising economic activity but does have serious defects which need to be rectified. These defects include monopoly power, and possible insufficient economic activity to maintain full employment. However these defects or imperfections can normally be corrected by government intervention. This school of thought predominated during the post-war consensus, and is named in honour of the economist John Maynard Keynes who was one of the first to argue the case for increased public spending to reduce levels of unemployment. The whole idea of a Keynesian approach to economics is that there should be a mixed economy with a large public sector plus other measures to support and encourage the private sector.

Radical/Marxist

Radicals believe that the market is *not* a good method of organising economic activity because its defects are so extensive, and so embedded that they cannot be rectified in the way that Keynesians suggest. A market economy will always get into crisis and periods of stability are merely passing phases linking crises which will occur at intervals. This school of thought follows a line of argument which stretches back to Karl Marx who was the first economist to suggest that the market system, or capitalism, ought to be replaced because its defects made it unworkable for the benefit of the majority in society.

These three descriptions are extremely brief and obviously do not do justice to the great works written by the founders and subsequent members of these schools of thought. Also, within the various schools there are wide variations of opinion on matters of detail.

It is impossible to say that any of these schools of thought represents 'the truth'. All argue from logical positions, and all can call forth evidence which they claim supports their view. This unfortunately makes it confusing for those studying economics for the first time. However to conceal the diversity of views would reduce the value of studying the subject in explaining the real world. The schools of thought will be mentioned at appropriate times in subsequent chapters, and certainly the intention is not to hide from any controversy which will arise. It should be recognised that a school of thought is often adopted which closely matches one's social and political values.

Summary

This chapter has introduced more formally the subject of economics and should certainly be read in conjunction with Part 1 on the built environment. The subject has been defined, and some of the basic problem areas underlying the subject have been identified. Methods for studying the subject were explained and finally the diversity of perspectives for studying economics were introduced.

The next chapter will begin a more detailed examination of economic principles starting with a microeconomic analysis of the economic process.

Tutorial questions

1. Explain the possible benefits of a publicly funded hospital building programme.
2. What are the advantages and disadvantages of new industry in an urban area?
3. Is the distribution of earnings determined mainly by the forces of supply and demand in the labour market?

2

The microeconomic process

Introduction

As described in Chapter 1, microeconomics examines individual parts of economic processes and builds them into a larger picture. Since the basic definition of the subject states that economics is about wealth creation, so the microeconomic process describes the wealth creating process.

As has been seen, wealth creation is known as the **production process**, that is, the means by which resources are combined to produce something else.

However production will not take place in isolation, and requires a preliminary and a subsequent event. Thus:

> *before production*, the resources necessary for production must be gathered, and
> *after production*, the wealth so created must be distributed.

This is shown diagrammatically in Fig. 2.1.

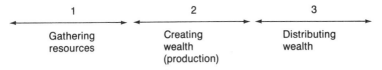

1	2	3
Gathering resources	Creating wealth (production)	Distributing wealth

Fig. 2.1   Simple microeconomic process

This three-stage process is an entity and consists of a central wealth creating process preceded and followed by a transfer of the ownership of resources or wealth. It is useful to think of this process as a basic 'building block' of microeconomic analysis, and this diagram or variants of it will be used frequently hereafter.

To proceed from here it is appropriate to examine how this

microeconomic process works in practice, that is, how the process is controlled and by whom. This means consideration of **economic systems**. It is already known that the market system is predominantly used in the UK economy. However alternative systems will be briefly considered here. The microeconomic process in the market system will be re-examined including consideration of the roles and processes within the system. Finally consideration can be given to the relationship between a single microeconomic process and other such processes in the context of the wider economic system.

Economic systems

An economic system is the mechanism by which the basic process of:

Gathering resources > Creating or producing wealth > Distributing wealth

is carried out. All economies, however basic, require an economic system. In pre-industrial economies the predominant system in Britain was the feudal system where decisions about what would be produced, how and for whose benefit were made by the 'lord of the manor', who held economic power through the ownership of land. Each peasant family would be allocated a piece of land to work, the produce from which would be distributed partly to the family and partly (the major part) to the lord. In other non-industrial societies the economic system may be based on the decisions of tribal chiefs or village elders.

In modern industrial economies there are theoretically two types of 'pure' economic systems, that is, the market system and the centrally planned system.

The market system

This system is sometimes referred to as **free enterprise** or **capitalist**. However the latter word also refers to a political as well as an economic system, so should not be used in this context. This system is usually associated with use in Western Europe and the USA.

In its purest form the market system relies on the free market forces of supply and demand which interact to ensure that the maximum wealth or welfare is created for the benefit of society as a whole. Market forces determine what is available and at what price.

Since the market system is predominantly used in the UK it will be the system mainly considered in this book. Chapter 3 will examine it in more detail.

The centrally-planned system

This system is sometimes referred to as the **command economy** or **communist**, although again the latter word also implies a political system as well as an economic. This system is usually associated with use in Eastern Europe, China and Cuba.

In its purest form the centrally planned system means that all resources are owned by the state, and are allocated not by supply and demand, but by a hierarchy of planning bodies ranging from strategic decisions at central level, down through regional, local and individual enterprise levels. Instead of prices being set by market forces, they are set by the planners in what they perceive to be the public interest. Similarly, the state controls distribution of wealth through public provision of goods and services, price subsidies and influence over incomes.

Economic systems and actual economies

The two 'pure' systems outlined above do not exist in reality because to some extent all countries have 'mixed' economies. It has already been seen that the UK economy, although predominantly market orientated, does have elements of public planning administered by central or local government.

It was seen in the case of Carbury, and indeed throughout the five-stage study of developing the built environment, that public planning frequently modifies or replaces market forces. The town planning system is of course an example of this.

Similarly in the so-called centrally planned economies such as the USSR, there is considerable and increasing use made of market forces. It was found that planning the economy in detail was virtually impossible, so consequently increasing numbers of decisions have been decentralised to the enterprises. Also private smallholdings are relied upon for a significant amount of agricultural output. In addition, the use of financial incentives and other 'capitalist' incentives to workers has increased over the years.

Central planning   A   B   C   Market

Fig. 2.2   Economic systems

Since pure market or centrally planned economies do not exist, it is better to show the various real systems as lying on a spectrum from pure market to pure planning as in Fig. 2.2.

In Fig. 2.2 'A' could represent the USSR which has predominantly a planned system but with some market forces; 'B' could represent the UK during the period of the post-war consensus, at the height of the mixed economy, when market forces predominated but with substantial public intervention; and 'C' could represent the UK in the 1990s after the break up of the post-war consensus, the change in the balance of the mixture of the economy through measures such as privatisation and a general expansion of the market philosophy.

The microeconomic process in the market economy

The market economy operates through the interaction of demand and supply, or buying and selling.

This means that certain roles have to be performed:

> **Demand** is seen as the role of the **Purchaser** (often referred to as the **Consumer**)
> **Supply** is seen as the role of the **Firm**.

This relates to the distribution of created wealth as in Fig. 2.1, and occurs after production.

There is also a buying and selling process during the gathering of resources before production:

> **Demand** is seen as the role of the **Firm**
> **Supply** is seen as the role of the **Owners of resources**.

Therefore the microeconomic process can be reformulated as in Fig. 2.3.

Figure 2.3 shows the three-stage microeconomic process with the addition of certain roles:

1. Owners of resources
2. Firm
3. Purchaser (or consumer).

48

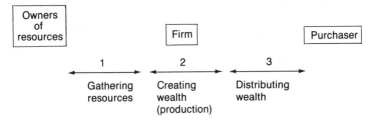

Fig. 2.3   Microeconomic process, including economic roles

It will be seen that the **firm** has a central role and is involved in all three stages of the process:

1. It buys resources before production
2. It carries out production to create wealth
3. It sells the wealth after production.

The meaning of this central role is a fundamental issue much debated. Does the firm control the microeconomic process, or does it respond passively to the needs of consumers? Conventional economic theory argues the latter, and indeed one of the main tenets of Monetarism is that the market economy ensures that firms serve society and not vice versa. This subservience of firms to consumers is known as **consumer sovereignty**. However critics of this theory argue that firms are more powerful, deciding what to produce and then manipulating consumers to ensure purchase. This issue will be examined under the market system in Chapter 3.

Performance of the microeconomic process

In Fig. 2.3 certain roles and processes have been identified — the **roles** are *owners of resources; firms; purchasers or consumers.* It is important to note that these are roles or functions and not individual people *per se.* For example an individual may perform all three roles at different times.

Thus a person may:

1. own resources such as his or her own labour
2. be part of a firm by working for it, and
3. be a consumer and buy the goods produced by firms.

These roles are sometimes referred to as **economic actors**, and since they are roles rather than specific individuals or organisations they are often treated in a fairly abstract manner. Thus firms perform the same roles or functions whether large or small, privately or publicly owned.

The processes are numbered 1, 2 and 3 in Fig. 2.3 and will be explained in more detail. Reference should be made to Chapter 1, particularly those sections entitled 'economic resources'; 'the allocation of resources'; 'production of wealth'; 'distribution of wealth'.

Gathering resources

Resources were classified in Chapter 1 as factors of production. Since these are sold (by owners of resources) and bought (by firms), this is a market process known as **factor markets**.

Since resources are acquired through markets they will have a **price** and will be available in certain **quantities**. The price/quantity relationship is an essential element in measuring the performance of any market, and will be examined more fully in Chapter 3.

As mentioned in Chapter 1 the three-way standard classification of factors of production has limited practical use. This is because firms do not actually buy 'pure' factors. In reality most resources are bought from other firms. This introduces for the first time the important point that the microeconomic process does not exist in isolation but is related to a wider context, an idea which will be explored later in this chapter under 'The microeconomic process in context'. Thus the output of one firm becomes the resources of another firm.

Thus a building firm uses resources such as:

1. bricks purchased from a brick manufacturer;
2. components purchased from components manufacturers;
3. plant purchased from plant manufacturers or hired from plant hire firms;
4. money 'purchased' or borrowed from money lending firms such as banks.

An exception to this is often *labour* which is distinguished from other resources in that:

1. It can only be hired not bought.
2. Under the normal contract of employment the firm buys a certain number of hours work, not necessarily a certain

50

quantity of work. The latter is mainly determined by the social influences on production discussed in Chapter 1.

In many cases even this exception does not apply. For example, building firms make use of labour-only sub-contractors, which in effect is the purchase of a given amount of work from a firm which is 'selling' labour.

Creating wealth

This is the combination of resources in the *production process* to create an item of wealth. This was introduced in Chapter 1 where the two sets of influences on the production process were divided into *technological* and *social*.

The performance of the production process is measured by **productivity**. This is a purely physical measure (that is, non-monetary) and is found by relating output to input:

$$\text{productivity} = \text{quantity of output} \div \text{quantity of resources used.}$$

Although this is conceptually the correct measure of productivity, it is not practicable to use because of the difficulty in obtaining a common unit for the denominator. This is because each resource may be measured in different units, for example, labour in hours, plant in capacity, bricks in thousands. The short cut adopted is to take the resource labour as the denominator because this can be more easily measured, for example, in terms of man hours or a similar alternative.

Therefore productivity is almost universally quoted in terms of output per unit of labour input. This means that use of productivity statistics can be misleading where comparison is not made between like and like. Such statistics are often used to 'prove' that, say, one country's industry is more efficient than another country's, or that privatised companies are more efficient than nationalised ones. Or, it may be quite possible to present the statistics in such a way that they prove the opposite.

What can be said about productivity is that it can alter due to changes in the two sets of influences on the production process, namely technological and social.

Technological

Improvements in productivity due to technological influences can occur due to improvements in the resources used. This often means new capital equipment, which can improve the ratio of output per unit of input of labour. Such improvements may also occur due to a better trained workforce. Improvements in productivity due to technological factors may have little to do with how hard people work.

Social

Improvements in productivity due to social influences occur when methods of work are improved to produce more per unit of labour. This may involve harder working due to incentives and/or closer supervision, or possibly these improvements may come about due to better working relationships or more flexibility.

Methods by which the management in a firm utilise these influences will be discussed in Chapter 4.

The production process has a very special and significant place in the whole microeconomic process because it is here, and only here, where a physical change actually occurs to resources. Therefore this is the ultimate source of wealth creation. What comes before (that is, 'gathering resources') and what comes after (that is, 'distributing the wealth') are simply mechanisms for changing ownership. Therefore they are often called **exchange processes**.

Distributing the wealth

As just stated, this stage is similar to 'gathering resources' in that it is an exchange process. Created wealth is sold by the firm to purchasers (often called consumers). This is also a market operation (called *product markets*). As with any other market the performance is measured in terms of *price* and *quantity*. As mentioned in Chapter 1 this post-production transfer of wealth through product markets is similar to the pre-production allocation of resources through factor markets.

The microeconomic process in context

As previously mentioned the three-stage microeconomic process is a basic building block of economic analysis and as such has a self-contained unity as shown in Fig. 2.4.

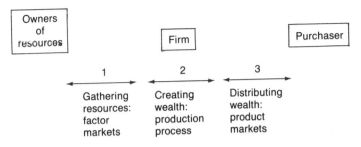

Fig. 2.4 Microeconomic process as a building block of economic analysis

However, this does not exist in isolation. Factor markets and product markets are essentially similar in that both are exchange processes. This similarity is emphasised particularly when it is remembered that the purchaser to whom firms sell their products is not always the final consumer. Many firms are engaged in producing what is known as **intermediate goods**. These are goods which are bought by other firms, as resources, to incorporate into their own production process. For example, most building materials are intermediate goods in that they are produced by, say, brick manufacturers, sold to housebuilders who will incorporate them into the final product to be sold to the consumer.

Therefore, many of the resources which a firm buys will be produced by other firms. In the same way, it is likely that many firms' products will be sold to other firms rather than to final consumers. It can therefore be seen that stages 1 and 3 in Fig. 2.4 are really the same. Figure 2.5 shows the relationship between two microeconomic processes.

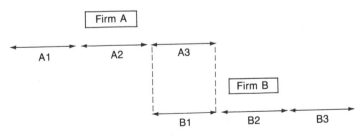

Fig. 2.5 Relationship between two microeconomic processes

53

In Fig. 2.5:

Firm A = a brick manufacturer
Firm B = a housebuilder

Process A1 — brick manufacturer acquires resources such as clay for making bricks.

Process A2 — brick manufacturer produces bricks, which become housebuilder's resources.

Process A3 — brick manufacturer sells bricks to purchaser who is the housebuilder.

Process B1 — housebuilder buys resources (bricks) from brick manufacturer.
(N.B. A3 and B1 are the same process).

Process B2 — housebuilder produces houses using bricks (and of course other resources similarly bought).

Process B3 — housebuilder sells houses to final consumers.

This shows the relationship between only two microeconomic processes. In practice the relationships can be more extensive and complicated. This theme will be returned to in Chapter 5 where in particular the association of many microeconomic processes into what are known as industries will be examined.

Summary

In this chapter, one of the important concepts (or 'basic building blocks') of economic analysis has been introduced. Although there are alternative economic systems, the market system predominates in the UK economy. Various economic actors (or roles or functions), and the various stages or sub processes in the microeconomic process have been examined. It has been seen how a single microeconomic process relates to another. However the next task is to expand the examination of important aspects of the microeconomic process. Hence the next chapter will look at the market system in more detail. This will include an examination of how markets are meant to work and what they should achieve. Following this, consideration will be given to one of the major actors in the process, that is, the firm.

Tutorial questions

1. Have the changes which have occurred in the UK economic system since 1980 been beneficial?
2. In a market economy is it likely that firms will generally produce what consumers want?
3. What problems will be encountered in seeking to measure the productivity of a construction firm?

3

The market system

Introduction

It has been mentioned that the UK economy is based on the market system. By now the reader should have a reasonable idea of what market forces are and how they may be amended or replaced by public intervention.

It should also be clear that a market can be any mechanism which brings together buyers and sellers to effect exchange. Thus it is an abstract concept which can take many forms — organised and tangible, or the opposite.

The theory behind the market system will now be examined in more detail, commencing with an introduction to basic market theory which is usually expressed by supply and demand curves, that is, the **market model**. The assumptions underlying this model will be carefully examined, especially in the light of the advantages for society which are claimed for the market system. This will lead to further discussions on the types of problems which occur with the market system in practice and how different kinds of real markets are classified. Finally some applications of market theory to the built environment will be examined.

Much of the material in this chapter will have already been covered informally in previous chapters. In particular, reference should be made to the material in Part 1.

Basic market theory

The market is based on the interaction of two forces:

1. Demand, that is, the buyer or purchaser
2. Supply, that is, the seller.

The interaction of these two forces determines the outcome or performance of the market, which is measured by:

Fig. 3.1 Market forces

1. Price
2. Quantity.

These simple relationships are shown in Fig. 3.1.

Basic market theory or *supply and demand analysis* is used to 'explain' market performance. The task now is to predict the behaviour of market participants in response to the outcome of price. The two participants in a market are the aforementioned forces of buyers and sellers, each of which will be considered separately and then jointly.

The behaviour of buyers in the market

Intuitively it can be said that normally:

> *more will be demanded at a low price than at a high price.*

This can be shown diagrammatically as in Fig. 3.2.

Figure 3.2 is drawn in the conventional form, with price on the vertical axis and quantity on the horizontal axis. Points on the graph show the relationship between price and quantity, or more specifically the quantity that will be demanded at each price. For example at point A, it is seen that the high price of P_1, yields a low demand of Q_1; at point B, it is seen that the low price of P_2, yields a high demand of Q_2.

If the two points are joined and extended this gives the line 'D' which is known as a **demand schedule**, or **demand curve**. This can be thought of as a planning device in that it measures the quantity that would be demanded at different prices.

The behaviour of sellers in the market

Intuitively it can be said that normally:

> *more will be supplied at a high price than at a low price.*

This can be shown diagrammatically as in Fig. 3.3

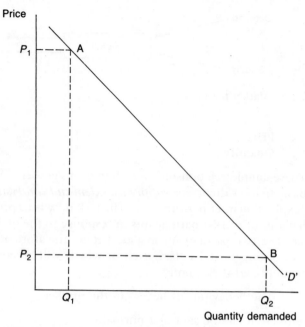

Fig. 3.2   Behaviour of buyers in the market

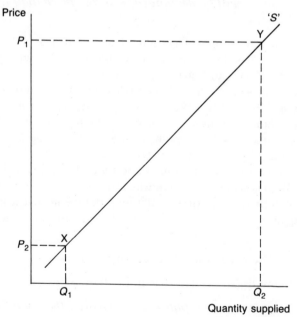

Fig. 3.3   Behaviour of sellers in the market

In Fig. 3.3, at point X, it is seen that the low price of P_2 yields a low supply of Q_1; at point Y, it is seen that the high price of P_1 yields a high supply of Q_2.

If the two points are joined and extended, this gives the line 'S' which is known as a **supply schedule**, or **supply curve**.

This too can be thought of as a planning device in that it measures the quantity that would be supplied at different prices. It is assumed that more would be supplied at a higher price as this would tend to increase the supplier's revenue.

The market model

It has been shown above how buyers and sellers respond to a range of prices. However a market requires the interaction of buyers and sellers, although it would appear on the face of it that the two sets of plans are incompatible.

However the theory of the market assumes that the plans of buyers and sellers can be made compatible by market forces as shown in Fig. 3.4.

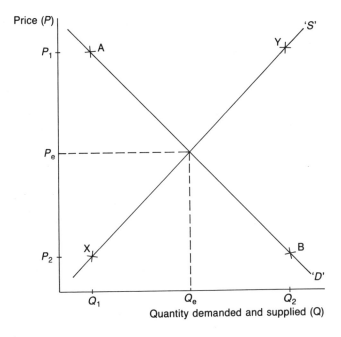

Fig. 3.4   The market model

Figure 3.4 takes the separate plans of buyers ('D') and sellers ('S'), and superimposes them onto the same axes. This shows that the plans of buyers and sellers are compatible at one point, known as the **market equilibrium**. At this point the price is P_e and the quantity both supplied and demanded is Q_e.

It would appear that the market has a way of bringing buyers and sellers into harmony at an equilibrium point. This and other assumptions of market theory will be examined to see if markets in the real world do perform in this manner.

Assumptions of market theory

As frequently mentioned, the belief is held by many that the market system is the best way of organising economic activity in Britain. It has also been seen that there are critical views of this belief. Assessment of these views depends on the validity or otherwise of certain assumptions underlying the way that the market is meant to work, as defined by market theory.

These assumptions are as follows:

1. The market is a harmonising force which brings together buyers and sellers at an equilibrium price and quantity without any wasted production.
2. The market operates in the best interests of society in that producers, or firms, respond to the wishes of consumers, that is consumer sovereignty exists. Furthermore resources are allocated and used in the most efficient manner. These benefits are guaranteed by what is known as **perfect competition**.

If these assumptions are valid then indeed the market is 'best' as was first contended more than 200 years ago when early economists argued that if everybody pursued their own 'enlightened self interest', the result for society would be favourable. In more recent times belief in these assumptions has led to support for a privatisation policy which in effect extends the market or market forces to more areas of economic activity. These assumptions can now be examined in more detail.

The market as a harmonising force

It has already been seen how the market is meant to harmonise supply and demand at an equilibrium price and quantity (see Fig.

3.4). Thus market forces balance out supply and demand at a market equilibrium which tends to be maintained. The equilibrium point can be thought of as a 'magnet' which draws buyers and sellers together. This is not to say that pressures, or disturbances, do not act on the market to alter it, but always a market equilibrium is not far away. These disturbances in the market will now be considered, as either minor disturbances, or major disturbances.

Minor disturbances

These are not fundamental or permanent, but are more of a temporary nature. Examples would be short term shortages or surpluses of products. The way the market deals with this can be understood by referring back to Fig. 3.4. If there is a shortage of a product then demand exceeds supply. An increase in price above P_e will reduce excess demand to make it compatible with supply, and so the market equilibrium is regained.

Similarly, if there is a surplus of a product then supply exceeds demand. A reduction in price below P_e will reduce excess supply to make it compatible with demand, and so the market equilibrium is regained.

In both these cases the market equilibrium is acting as a 'magnet' for harmonising the market, with movements in prices helping to restore order. Therefore it is *flexible prices* in a market which lead to the restoration of equilibrium after a minor disturbance.

Major disturbances

These are of a much more fundamental or permanent nature than those described above. They usually result from an underlying change in the conditions of demand or supply, for example,

1. Demand changes are brought about by changes in incomes, tastes, or the prices of substitute or complementary products.
2. Supply changes are brought about by changes in costs of production due to technological change, price and availability of resources and levels of taxation.

It has already been seen that changes in price affect the position on the demand or supply curves (see Fig. 3.4). However changes in the conditions of demand or supply, such as those just mentioned, result in a change in the position of the demand and supply curves themselves.

61

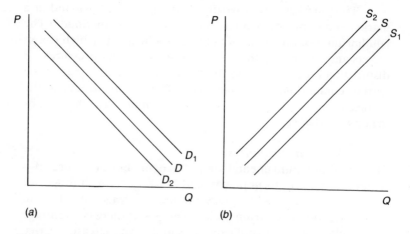

Fig. 3.5 (a) Shifts in demand curve, (b) Shifts in supply curve

Thus in Fig. 3.5(a), the demand curve shifts:

1. From D to D_1 as a result of increasing tastes for the product, higher incomes, or increased price of substitute or competing goods.
2. From D to D_2 as a result of reduced tastes for the product, lower incomes, or reduced price of substitute or competing goods.

And, in Fig. 3.5(b), the supply curve shifts:

1. From S to S_1 as a result of reduced costs due to improved technology, better and cheaper availability of resources, or lower taxation.
2. From S to S_2 as a result of increased costs due to shortages of and/or more expensive resources, or higher taxation.

When shifts in demand and supply curves occur, it means that more or less of a product will be produced and that a change in the use of resources has occurred.

Thus in Fig. 3.6 the original market equilibrium of P_1Q_1 has been disturbed by an increase in demand for the product caused by increased tastes for it. This disturbance is too great to be dealt with by a simple price adjustment. Instead the amount of resources used to produce this product are increased. This is shown diagrammatically by a shift in the demand curve from D

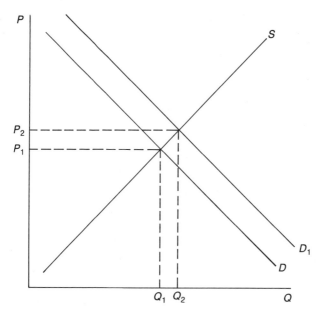

Fig. 3.6 Change in market equilibrium

to D_1, with a new market equilibrium at P_2Q_2. Therefore, as a result of a major disturbance in the market, market theory assumes that there will be a *reallocation of resources*, and a new market equilibrium.

Elasticity of demand

Before leaving this assumption of the market as a harmonising force, there is one more concept to introduce. It has already been seen that there is a relationship between price and quantity. For demand, this is an inverse relationship because as price goes up demand goes down, and as price goes down, demand goes up. For supply, this is a direct relationship because as price goes up supply goes up, and as price goes down supply goes down. However the magnitude of these relationships is also of interest. For example, by how much does demand go down when price goes up by a given amount? This is measured by what is called elasticity of demand (or supply).

The general formula for elasticity of demand is:

$$\text{Elasticity} = \frac{\text{percentage change in quantity demanded}}{\text{percentage change in price}}$$

Where this is low (less than 1), demand is said to be inelastic; and where this is high (greater than 1), demand is said to be elastic.

The degree of elasticity of demand tends to be influenced by factors such as the availability of substitutes, how essential the product is, and how large a proportion of total spending this product represents. To take a simple example, salt has an inelastic demand because there are few substitutes, it is a fairly essential item, and it forms a small proportion of the typical consumer's budget.

Elasticity of demand is shown diagrammatically by the slope of the demand curve, as shown in Figs. 3.7(a) and 3.7(b).

The analysis of elasticity of supply follows a similar pattern, with the degree of elasticity depending on how quickly supply can be increased. Therefore time tends to be the main determinant of elasticity of supply. In the immediate period supply may be fixed, giving a perfectly inelastic supply (shown by a vertical supply curve), while as time progresses supply becomes more elastic.

The concept of elasticity has several applications, as will be seen later (for example, see section on 'markets and the built environment' at the end of this chapter). In the meantime this completes the study of the first major assumption of market theory, that is, that the market is a harmonising force. The second assumption can now be considered.

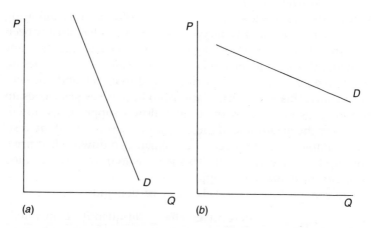

Fig. 3.7   (a) Inelastic demand, (b) Elastic demand

The market as a servant of society

This assumes that not only does the market make compatible the disparate plans of buyers and sellers (as in assumption 1), but also that the outcome of the market economy leads to the maximum benefit to the members of society, that is, to consumers.

Thus it is assumed that freely operating markets will ensure the efficient allocation and use of resources. In addition, consumers, by their actions in the market place, register preferences as to what should be produced, and that firms respond passively to these preferences by allocating resources and producing accordingly.

These assumptions regarding the benefits of the market to society will be valid if certain conditions are present in the market. These conditions are encapsulated in the ideal market model which is known as **perfect competition**.

The main conditions for perfect competition are as follows:

Many firms
There should be many firms in the market. This is the generally accepted definition of competitive conditions, that is, where many firms are striving with each other to gain favour from customers. As well as there being no dominating sellers in the market, it is also important that there should be no dominating buyers, particularly in market transactions between firms.

Free entry
There should be free entry into (and exit from) the market, that is, there should be no **barriers to entry**. This condition is to ensure that competitive conditions can be maintained over time. With free entry and exit, efficient new firms can enter the market to keep up the level of competition, or, alternatively, existing firms who have become inefficient can 'withdraw'.

Mobility of resources
Free entry to and exit from the market is important not only for ensuring efficiency, but also in response to changing patterns of consumer demand (that is, one of the major disturbances discussed earlier in the chapter). As was seen, these changing responses are accompanied by the reallocation of resources. Therefore perfect competition requires complete mobility of resources, so that resources can be transferred from one activity

to another in response to the wishes of consumers. When an increase in resources for an activity is required this may come from existing firms increasing supply or by new firms entering the market. When fewer resources are required existing firms cut supply and/or some firms leave the market.

Perfect knowledge

There should be perfect knowledge of the market. It is important that both buyers and sellers know what the market has to offer. Buyers must know what each firm is selling and at what price, and sellers must know what buyers want and what they are prepared to pay. This enables rational decisions to be made and for the market to harmonise. For perfect knowledge to exist perfect competition requires that there should be **homogeneous products**. This means that all firms operating in a particular market are selling identical products, with the consumer being indifferent to anything other than the price. For example, a consumer buying cauliflowers in a street market would be indifferent about the farm from which they came. This ensures that all firms in the market are competing on price alone, with no scope for influencing the consumer, or blurring knowledge through advertising, brand names and the like.

Perfect competition and price

There are a number of stringent conditions which have to be met for perfect competition to operate, and the full theoretical benefits of the market to be achieved. It was mentioned previously that the main method of specifying the outcome or performance of a market is by market price. Under perfect competition all firms have to compete vigorously with each other. This has the effect of competing the market price down to such an extent that if it fell any lower it would not be possible for firms to make any profit and so they would not produce. Therefore the market price is competed downwards until the costs of production are just being covered. This 'basic cost' has to allow for a minimum profit which enables the firm to stay in business, a concept which will be fully discussed in the next chapter. Therefore any firm which was not efficient enough to produce and sell for the market price would be unable to stay in business. Furthermore where demand is increasing then firms will be attracted into the market by the prospect of profits. There may be a period when prices are higher than they need be (that is, above costs of production), but perfect competition ensures that new firms can enter the market to compete market price downwards. Thus all firms in the market ultimately have to accept the market price, and this price will be at the lowest possible level consistent with the most efficient firms being able to stay in business.

The model of perfect competition is used to illustrate what the ideal market situation would be like, and how it would benefit society. This and the other assumptions of market theory lend strong support to the market system. The practical outcome of this must now be examined.

The market system in practice

Few people believe that the market system actually performs in the way explained above. It is unlikely that even in the most favourable conditions imaginable it would be possible to achieve *all* the benefits predicted by market theory. The question really becomes whether a freely operating market system would allow these benefits to be substantially achieved. In other words, is it possible to move towards market equilibrium and perfect competition?

The answers to this depend entirely on one's perspective as defined by the schools of thought described in Chapter 1.

Monetarists

Monetarists argue that the problems with the economy stem from obstacles in markets caused by government activity, trade unions and other forms of control. As long as these obstacles could be removed, then the market economy would operate more or less in the way depicted by market theory, with all the associated benefits. This has been the line adopted by the government since 1979 with the objective of making the market as free as possible by a variety of measures such as privatisation and changes to employment law.

Keynesians

Keynesians argue that although the market is basically a sound system it does suffer from **imperfections** such as monopoly power which would occur even if the market was made as free as possible. In other words the free market alone cannot achieve the benefits shown by market theory. Therefore it is essential that there is strong public intervention to correct market imperfections, or replace the market where necessary. This was broadly the line adopted by the majority of post-war governments until 1979. This Keynesian period witnessed a growth in the public sector and the emergence of a mixed economy, a trend reversed since 1979.

Radicals

Radicals argue that the supposed benefits of the market system are an illusion. Rather than having removable imperfections the market actually suffers from deep-seated and severe failures which cannot be corrected by anything other than widescale public intervention. Thus monopoly power and inequality are seen as entrenched features of the market system and not removable without a scale of public intervention which would amount to reducing the market to a relatively minor role in the economy.

Of these three views the Monetarists and Keynesians have in common that both operate within the framework of the market and believe that the benefits predicted by market theory can in some large measure be achieved. The Monetarists and Radicals have in common that both believe that the market system has its own dynamic and its own set of rules which cannot be tampered with in the Keynesian manner. Therefore the market system either has to be adopted wholeheartedly, or substantially replaced.

To gain a wider understanding of the market system in practice it is necessary to examine the assumptions of market theory and in particular to see how the conditions for perfect competition reflect, or could reflect, the real world. Each of the conditions will be discussed in turn together with the imperfections which may attend them.

Many firms

This is the usual test of competitiveness with market price being competed down to the lowest possible level, consistent with the firm covering its basic costs. However the imperfection which arises is **monopoly power**, where there may only be a few firms in a market (a complete monopoly where there is only one firm is rare). In the case of a few firms (a condition known as oligopoly) there is the possibility that the firms may act in collusion to raise prices above basic costs thus exploiting the consumer. There is also the possibility that monopoly firms do not have the incentive to be efficient, resulting in a waste of resources.

Free entry into the market

This is necessary to allow for competiton to be maintained over time. However a group of firms might maintain monopoly power through the imperfection of **barriers to entry**. These prevent new firms entering the market. They can take many forms including the following.

Techonological barriers

These apply to those industries where the cost of capital necessary to set up are so great that it acts as a strong deterrent to competition. This is because the costs per unit of producing certain items reduce dramatically when large amounts are involved. Therefore production on a smaller scale would involve high costs of production per unit. This ability to reduce costs per unit as production increases is known as **economies of scale**, and applies to large scale manufacturing industries such as steel and motor vehicles. The effectiveness of economies of scale as a barrier to entry depends on the size of the market. The smaller this is then the fewer firms will be able to produce at the scale necessary for minimum cost per unit. Where the market can support only one or at any rate only very few firms then this situation is sometimes referred to as **natural monopoly**. This approach can be extended to include **public utilities** such as gas, electricity, telecommunications, railways and water, where many firms competing would be impractical as well as wasteful. The ownership of natural monopolies and public utilities varies — they may be publicly owned; or they may be privately owned, but with some public regulation to prevent monopolistic exploitation of the consumer. In Britain the trend since 1979 has been from public to private ownership, the belief of the government being that the advantages of the market can be achieved by privately owned utilities even if they are monopolies.

Technological barriers to entry are the only 'natural' ones. The remainder are created.

Artificially created high costs
Where there are no high technological costs to deter new competitors, other barriers may be found. One way is to increase costs artificially by high advertising costs and multiple brand names. Thus potential new entrants to the market would need to spend up to the same level on advertising to have any chance of making an impact on the market. This effect is accentuated where the existing firm sells many brands which are broadly similar. The effect is that new firms would be competing against not just one but several brands and so the advertising costs would be that much greater. One example of this method is the soap powder industry where there are only two major firms dominating the market, each with many brand names.

Before leaving the question of artificially created costs a further point is that barriers to entry will often involve a high cost to the firm setting them up. Thus the firm has to weigh up whether it is worthwhile incurring extra costs for the sake of eliminating competitors. The real test is what will be the effect on the firm's profits — that is, will the *cost* of the barriers be outweighed by the extra *revenue* gained by having monopoly power?

Other cost advantages
This covers any other reason which gives existing firm(s) an advantage over potential competitors. This could include ownership of or access to cheaper supplies of factors of production. Another cost advantage which a large firm may have over a small one is that they may be able to obtain finance more easily and at lower rates of interest because the assets which firms own are used as security.

Limit pricing
Limit pricing and excess capacity are both ways of manipulating the two measures of market performance, that is, price and quantity. Limit pricing (also sometimes called predatory pricing) is the system whereby existing firms try to discourage newcomers by temporarily cutting prices thus reducing profit margins and 'squeezing out' competition. This is particularly effective if the existing firms have plenty of assets and can afford to suffer very low profits or even a loss in the short term, something which much smaller firms could not afford to do for any length of time. This strategy may be adopted by firms either to deter new competitors, or to hinder a competitor who has already entered

the market and threatens to upset existing monopolistic pricing arrangements. For example a group of large firms faced by competition from a new firm seeking to enter the market by undercutting prices, may respond by cutting prices themselves even further. This could force the new firm out of business. In common with artificially created high costs, the practice of limit pricing is costly and the existing firms must consider whether it is worth the short term loss in profits to keep out competition.

Excess capacity

This is the practice where existing firms invest in more productive capacity than they really need. It involves manipulating the quantity measure of market performance just as limit pricing manipulates the price measure. Maintaining excess capacity can deter potential competitors, because they would be aware that the market could easily be flooded thus reducing prices and profits if they tried to enter. Thus the existence of excess capacity could act as a visible deterrent to new competitors particularly where the time lag between deciding to enter and actually entering the market is significant. This could be the case in manufacturing where the time taken to build a factory and install plant could be very lengthy. In the commercial property market empty office space could deter new entrants because of the time taken to design and build new office blocks, or to refurbish existing ones.

Once again, the cost of maintaining excess capacity is quite high, and the existing firm(s) would need to decide carefully whether it is worthwhile.

To summarise, there are a number of possible reasons why entry to the market may not be completely free. This is not to say that these barriers to entry will prevent the benefits of the market being achieved. The natural monopolies may be under effective public control and the artificially created barriers may not always succeed. Barriers to entry will reappear later in the chapter when considering the classification of market conditions.

Mobility of resources

As seen, a reallocation of resources is necessary when:

1. Changes occur in consumer demand. A shift in the use of resources occurs to enable a new market equilibrium to be obtained.

2. There is entry to or exit from the market. This requires a smooth reallocation of resources.

In reality, immobility of resources is a major imperfection in the market. This will be briefly described under the usual three way classification of factors of production as defined in Chapter 1.

Land

Not only is it impossible physically to move land, but its change of use may be difficult to achieve and occurs only slowly. For example, to change the use of a piece of land from, say, residential to commercial involves the time taken for demolition, design, approvals and construction. In the case of a controversial development, say to build housing on a green-field site, the time taken to obtain approval could be lengthy, with an uncertain outcome.

Labour

This may be immobile in two important respects:

1. People may not be willing or able to move physically to different areas, where there may be work. This may be due to family ties, and/or to the cost of moving (including rehousing) making this difficult or even impossible.
2. People may not have the necessary skills for the new demands in the market. To train additional people in the required skills may take some time.

Capital

This represents long term assets, many of which cannot be moved or easily adapted to new uses. To counteract this problem, modern factories and offices are often built on an open plan basis, creating flexibility of use, thus improving mobility.

This immobility of resources can be a serious problem in the market system. Certainly in the short term many resources are inelastic in supply which means that supply cannot be increased significantly even with an increase in price. This makes it extremely difficult for market adjustments to take place in line with consumer demands. This is an important theme in considering built environment issues, and will be raised again subsequently at the end of this chapter.

Perfect knowledge

Buyers and sellers in the market must be able to make rational decisions, and this requires perfect knowledge of the market. As seen, an important aid to this is homogeneous products where all competing firms are producing and selling the same product.

In practice, knowledge is imperfect. Not only may firms find difficulty in knowing exactly what consumers want, but consumers themselves may not know either. This is because there is a great range of goods available, some with a high degree of technical sophistication. For perfect knowledge and rational decision making homogeneous products are required. However what usually exists is **product differentiation** heavily backed by advertising. While some advertising is undoubtedly informative to the consumer, a great deal is persuasive giving the consumer the feeling that a particular product is indispensable. Successful advertising often uses brand names designed to create a special image for a product thus boosting sales. It has already been seen above how brand names can be used to create barriers to entry.

Imperfect knowledge by consumers may mean firms are able to manipulate demand and diminish consumer sovereignty.

As mentioned above, perfect knowledge is a pre-requisite for rational behaviour by consumers. In particular it is fundamental to the working of the market system that consumers respond to prices in a knowledgeable and rational manner. However what consumers regard as rational is not a fixed timeless idea. One area in which behaviour has changed is in the apparent willingness to borrow more money at a higher price (that is, rate of interest) than would have been the case in an earlier era. This unpredictability has important implications for policy makers in trying to run the economy. The effects of this will be examined in Chapter 7.

In summary it can be seen that the four features of perfect competition — many firms; free entry; mobility of resources; perfect knowledge — in practice may each suffer from imperfections. These imperfections may apply to a greater or lesser extent in real markets, and so it is necessary to have some way of classifying markets according to how closely they resemble the market ideal of perfect competition.

Classification of market conditions

As seen, markets in practice may not conform to perfect competition, and so the benefits predicted by market theory may not be present. To tell how far from perfect competition a given market is, there is a need to classify it. Two methods of classification will be described, both of which show variations from perfect competition.

Neo-classical market structures

This is the more commonly used classification and consists of a range of four options with perfect competition at one extreme, and monopoly at the other, with two intermediate options called monopolistic competition (or imperfect competition), and oligopoly. These four special cases may be defined according to the way in which the four market variables apply.

These variables are:

1. Number of firms
2. Whether there is free entry into the market
3. Whether there is mobility of resources
4. Whether there is perfect knowledge.

The market classification can be shown as follows:-

	Perfect competition	*Monopolistic competition*	*Oligopoly*	*Monopoly*
(*a*)	Many firms	Many firms	Few firms	One firm
(*b*)	Free entry	Free entry	Barriers to entry	Barriers to entry
(*c*)	Mobility of resources	Mobility of resources	Immobility of resources	Immobility of resources
(*d*)	Perfect knowledge	Imperfect knowledge	Imperfect knowledge	Imperfect knowledge

By departing from perfect competition, the market can be said to be less competitive because increasing numbers of imperfections are introduced. The first imperfection occurs in monopolistic competition where imperfect knowledge occurs through brand names backed up by advertising as previously described. This can cause some irrational consumer behaviour. Moving along to even less competitive conditions there are fewer firms, and the introduction of barriers to entry. Ultimately there is monopoly with only one firm. In reality most markets are either monopolistic competition (where there are many firms) or oligopoly (where there are few firms). The dividing line between the two is not clear but it would seem that in actual industries there has been a steady drift towards oligopoly, a point which will be explored in more detail under industrial structure in Chapter 5.

These standard classifications of market conditions are used to predict the behaviour of the firms which operate in them. The problem is that the most common market form in practice (oligopoly) is the most difficult to predict. With perfect competition and monopolistic competition it can be predicted that there will be competition, guaranteed by the large number of firms. With monopoly it is equally predictable that competition will not exist since there is only one firm. With oligopoly there are a few firms which means there might be competition or there might be some kind of collusive arrangement to set prices. To help understand this an alternative method of market classification will be used.

Degree of monopoly

This method of classifying markets uses a sliding scale starting from perfect competition and gradually moving away from it. It was mentioned before that the main outcome of perfect competition is that all firms must charge a price equivalent to the basic cost of production. This includes the actual cost of production plus a 'normal' profit which is enough to enable the firm to replace its capital which is wearing out. Therefore this perfectly competitive price (equivalent to basic cost) is the minimum which would allow the firm to stay in business. Any price below this would mean that the firm could not replace its worn-out capital and so it would eventually go out of business. Thus the advantage of perfect competition to the consumer is that firms will enter the market to compete the price down to this perfectly competitive price.

The degree of monopoly measures the deviation from perfectly competitive price, that is, the mark up on basic cost. The higher the mark up, then the higher the degree of monopoly. This concept is useful because it concentrates on the main indicator of market performance, that is, price.

There are three determinants of the degree of monopoly. These are:

1. Number of firms
2. Extent of collusion
3. Strength of demand, for example, as measured by elasticity of demand.

Clearly the number of firms affects the degree of monopoly. However as observed when considering oligopoly, high mark up pricing may only be possible where the firms are able to act with some measure of agreement or collusion. This depends not only on how many firms there are, but on what the strength of demand is. Thus if demand is strong (that is, inelastic) firms are much more likely to be able to obtain high prices than if demand is weak (that is, elastic).

Changes to the degree of monopoly can occur over time and this will happen if the conditions underlying one or more of the determinants change. Thus the degree of monopoly will become greater if, for example:

1. the number of firms reduces say due to mergers, takeovers and bankruptcies; or
2. demand strengthens due to, say, the increased spending power of full employment or an increase in tastes for a particular product.

Alternatively, the degree of monopoly will reduce (that is, competition will increase) if, for example:

1. new firms enter the market; or
2. demand weakens due to a recession.

Forces which increase the degree of monopoly tend to involve more collusion and vice versa.

To take some examples, the degree of monopoly in some sectors of the construction industry may have tended to increase due to mergers and takeovers reducing the number of firms. In the oil industry the degree of monopoly may have tended to reduce because although there are still only a few firms, the strength of world demand for oil has slackened. Thus at any one time there may be forces affecting the degree of monopoly in either direction.

Another possibility is that rather than the degree of monopoly increasing or decreasing for the whole of an industry, there may be some polarisation taking place. For example a competitive industry with large numbers of medium size firms may evolve over time into an industry with a few very large firms (that is, *the core*) and many very small firms (that is, *the periphery*). This would appear to mean that the degree of monopoly has increased overall in that few firms dominate the industry, but within the industry the degree of monopoly has reduced in that many small firms are competing with each other for work from the large firms. This core/periphery structure has evolved in many industries and in particular appears to define the main contractor/sub-contractor relationship typical of the construction industry in recent times.

These two classifications of market conditions have been discussed in the context of market theory and how the market is meant to benefit society. The degree of monopoly in particular, including the core/periphery concept, will appear again in the next two chapters — on the firm, and on industrial structure.

Markets and the built environment

The diagram of the basic market model (Fig. 3.4) shows moderately sloped supply and demand curves, based on the assumptions of market theory. In such a model adjustments can take place, as in Fig. 3.6 without dramatic changes in price and quantity. It needs to be asked whether such a model is appropriate to the built environment. It was seen in Fig. 3.7(*a*) and (*b*) that demand (or supply) curves may be elastic or inelastic rather than moderately sloped. Probably the most notable feature of markets in connection with developing the built environment is the inelastic supply of land, be it for housing, commercial buildings, or road space. Inelasticity involves:

1. Limitations of the amount of suitable land available
2. The time taken to bring land into use.

The effect of this is that the supply of new development (or redevelopment) is slow in relation to demand, that is, supply is inelastic. Insofar as it is possible to use the market model to explain the development of the built environment, the diagrammatic representation would look more like Fig. 3.8 than Fig. 3.4.

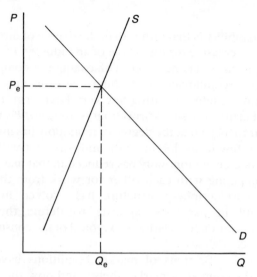

Fig. 3.8 Market model appropriate to development of the built environment

With a model such as shown in Fig. 3.8, how does the market perform, say, in response to an increase in demand? To illustrate this two common examples from the built environment will be considered.

Housing

The demand for new housing in many parts of the country could be flexible relative to supply, which is inelastic due to shortage of suitable land and the time taken to build units for the market. Fig. 3.9 shows what happens when there is an increase in incomes causing the demand curve for housing to shift from DH to DH_1. It can be seen that the result is a very sharp increase in prices, much more than the small adjustments shown in Fig. 3.6.

Therefore it can be said that because of inelastic supply relative to demand, the housing market does not stabilise smoothly and is characterised by *escalating prices*.

Roads

The amount of roads available can be thought of as the supply of road space, and the number of vehicles wishing to use the roads as the demand for road space. The 'market' for road usage has

78

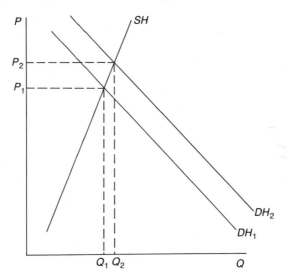

Fig. 3.9   Effect of increase in demand for housing

similar characteristics to housing in that demand appears to be ever rising, that is flexible, while supply is very slow to increase, that is inelastic. Under the normal rules of the market this should lead to a rapid increase in the price for using roads, as is the case with housing (see above). However, there is no direct price paid for road use and payments are not commensurate with the actual amount of usage. Therefore, no adjustment along the price axis of the market model is possible. The only possibility is some 'adjustment' on the quantity axis. The practical expression of this is heavily congested roads and dilution of the quality of travel.

Therefore since there is no money price paid by the road user *congestion* is the 'price' paid by society.

Therefore inelastic supply is a major imperfection in the markets connected with developing the built environment. In Part 3 (particularly Applications A to E) this will be considered further together with other problems of the market including externalities, and distribution issues. Solutions to the problems will also be considered.

Summary

This chapter has described the market system in terms of what it is meant to do and what advantages it is meant to give to society. This is depicted by basic market theory or *supply and demand analysis*. To understand how this works the assumptions of market theory were examined and then compared with the market system in practice. There are a variety of views on how well the market system serves society and these were briefly reiterated. The conditions for perfect competition were examined together with the imperfections which occur in practice such as monopoly power, barriers to entry, immobility of resources and imperfect knowledge. These imperfections operate to varying degrees, so it was necessary to introduce the methods of classifying markets according to how closely they resemble perfect competition. Finally some brief examples of markets in the built environment were given.

The market system has been dealt with as far as is possible within the framework of basic market theory. Concepts such as market structure and the degree of monopoly will be used again in subsequent chapters. Also market theory will be used when further applications to the built environment are discussed. This was introduced in the last section when a preliminary study of housing and roads was undertaken. As mentioned, this will be extended in Part 3, particularly in Applications A to E.

Tutorial questions

1. Does privatisation benefit society?
2. Are economies of scale significant in the construction industry?
3. Is immobility of labour a serious obstacle in the construction industry?

4

The Firm

Introduction

In previous chapters the firm has appeared as an important actor on the economic stage. When examining the microeconomic process in Chapter 2 it was seen that the firm has responsibility for production of wealth, a role which is expanded to include acquisition of resources before production, and the distribution of wealth after production. Thus the firm has a central role in the microeconomic process. However in Chapter 3 it was seen that in market theory the firm represents the supply side of markets, and in the ideal situation of perfect competition is passive to the needs of consumers. That study of market theory acknowledged imperfections in the market such as monopoly power, but the implication was that such imperfections can be removed so that the perfectly competitive situation of consumer sovereignty can be approached.

This chapter will study the role of the firm in more detail, and in particular assume the firm to be a much more active participant in the microeconomic process. The assumption will be made that since the firm is responsible for wealth creation (that is, production), the objectives of firms have a significant if not dominating influence on the economic activity that takes place. The chapter will also recognise the fact that a great deal of market transactions in the economy occur not between firms and consumers but between one firm and another. For these reasons the chapter will start with consideration of the firm's objectives. Particular attention will be given to profitability. The nature of profit will be examined together with ways of measuring the performance of the firm, for example, through company accounts. The various factors which influence the firm's performance will also be examined, and will involve an analysis of the various constraints on the achievement of the firm's profitability objective. It will be assumed that the firm is not passive to the market but capable of taking measures to improve its own market position. This will pave the way for discussing industrial structure in Chapter 5, a concept first mentioned in Chapter 3 when various market conditions were classified.

Objectives of the firm

The first requirement of any firm is survival. This must be put into a time scale — that is the survival of the firm in both the short term and the long term.

Short term survival

In the short term a firm must be able to pay its bills. This means that it must be able to obtain sufficient cash or **liquidity** to pay for labour, materials, plant hire and energy. The funds necessary to allow the firm to stay afloat in this way are known as working capital. The usual sources of these funds are bank overdrafts and trade credit. It is quite possible that a firm may go out of business (that is, go into liquidation) even if its long term prospects are good. This cash flow difficulty is often thought of as a particular problem in the construction industry where payments on contracts are normally made monthly, whereas many bills have to be paid weekly. A loss of support from the bank can have severe consequences. This problem will be studied in greater detail in Part 3 Application K.

Long term survival

In the long term a firm needs to be able continually to renew the cycle of production, as depicted by the microeconomic process (see Fig. 2.4). Thus the firm has to gather resources, produce the product and finally sell the product. At the end of this there must be a surplus to regenerate the whole process, and in particular the business has to be kept intact by replacing those items of fixed capital, such as plant and machinery, which are wearing out. This surplus is the difference between the revenue from sales and the costs of production, and is commonly called profit. Thus **profitability** is the vital long term objective of the firm. If the firm cannot make a profit it cannot renew the cycle of production for long and cannot survive. Of course a firm may borrow funds

82

externally to finance its activities, for example through loans or share issues. However such funds will not be available unless the lender or investor is satisfied that repayment plus a return will occur. Ultimately this can only come from profits. Therefore profits, or the prospect of profits, are essential for long term survival.

Thus the firm has the twin survival objectives of liquidity and profitability. The latter takes some precedence since a firm may survive for a short time but ultimately has to remain effective if it is to become a permanent feature of the economic scene. Whether a firm is granted, say, overdraft facilities to ensure liquidity will depend on the firm's expected long term performance on profitability. However it cannot be assumed that profitability guarantees survival. There could be many reasons why a bank may withdraw short term funding from a firm even if its prospects are quite good. Banks tend to be cautious and usually adopt a risk-averse strategy. They prefer to lend to firms with assets since these act as security against funding. Building firms are vulnerable to this cautious approach from banks because they have fewer saleable assets than, for example, manufacturers. Therefore building firms may still be liable to go into liquidation even though they have a number of potentially profitable contracts in hand.

Is the firm a profit maximiser?

It has been seen that profitability is the essential requirement for a firm to survive. Conventional economic thinking goes further and argues that the sole objective of the firm is profit maximisation. There has been some dispute over this down the years, and in particular it has been argued that in a large firm the objectives of those who work for the firm, such as middle managers, will outweigh the profit maximising objectives of the firm's owners, that is the shareholders. This may be possible because of the separation of ownership and control in large firms. Here, control may rest with middle management who may have different objectives from shareholders.

Whether this is accurate or not is unimportant at this stage because it has been established that profitability is essential even if it is not maximised. This whole question of whether the objectives of a firm may be modified by those who work for it will be more fully examined later in this chapter.

The nature of profit

Having recognised that profitability is the most important objective of the firm, it is now necessary to explore the meaning of this in more detail.

A simple formula which can be used is:

Profit = **Revenue** from sales − **Costs** of production

In abbreviated form this is:

$$P = R - C$$

An important consideration to remember is that revenues and costs are two independent variables and profit is simply the difference between them. Therefore in seeking to explain what determines the level of profit, it is not possible to answer this without considering:

1. What determines costs and
2. What determines revenues.

There are two stages to making a profit, which can be related to the diagram of the microeconomic process as represented by Fig. 4.1.

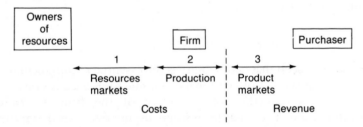

Fig. 4.1 Profit making and the microeconomic process

In addition, the cost and revenue aspects of profit may be further analysed by reference to Fig. 4.2.

The two stages to profit making are as follows.

Generating potential profits

There is a need to produce as cheaply and efficiently as possible. This may be thought of as generating the potential for profits and involves minimising the costs of production.

84

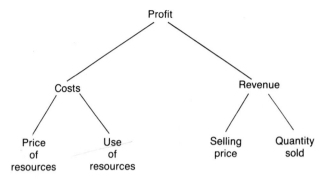

Fig. 4.2 Analysis of profit

The costs are incurred, as shown in Fig. 4.1, through:

1. The resources (or factor) markets, which determine the price paid for resources.
2. The production process which determines the effectiveness of using resources, that is productivity.

Therefore ideally the firm should aim to:

1. pay as little as possible for resources, and
2. use them as effectively as possible.

Of course these two aims may well be in a trade-off position as shown in Fig. 4.2 in that paying more for resources may result in a better performance and vice versa. It is the overall cost which is important and as stated this depends not only on how much is paid for resources, but how well they are used. For example it is of little use buying cheaper facing bricks if the wastage factor more than outweighs the saving. And, it may be more sensible to pay higher wages to skilled and motivated workers if this gives a better performance and ultimately lower costs. So, costs are one component of profit, and minimising costs is the first stage of profit making.

Realising profits

There is a need to sell effectively in the market. This may be thought of as realising profits (that is, realising the potential generated through producing at low cost), and involves maximising sales revenue. These revenues are determined, as shown in Fig. 4.1, through selling in the product markets:

85

1. as much as possible,
2. at as high a price as possible.

Again as shown in Fig. 4.2, there may be a trade-off because, as shown in Chapter 3, price and quantity sold have an inverse relationship, indicated by the downward sloping demand curve (see Fig. 3.1). Thus at high price less will be demanded than at low price. Revenue is price × quantity, and it is the relationship between price and quantity which determines revenue. This depends on the elasticity of demand (see Chapter 3). With an inelastic demand (Fig. 3.7(a)), increasing prices will tend to increase revenues, but with elastic demand (Fig. 3.7(b)), they will tend to reduce revenues. As revenues depend not only on the price charged but also on the number sold, care must be taken not to increase the price beyond the point where the quantity sold falls more than proportionately thus reducing revenues.

To summarise, profit making is a two stage process which involves both producing as cheaply and efficiently as possible (that is, minimising costs) and selling as effectively as possible in the market (that is, maximising revenues). A firm must pay attention to both aspects in order to perform well. It makes little sense to produce at low cost if the goods cannot be sold. Similarly it makes little sense opening up markets for selling the goods if they cannot be produced at an appropriate cost. What is important is for the firm to try to maximise the difference between revenues and costs. Each must be considered separately because there is no guarantee that the conditions which allow low cost production will occur at the same time as conditions for high sales revenue.

Measuring performance

The firm's performance is measured through financial data, as shown in company accounts. These are published each year and are of interest to potential investors, suppliers and customers of the firm. Their purpose is to indicate how well the firm is meeting its objectives and they are arranged so that information on profitability and liquidity can be extracted. Two of the most common parts of company accounts are the balance sheet and the profit and loss account.

86

The balance sheet

This shows the firm's assets and liabilities *at a moment in time* at the end of the accounting year. To reflect the objectives of profitability and liquidity the information is arranged under long term and short term (or current) headings. Various inferences about the firm's performance may be drawn from these accounts. For example the ratio current assets:current liabilities is an indication of the firm's liquidity. A brief outline of a balance sheet could be as follows:

Liabilities	*Assets*
long term	long term
share capital	land and buildings
loans	plant and machinery
current	current
creditors	stock
short term loans	debtors
overdraft	cash

The profit and loss account

This shows the firm's performance over a *period of time*, normally a calendar year.

A typical format might be as follows:

     Sales Income
− Cost of Sales
= Gross Profit
− Operating Costs
= Net Profit

In the above profit and loss account, the final figure is net profit. From this are deducted dividends and taxation to determine how much of the year's profit will be retained in the firm for long term funding.

Of course, financial accounting as a way of measuring performance is a highly specialised function which will not be discussed further here.

Having seen how the performance of a firm is measured, the various factors which influence this performance will be discussed.

Determinants of the firm's performance

The main objective of the firm is to make a profit, since without this the firm cannot survive in the long run. To assess how the firm performs it is necessary to examine the various factors which affect the firm's achievement of profitability, and to examine the various constraints on profitability. These constraints will be considered under three headings:

1. Constraints due to the firm's *market position*
2. Constraints due to *internal factors*, for example, from those who work for the firm.
3. Constraints due to *public policy* provisions.

Constraints 1 and 3 will be dealt with fairly briefly here as they receive consideration elsewhere (for example, in Chapters 3 and 7). In each case the effect of these constraints will be considered with particular regard to profitability. The ways in which firms respond to these constraints will also be examined.

As a general rule, reference to the formula:

$$Profit = Revenue - Costs$$

indicates that profits are improved by increasing revenues, and/or reducing costs.

Market constraints

It can be seen from the microeconomic process (see for example Fig. 4.1) that firms buy their resources through factor markets and sell their products through product markets. Therefore the firm's position both as buyer and seller in the markets will greatly affect its profitability. This position depends on the *extent of competition* which the firm faces. In Chapter 3 it was argued that the more competitive a market, then the lower the price and profit margin tends to be. In the extreme case of perfect competition the price is competed down to the point where costs are barely being covered, and the firm just stays in business. Therefore, it could be said that the firm would much prefer not to be in such a marginal position, but would actually like to obtain a degree of monopoly for itself (see Chapter 3) in order to increase its prices and profits. When a firm improves its market position this usually leads to higher profits through increased revenues.

If a firm wishes to improve its market position by increasing its degree of monopoly it must consider the relevant factors. The degree of monopoly is determined by:

1. the number of firms,
2. the extent of collusion,
3. the strength of demand.

as explained in Chapter 3. Therefore a firm may seek to make these factors work to its advantage by, for example:

1. Reducing the number of firms by mergers, takeovers, and setting up barriers to entry if possible.
2. Engaging in product differentiation promoted through advertising, to strengthen demand for its products.

All these factors affect the structure of the industry in which the firm operates. Firms engage in these market strengthening practices to improve profits, either through increasing revenue and/or reducing costs. A fuller discussion of mergers and takeovers will occur in Chapter 5.

Internal constraints

There is often a tendency to treat the firm as a unified entity with everybody in the firm sharing a common goal of maximising profit. However examples have been seen in the production process of how human behaviour may be variable and unpredictable. In reality the firm is a collection of people not necessarily sharing the same objectives. In this section the study will firstly, consider the constraints on profitability from those within the firm, and secondly, consider ways in which the firm responds to such constraints.

Almost without exception, the employees of a firm, whatever their rank or position, will seek to obtain high remuneration for themselves. Wages and salaries represent a cost of production to the firm, and the higher they are, the greater the constraint on profitability. A number of factors influence the level of wages including labour market conditions such as unemployment, and whether there is collective bargaining.

In addition to remuneration, particular groups of employees

may be able to exercise further constraints on profitability. In most cases internal constraints affect profits by increasing costs. Two groups of employees who might exercise constraints through not necessarily sharing the profit maximisation objectives of the firm are:

1. middle management, and
2. production workers.

Middle management

This includes the various managerial and supervisory grades below the level of board of directors. Unlike the board, middle management does not have the same direct duty, imposed by the owners (shareholders), of striving for profit maximisation. In a small company this may not be a factor because the owner(s) may also control and manage the firm. However in a large publicly-quoted firm there may be a *separation of ownership and control*. This means that the owners of the firm (shareholders), being so diffuse, have little control over the firm, this control being exercised by the managerial structure. Thus managers may pursue objectives of their own choosing rather than profit maximisation. Such objectives have been claimed to include the following.

Sales maximisation   The sales revenue of the firm is expanded literally at any cost. This can lead to problems such as breakdowns in machinery or expensive overtime working, each of which add to costs, and therefore may reduce profits.

Growth   This is a long term objective which may ultimately result in the firm having more market power, but in the short term it may depress profits.

Managerial utility   This is a multiple objective with a number of aspects which increase the well being of management, including profit, sales, number of staff, fringe benefits, and power of discretion over spending the firm's money on projects.

Behavioural theories   These theories seek to explain that management pursue policies which try to strike a balance between all the interests connected with the firm. Apart from shareholders, other interests include employees, customers, creditors, the local community, and society at large.

It has frequently been suggested that objectives such as the above represent alternative theories of the firm to profit maximisation. These theories suggest that middle managers wish to pursue objectives other than profit maximisation. A criticism of this view is that managers will have no such desire. This is because they may be shareholders themselves, and also may be heavily influenced by the profit ethic. It seems likely that developments since the early 1980s, such as profit sharing, management buy-outs, and the general business environment would tend to make managers more profit orientated. Even so, middle managers may still be unable to pursue alternative objectives even if they wanted to. This may be due to outside influences such as stock market constraints (assuming the firm is a public limited company). This will be considered later in the chapter.

Production workers

This includes all those who work at the 'sharp end' of production and in the supporting administration. In other words it is those who are usually referred to as 'workers'. Apart from good levels of wages and salaries, workers may have other objectives which are related to the way in which the work is actually carried out. These objectives may vary but could include matters such as craft workers having the freedom to carry out their work in a way which they choose; having sufficient manning levels and breaks which make the work less intense; having clear divisions or demarcation between jobs to maintain job control and security. The effect of these may be to reduce the level of productivity below the maximum achievable and so increase the costs of production, thus reducing profits.

The means by which workers may try to exercise the above constraints may be through individual or collective methods. In many jobs, the salary and conditions applicable will be a matter of individual negotiation between worker and employer. This is particularly the case with white-collar workers in small firms. The worker's bargaining power will probably depend on how easy it would be to find alternative employment, and/or how easy it would be for the employer to find a replacement worker.

A great deal of negotiation in the UK economy is collective rather than individual. This can either take place on an official basis through trade unions and collective bargaining, or on an unofficial basis through rank and file groups of union members or through groups of non union members. Official collective bargaining may agree matters such as basic pay and holidays at a national level, but these agreements are frequently modified at local, plant or company level by supplementary agreement. Typically, pressure has been applied by groups of rank and file workers at plant or workshop level to improve their position with regard to matters such as manning levels, demarcation, and bonuses. Such working practices are often referred to as restrictive practices, and are sometimes regarded as questioning the 'right of management to manage'. Many industrial disputes are concerned with matters such as these rather than with pay. Often there may be a disagreement between the trade union officials, and the rank and file workers and their leaders (shop stewards) about how to get the best deal from the employers. It has been quite common over the years for rank and file workers to be more militant than the officials, and they have been quite willing to take unofficial industrial action.

The constraints exercised by middle management and/or production workers will have the effect of increasing the costs of production and thus reducing profits. **It is now possible to consider how firms respond to the various constraints**. Some of these responses are designed to improve the firm's market position as well as tackle internal constraints. These responses include:

1. Relying on outside influences.
2. Adopting a multi-divisional structure.
3. Choosing appropriate production methods.

Relying on outside influences

The environment in which the firm operates will affect its relationship with its employees. It was mentioned earlier in this chapter that labour market conditions will strongly influence wages and salaries. This is a major outside influence. In addition, where a firm is a public limited company (that is, its shares are sold on the Stock Exchange), this too can affect the behaviour of employees in the firm. Consideration will be given to whether the firm can make use of these two external influences in responding to constraints.

The labour market The labour market, like any other market, has both a supply and demand side — firms demand labour, and workers supply it. If a simple unified labour market

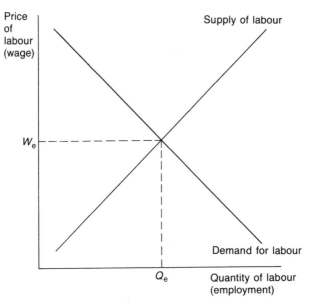

Fig. 4.3 Simple labour market model

existed, it could be shown as a simple market model, as in Fig. 4.3 (which is similar to Fig. 3.4).

In Fig. 4.3 the market will be balanced at a wage of W_e with Q_e being the number employed. If this were true for the whole economy, the total employment (or unemployment) would be determined by wage levels. This is a matter of strong contention between the various schools of economic thought, and will be discussed further in Chapter 6. However it can be seen that when the labour market is depressed, (that is, with high unemployment) this puts the firm in a relatively strong bargaining position *vis-à-vis* its existing or potential employees. This will affect wage levels as unemployment indicates that labour supply exceeds labour demand with workers competing for jobs. Similarly the conditions of employment and hence productivity will be affected. For example high levels of unemployment mean workers would be less able to enforce restrictive practices, or challenge management's right to manage. Clearly the overall condition of the labour market will affect the relationship between firms and employees. In particular, wage levels and productivity, and hence the costs of production will be affected.

However within the overall, or macro, condition of the labour market there may well be micro variations. In times of general unemployment there may be specific shortages of workers, particularly with regard to **skill** and/or **location**. For example, it may be difficult to find carpenters in London despite high levels of unemployment nationally. This problem was first encountered when considering the market imperfection of immobility of labour in Chapter 3. The effect of such variations in the labour market is that different wages and conditions may prevail in different parts of the country. Therefore firms will face different levels of costs depending on their geographical location.

The other major players in the labour market which could affect wages, productivity and hence costs are the trade unions. Their role is much debated. To some (particularly Monetarists) they are an interference in the labour market, while to others they are defenders of workers' rights and essential if the balance of power between employers and employees is to be maintained. During much of the post-war period the role of trade unions expanded based on the belief that a collective of workers was a more even balance to an employer than an individual worker. Collective bargaining between employers and unions became the norm. This has changed since the beginning of the 1980s. Trade union membership has tended to fall, collective bargaining is less common and there is generally more emphasis on the individual contractual relationship between the worker and employer.

Some of these labour market issues will be considered further when production methods are examined, since the hiring of labour through the labour market and the use of labour in the production process are for practical purposes indistinguishable. In Part 3 Application J further consideration will be given to aspects of labour in the construction industry.

The stock market The labour market conditions described above will influence the wages and conditions of all employees, both middle management and production workers. In the case of a public limited company, there is also the possibility of stock market constraints. These might be effective in restricting the freedom of middle management within the firm. Where the firm is not maximising profits, possibly by, say, pursuing alternative objectives, the value of the firm's shares could drop making the firm vulnerable to takeover. In such an event managers would be likely to lose their employment. This risk would discourage them from pursuing any objective other than profit maximisation. Of course for this constraint to be effective the stock market must operate in a manner similar to perfect competition (see Chapter 3) with investors having perfect knowledge of the profit levels a firm should be achieving given its asset base. This assumption of perfect knowledge may not be realistic, and the owners of the firm may not be able to rely on the stock market ensuring that profit maximisation will be achieved. The fear of takeover is something that could concern all employees, since loss of livelihood could follow.

Adopting multi-divisional structures

The traditional structure of the firm is based on the unitary (or U-form) structure. Below the board of directors the firm is divided into various functions such as is shown in Fig. 4.4.

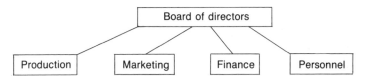

Fig. 4.4   Traditional structure of the firm

The weakness of this structure is that the various functions do not represent a line of accountability in terms of achieving the profitability objectives of the firm. The various functional departments may spend or earn money, but this is not necessarily related to any particular product or service. Each department does not correspond to all or part of a microeconomic process model, as in Fig. 4.1, with no direct relationship to either the costs incurred in producing a product, or the revenues received from selling a product. The actions of employees (middle management or workers) in a department may not be accountable, and waste or increased costs to the firm may go undetected, or at least without any sure way of identifying the source of the increased costs.

The multi-divisional structure (or M-form) is designed to overcome these problems. Although originally conceived as the best way of managing large multi-national companies, its application to smaller firms is becoming increasingly common. Below the board of directors the hierarchy is split into divisions, each based on a profit centre or cost centre which relates to

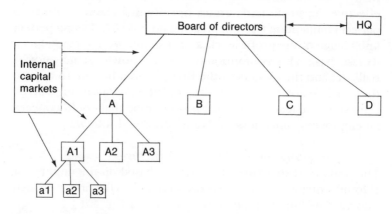

Fig. 4.5   Multi-divisional structure of the firm

particular products, regions or countries. This can be shown as in Fig. 4.5.

If Fig. 4.5 represented a multi-national company:

> A, etc. could represent different continents
> A1, etc. could represent different countries
> a1, etc. could represent different factories making a particular product.

If Fig. 4.5 represented a large construction firm:

> A, etc. could represent different regions.
> A1, etc. could represent different types of work
> a1, etc. could represent different sites.

Any amount of subdivision is possible, but in each case a division must represent all (profit centre) or part (cost centre) of a well defined microeconomic process related to a product or some other part of the firm's activities.

With this multi-divisional structure it is easier for the board of directors to maintain control and ensure that profit maximisation is pursued. The methods of control are as follows.

1.   The staff at head office (HQ) advise the board on the targets to be given to the various divisions. These targets will be expressed in terms of profit or cost, and will be based on what should be achievable given the resources at the disposal of the division, and the market in which

it operates. In a large firm this target setting function may be known as **corporate planning**.

2. The board of directors will set up **internal capital markets** within the firm, especially between itself and the divisions. Each division will be advanced capital funding in accordance with its profit or cost target. Failure to meet targets may result in the transfer of funds, and ultimately the closure of particular divisions. Thus the board acts in a similar fashion to a bank, albeit a better informed one.

An important feature of the M-form structure is that decision making is decentralised. The board sets financial targets and broad strategic guidelines relating to products. It may also provide back up services such as research and development, but generally the divisions are autonomous, deciding for themselves how targets will be met.

It is believed that this structure ensures adherence to profit maximisation. The source of any increased costs and/or lack of profit are more easily identifiable, reducing the autonomy of middle management to pursue other objectives since this may result in withdrawal of funds or even the closure of the division with resulting loss of employment. Production workers may feel more vulnerable given that production may be switched to another factory, or even another country.

The board of directors is thus better able to ensure that terms and conditions exist which are more likely to improve the profitability performance of the firm.

Choosing appropriate production methods

The importance of the production process has already been mentioned. In Chapter 1 a distinction was drawn between the technological and social influences on production. In Chapter 2 the concept of productivity as a measure of the performance of the production process was introduced. Earlier in this chapter it was seen that improving productivity reduces costs which in turn enables the firm to achieve its main objective of profitability.

Productivity performance is one of the components of the costs of production and a major determinant of profitability. Productivity is an important variable because it measures the performance of the production process, the ultimate source of wealth creation and hence profit. Consequently the firm must pay great attention to selecting the correct production methods. This is particularly so since changes in production methods are difficult to implement. Other cost factors such as wages may be more easily varied.

The term production methods needs further explanation. From a technological point of view it represents the particular combination of resources used. This may be defined for example in a production function. It would particularly include the type of plant and other capital equipment used, and whether the production method is capital intensive or labour intensive. A change in production method may be difficult to introduce where this involves using modern machinery (or new technology) since this often results in a reduction in labour requirements.

In addition to technological factors there are also social matters such as the conditions of work and conditions of contract to be considered. For example, the normal contract of employment specifies hours of work rather than amounts of work. Such a contract has little control over productivity. However a contract based on self-employment would link pay to productivity more closely. In order to increase productivity a firm may change the contractual rather than the technological aspect of production methods. This is common in the construction industry where most employment is on a self-employed or labour only sub-contract basis, with lump sum payments made for specific quantities of work.

When considering the choice and implementation of production methods the firm needs to examine both technological and social problems. From the technological point of view a firm may seek to install the most efficient capital equipment provided the market for the firm's products warrants the necessary investment. However the key to successful production is the relationship between the firm and its workforce. The most efficient machine is of little use without people to operate and maintain it. As previously mentioned, people or labour can be variable or unpredictable.

There are a number of aspects of **variable labour**.

Variable quantity of labour   In Chapter 1 it was seen that production is often characterised as variable labour applied to capital or land which is fixed in the short run. If an example is taken of an acre of land and a single worker, this one unit of labour will have to perform all tasks. If an additional unit of labour is employed, each can specialise in particular tasks, giving increased efficiency. Additional units of labour can be added, and increased efficiency attained, provided the work can be subdivided into additional separate tasks (a process known as the division of labour). Eventually when additional new tasks can no longer be found (that is, the division of labour is exhausted) each further unit of labour merely assists with existing tasks, and the rate of increase of production will diminish. This is in essence the conventional economic theory of production in the short run (often called the Theories of Diminishing Returns or Diminishing Marginal Productivity).

In the long run, all resources are variable enabling the firm to choose whatever combination of labour and other resources best suits its needs. A firm can choose a production method which is capital intensive (for example, modern machines and less labour) or labour intensive (for example, more labour with few machines). In these theories there tends to be the assumption of *homogeneous labour*, with one unit of labour being identical to another. Therefore a firm buying units of labour in the labour market need only decide on the quantity required. However to consider labour as variable only in quantity is but part of the whole picture.

Variable quality of labour It has been seen that the purchase of a given number of units of labour does not guarantee a given amount of production under the usual contract of employment conditions. Labour varies greatly in terms of physical and mental capacities for work, by reason of varying levels of education, training, skills and indeed inclination. This last point hints at a fundamental contradiction in human behaviour which must be taken into account by the management of firms in their relationships with their employees. People will exhibit a mixture of characteristics in their attitude to work. Some are positive from the point of view of efficient production, and some are negative. In a positive vein, people have the desire to do something valuable with their working lives and achieve something of which they can be proud. Therefore they want to work effectively. On the other (negative) hand, people may be resistant to authority and may not feel inclined to work hard to make money for others. Therefore they do not work effectively. All people have these positive and negative inclinations in varying measures. The way in which management responds to these characteristics is an important determinant of the outcome of the production process.

Choosing appropriate production methods is an essential task for the management of the firm, with the most suitable choice being beneficial for productivity, costs, and hence profits. As with other aspects of the real economic world there is no single answer to the question of what constitutes the most appropriate production method. There are different management styles and different characteristics of the workforce to be taken into account. There are many possible outcomes. For example, management may vary with regard to their attitude on matters such as:

1. Do workers exhibit primarily positive or negative qualities? Are they willing to work or do they have to be coerced? Or as management theorists might put it, which methods of motivation are required?

2. The role of trade unions. Some managers believe that unions have an important role and that collective bargaining should be encouraged, while others believe that unions are a hindrance in the labour market and the workplace, being responsible for excessive wage levels and inefficient working practices.

3. Workers participation. Some managers believe that workers should take a wider role in organising their own work, while others believe that 'managers are there to manage' and 'workers are there to work', and that never the twain shall meet.

Depending on management's attitude on these and other matters, a variety of approaches to production will be possible. However the same approach may not be taken with all those who work for a firm. In the last chapter it was shown how many industries have evolved a core/periphery structure. Similarly a firm may regard part of its workforce as core with good wages, working conditions and responsibilities, and others as peripheral with lower wages and poorer conditions. Often these peripheral workers may be outside the firm, in a sub-contract or casual relationship.

Management adopt strategies which they believe will lead to greater productivity and hence profit. Apart from core/periphery distinctions as mentioned above, other strategies adopted may include reducing the skill element of the work so that it can be more easily mechanised, with the machine rather than labour setting the pace of work. This is known as **de-skilling** and is a long established technique based on the ideas of scientific management.

These management strategies adopted in the production process need to be examined in greater detail. In Part 3, Application M, consideration will be given to management approaches to production in construction and will make comparisons with other industries.

Public policy constraints

Following consideration of constraints imposed by the firm's market position, and constraints imposed by internal conflicts, the constraints on the firm's performance imposed by society through public policy can now be examined. Only a brief summary of these constraints will be given here, since a wider examination of policy issues will appear in Chapter 7.

In the context of constraints on the firm's profitability performance, it should be said that public policy may affect either the revenue or cost sides of the equation. This may be the result of policies which affect the economy as a whole and firms in general, or through policies which have specific effects on particular firms or types of firms.

Policies which affect revenues might include:

1. Those which affect aggregate demand in the economy (see Chapter 6)
2. Those, such as taxes and subsidies, which affect demand for particular products. For example the demand for houses, and hence the revenue of housebuilders, is affected by tax relief on mortgages.
3. Those which affect the extent of competition in the economy generally or in a particular market. This includes competition policies operated through the Office of Fair Trading and the Monopolies and Mergers Commission.

Policies which affect costs would include:

1. Interest rates, which affect the cost of borrowing.
2. Regulations which directly affect the costs of production. Some examples were given in Part 1 relating to development of the built environment, including

101

planning controls, building regulations, health and safety legislation and employment law.

As shown by the brief list of policies above, some have general and others more specific application.

Summary

This chapter has examined the firm as an active participant in the microeconomic process. The firm's objectives were taken as a starting point. The overriding objective of the firm is to survive by ensuring liquidity in the short term and profitability in the long term. Profitability was taken as the main practical objective. To achieve this the firm has to produce as cheaply and efficiently as possible, (that is, minimise costs of production) and/or sell effectively in the market (that is, maximise revenues). Given the essential objective of making a profit, there are three main sets of constraints on achieving this — that is, market, internal, and public policy. The firm may seek to counteract these constraints by several methods including adopting a multi-divisional structure and organising its production in an appropriate manner.

In the following chapter the firm and its microeconomic process will be put into a wider context. In particular this will involve studying industry and industrial structure.

Tutorial questions

1. Are all construction firms equally vulnerable to cash flow problems?
2. Is productivity in construction determined purely by technological factors?
3. What are the benefits of the multi-divisional structure to the large construction firm?

5

Industry and industrial structure

Introduction — the microeconomic process in context

Most of the analysis to date has been based on the individual firm's microeconomic process first introduced in Chapter 2 as a basic 'building block' of economic analysis. It was seen that these processes link together into larger relationships (see Fig. 2.5). In fact the microeconomic process can be built into a hierarchy of relationships, thus:

> Each firm (and its microeconomic process) is part of an **industry**, which is part of a **national economy**, which in turn is part of the **international economy**.

This chapter is mainly concerned with the first stage in the hierarchy, and will involve using knowledge of markets and firms in a wider context. But first, brief mention will be made of the higher levels.

The national economy is usually regarded as too large and complicated to study using the microeconomic method. Instead the macroeconomic method is used. This involves taking a 'top downwards' view of the economy as a whole. This is the main topic to be studied in Chapter 6.

It is generally recognised that the economy has become increasingly international in character. A detailed study of this trend is outside the scope of this book, but brief mention will be made of some of the more important aspects.

1. The UK economy is 'open' in that much of what is produced is exported and much of what is used is imported. The external balance of the economy will be discussed further in Chapters 6 and 7.
2. There are a number of international organisations operating at the level of the state. These may have wide

economic and political scope as with the EEC, or they may fulfil a much narrower purpose such as controlling the price and/or output of a commodity as with OPEC.

3. Many natural resources and raw materials are bought and sold in world-wide markets often called commodity markets. Market forces, described in Chapter 3, take on an international dimension. Many countries' economies are heavily dependent on commodities such as oil, copper or coffee beans and any significant reduction in world prices can put severe pressure on the country in question.

4. The particular issue of the world's natural resources includes the depletion of energy, and environmental pollution. As mentioned in Chapter 1 the market mechanism is essentially short term and takes little account of long term considerations.

5. Most firms of significant size operate internationally. They are usually called multi-national, or transnational companies. To understand how they operate it is necessary to consider the general studies of the firm (see Chapter 4). In particular it was seen that firms often organise themselves using a multi-divisional or M-form structure. This lends itself especially to multi-national companies. The trend towards transnational operations may increase particularly in the light of the single European market projected to come into effect in 1992.

The main focus of this chapter is industry. Under this general heading there are a number of topics to be considered, including:

1. definition of an industry
2. industrial structure — what it is; how and why it changes
3. market structure — what it is; how and why it changes.

Definition of an industry

An industry is simply a collection of microeconomic processes, as identified in Fig. 2.5. This shows the relationship between two processes, although of course in reality an industry will be much more complicated.

It is useful to think of an industry as having vertical and horizontal dimensions.

1. *Vertical.* Before a product is purchased by the final consumer, it will have gone through a number of stages

of production, each of which will have added some value to it. Raw materials are extracted, made into components, assembled into products, and sold to the final consumer.

2. *Horizontal.* At each stage of the process there will be a number of firms operating, giving the industry its horizontal dimension.

However industries are not normally as uncomplicated as this, and indeed most have permeable boundaries. For example, in defining the construction industry quite a few difficulties would be encountered. Does the industry include only contracting firms? What about design consultants, materials manufacturers, component manufacturers, plant manufacturers and hirers, builders' merchants, building departments of local authorities or commercial organisations? A diagram showing the structure of the construction industry would be very complex. Fig. 5.1 is a simplified version of the industry but it is still quite complex.

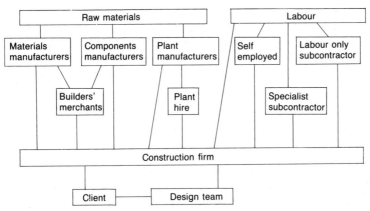

Fig. 5.1 Simplified structure of the construction industry

In reality an industry is a convenient method of defining the economic activities of a range of firms which have some commonality in their operations. It provides reference points for statistical information which can be interpreted in order to give an understanding of how the economy is faring and to provide a common basis for research.

By defining industries the concept of **industrial structure** can be utilised. This studies the importance of, and inter-relationships between, individual industries or groups of industries. A related concept is **market structure** which is more concerned with studying the extent of competition or monopoly either within an industry or in the economy as a whole. For example the extent of competition at a particular horizontal stage in an industry can be studied. In this light it can be seen that the supply of common bricks to the building industry is subject to a high degree of monopoly.

Obviously if everybody used their own definition of what constituted a particular industry, research would be extremely difficult. Fortunately there is a widely recognised framework devised by the government department which collects statistics on industry. This framework is known as the **Standard Industrial Classification (S.I.C.)**. It lists all industries and sub-industries on a number of levels. Broad sectors of the economy such as primary industries (agriculture, mining); secondary industries (manufacturing); tertiary industries (services) will be found at the top level. Below this there will be, say, particular manufacturing industries. The fifth and last level of classification may cover individual product types.

Clearly the S.I.C. is a useful device for collecting information about the economy, but it must be noted that since industries have permeable and overlapping boundaries there is some degree of anomaly in defining what constitutes an industry.

Industrial structure

As previously defined, industrial structure studies the importance of, and the inter-relationships between, individual industries or groups of industries. Despite the difficulties of defining an industry, it is nevertheless necessary to measure the contribution that particular industries or sectors make to the economy. This can be measured in terms of matters such as

1. output
2. employment
3. exports.

Information which has been gathered over a period of time can assist firms, workers, investors or the government to predict the prospects of industries.

It is important to understand changes in industrial structure. Since the Industrial Revolution, when manufacturing replaced agriculture as the dominant industry, the UK has imported a great

106

deal of food and raw materials, and exported great amounts of manufactured goods. Therefore the strongest part of industrial structure throughout the nineteenth and for most of the twentieth century has been manufacturing.

Recent years have seen a decline in traditional manufacturing, to the extent that more manufactured goods are now imported than exported. This applies to both consumer goods such as cars and electrical goods, and capital goods such as machinery and commercial vehicles. This process has been described as **de-industrialisation**. Some people believe that market forces will ensure that other industries will take the place of traditional heavy manufacturing. These new industries include 'high tec' and service industries. Critics believe that these new industries will never be able to replace the job losses of traditional industries especially as there may be a discrepancy between the geographical location of the two.

There are a number of explanations suggested for de-industrialisation some of which take an optimistic view of its possible consequences and some a pessimistic view. For example:

1. The decline of large-scale manufacturing industry and its replacement by more specialist manufacturing and services is a natural stage in the development of industrialised society.
2. The decline in manufacturing is short term and reversible when world market conditions improve.
3. The decline in manufacturing is a long term and possibly irreversible trend which has deepened throughout the twentieth century. The decline has been caused by the failure of firms to invest, of the City to provide risk capital, and of governments to give proper support through planning and other measures. In recent years this latter point has been reinforced by a government guided by Monetarist principles, entailing a reliance on market forces with a minimum of public intervention. Those who propose this explanation of Britain's industrial decline advocate a large programme of public intervention particularly public investment to regenerate British industry.

When considering the changes which have occurred in industrial structure attention should be paid to the international aspects mentioned earlier. The role of multi-national companies is of particular importance since they are able to move resources between countries.

In the late 1980s dispute has arisen about whether the increased support for market forces has improved the performance of UK industry. Evidence in support of this claim is provided by Monetarists, although Keynesians and other critics feel the evidence is inaccurate and ambiguous. This question will be considered further in Chapter 7.

Market structure

As previously defined, market structure studies the extent of competition or monopoly in an industry or in the economy as a whole. This is closely linked with previous material on the market system and the firm in Chapters 3 and 4. Under this heading the basic methods of classifying market structure will be reiterated and the mechanisms by which market structure changes will be examined. Given that British industry has been characterised by an increasing degree of monopoly over the years, it is necessary to examine the reasons for this, and in particular the role played by the firms' objectives (as discussed in Chapter 4) in bringing this about.

There are two methods of classifying market structures. Firstly the neo-classical method describes four special cases of market structure which range from perfect competition to monopoly. Secondly, the degree of monopoly method measures variations from perfect competition based on the mark up of price on basic cost.

There are various mechanisms whereby the market structure of a particular industry may change over time. These mechanisms have mainly been used to increase the degree of monopoly in a particular industry. Once a degree of monopoly has been achieved, barriers to entry (see Chapter 3) may be set up to maintain this position.

The mechanisms by which the degree of monopoly is increased, (that is, competition reduced), will be considered mainly, although it should be recognised that it is possible to increase competition by new firms entering the market. A similar effect may be achieved when overseas competition is introduced.

The mechanisms by which the market structure of an industry becomes more monopolised (or concentrated, as it is often called) may depend on changes in market conditions. However, mainly to be considered here are changes based on the actions of firms, including the following:

1. internal growth
2. mergers
3. takeovers
4. diversification
5. consortia.

Internal growth

This occurs when a successful firm expands either by ploughing back its profits into the business, or by acquiring capital through loans or sales of shares.

Mergers

These occur when two or more firms agree to combine into one firm with the hope of improving their joint performance. Quite often there may be a prime mover or senior partner in the merger, seeking the assets of a 'junior' firm. Assets might be physical (land, buildings and machinery), human (a skilled workforce), or intangible (goodwill or brand names).

Takeovers

These differ from mergers in that they are usually contested. In this situation the 'senior' firm bids for the shares of the 'junior' firm. The directors of the junior firm advise the shareholders not to sell. It is probable that the attraction will be the physical or intangible rather than the human assets of the firm, because following a successful takeover, the senior staff of the firm taken over would probably resign.

Mergers and takeovers can occur in either the horizontal or vertical dimension of an industry. Horizontal integration occurs when firms at the same stage of the industrial process amalgamate, for example two brick makers or two housebuilders. Vertical integration occurs when firms at different stages of the industrial process amalgamate, for example if a brick maker takes over a housebuilder.

Diversification

This occurs when a firm expands into a different sphere of activity from that in which it is currently engaged. For example, a brick manufacturer may diversify into road haulage. In some instances diversification may increase competition, as although the main objective is to increase the power of the firm, this action may also have the effect of introducing new entrants into some other market.

Consortia

This is a more informal arrangement where two or more firms enter into an association short of merger. Such an arrangement might be for a particular one-off purpose, or on a more long term basis. Examples exist in the construction industry and will be considered in Part 3 Application L.

Undoubtedly many UK industries have become increasingly monopolised over the years, usually by means of the mechanisms mentioned above. Not only have some industries become dominated by a few firms, but also there has been a polarisation between sizes of firms in some industries at different stages of an industrial process. For example, the construction industry of the immediate post war period was characterised by large numbers of medium sized general builders. Today there are relatively few very large firms, and a large number of very small firms. The small firms are in strong competition with each other and are often in a sub-contracting relationship with large firms. These large firms have a high degree of monopoly, and can drive a hard bargain with the competitive fringe of sub-contracting firms. Within the construction industry there are core and peripheral firms, a concept first introduced in Chapter 3. It should be recognised however that these core/peripheral relationships are not fixed. In certain market conditions sub-contractors may be in short supply and can drive a hard bargain with main contractors.

Given that there has been a trend towards more monopolised market structures in many industries, it is necessary to consider why this has occurred. As a starting point the objectives of firms (as discussed in Chapter 4) and their influence in changing market structures will be considered. In addition it can be seen how other factors such as public policy may also have influenced the situation.

Firms' objectives and changing market structure

As discussed in Chapter 4, the overriding objective of the firm, to ensure long term survival, is profitability. The formula for profitability (see Chapter 4) is:

$$\text{profit} = \text{revenue from sales} - \text{costs of production,}$$

or $P = R - C$

It was seen that revenue and costs are two independent variables. Any action which the firm takes would be designed to increase revenues, and/or reduce costs.

Therefore the factors changing market structures resulting from the firm's desire to reduce costs and/or increase revenues can be examined.

Market structures and reduced costs

The firm may engage in mechanisms to increase monopoly for the following reasons:

1. To enjoy the benefit of economies of scale. This involves taking advantage of lower costs of production per unit by producing on a larger scale. Where such economies are possible mergers between firms could create larger production facilities.

2. To take advantage of more extensive infrastructure such as transport and communications which make it easier to run a multi-plant firm. Thus lower costs are possible due to factors outside the production process, and consequently are known as external economies of scale (to distinguish from production economies or internal economies of scale as mentioned above).

3. A larger firm using the multi-divisional or M-form structure (see Chapter 4) may set up internal capital markets, reducing transaction costs within the overall firm. This would apply particularly where a firm is diversified and vertically integrated. In such a situation the possibility of 'internal trading' may enable the firm to take advantage of different tax regimes in different countries.

4. A vertically integrated firm may be able to ensure its supplies of raw materials or components which may otherwise be expensive or even unobtainable in certain circumstances.

111

Market structures and increased revenues

There are a number of revenue advantages which may accrue to a firm if it seeks to increase its size by engaging in mergers and takeovers. These could increase revenues either directly or indirectly.

1. In simple terms a firm would increase its market power by amalgamating with competitors, because the conditions for increased degree of monopoly and larger mark up of price on cost would be improved. The degree of monopoly will be increased because there will be fewer firms in the market, making it easier to have some kind of collusive arrangement on prices.
2. Diversified firms in particular would be better able to spread risks and not be so reliant on a single market.
3. A diversified or vertically integrated firm may have the possibility of 'tie-in' sales. For example, car components would have to be purchased from the car manufacturers, who are thus able to increase their revenues.

Public policy and changing market structure

The generally accepted feeling is that monopoly power is not desirable for society as it enables firms to increase prices, restrict output and exploit consumers. Competition is believed to lead to reduced prices, more efficiency, and more choice for the consumer (see Chapter 3).

However matters are not quite so simple. It has been seen that the firm is motivated to increase in size in order to increase profits. This may be done by either increasing revenues or reducing costs.

In the case of increasing revenues this is without doubt undesirable for society because the firm is increasing its profits without contributing anything to society in terms of reduced prices, or more efficient use of resources. However in the case of reduced costs there may well be a benefit to society in certain circumstances. For example:

1. If a firm grows larger to take advantage of economies of scale, the resulting reduced costs could to some extent be passed on to consumers as reduced prices. This might even result in lower prices than would be possible under

more competitive conditions. This is because smaller (competitive) firms could not take advantage of economies of scale and would therefore have to produce at a higher cost.

2. Larger more powerful firms may be better able to compete in a world-wide market. This could benefit the country in terms of export performance and balance of payments.

For these reasons mergers have not always been seen as undesirable. Indeed there have been times when governments have encouraged them as a way of rationalising industries. Mergers have also been promoted as a way of making better use of resources and giving strength in export markets. A further possible advantage of mergers is to ensure the survival of a home-based industry where the existing smaller firms could not compete with overseas giants. However with the trend towards large multi-national, multi-divisional firms (see Chapter 4) there must be some doubt whether governments can exercise enough control over them to achieve these benefits for their country's economy.

Summary

This chapter has progressed from the basic microeconomic process to consider wider aspects of industry. This can be thought of as groups of related microeconomic processes. Before examining industry, even wider aspects of the national and international economy were briefly mentioned. Some of these will be studied further in subsequent chapters.

The study of industry involves defining an industry, industrial structure, market structure, and examining how and why these structures change over time. The term industry is used as a convenient way of drawing the boundaries around a collection of horizontally and vertically related microeconomic processes, and forms a basis for collecting data and analysing the performance of aspects of the economy. Since industries overlap considerably the government's Standard Industrial Classification is useful for categorising economic activities.

Industrial structure studies the importance of individual industries, groups of industries and how they relate to each other. It is especially important to know the contribution that particular industries or sectors make to matters such as output, employment and exports. It is also important to know how this changes over time. In the case of the UK the de-industrialisation debate is of current concern. Some of the reasons why the decline in traditional manufacturing industry should be viewed with concern were debated.

Market structure studies the extent of competition or monopoly in an industry, sector or the economy as a whole. It was seen that there are various mechanisms through which market structure may change, notably through internal growth, mergers, takeovers, diversification and consortia. The trend of most industries has been towards greater concentration. The main reasons for change can be traced to the objective of the firm to make a profit. Since profit results from revenues minus costs, it can be expected that firms will engage in mergers and takeovers where there is a prospect of either increasing revenues, and/or reducing costs. The attitude of public policy to mergers and takeovers is ambiguous. Although monopoly power is generally considered to be undesirable, there may be advantages to society in certain circumstances through economies of scale and increased strength in export markets.

This chapter has mainly used the microeconomic method and drew heavily on previous chapters, especially Chapter 3, the market system, and Chapter 4, the firm. In the next chapter the national economy, or the economy as a whole, will be examined mainly using macro methods.

Tutorial questions

1. What impact is a single European market likely to have on the structure of the UK construction industry?
2. Does the decline in traditional UK manufacturing industry matter?
3. To what extent can the construction industry be described as monopolistic?

6

The national economy

Introduction

As seen in Chapter 5, economic activity can be studied on a number of levels. For example, each firm (and its microeconomic process) is part of an industry, which is part of a national economy, which is part of the international economy.

In Chapter 5 consideration was mainly given to the study of economic activity at the level of industry. In this chapter the main area of study will be the national economy. Until now the microeconomic method has been used which takes a 'bottom up' view. However this method is too complicated to use for the economy as a whole. Instead use is made of the macroeconomic method which takes an overall or 'top downwards' view. For this reason a study of the national economy is often called macroeconomics. However it must be emphasised that macro and micro are two methods of studying aspects of the economy. As far as the UK economy is concerned, macroeconomics bases its methods on studying markets as does microeconomics. But whereas microeconomics studies individual markets and firms, macroeconomics studies the behaviour of markets and firms at a broader or aggregate level. To understand macroeconomic problems it is often necessary to use microeconomic methods. For example, the macroproblem of unemployment is often analysed using a microapproach to the labour market.

The chapter will be in several parts:

Firstly, the various problems which are generally regarded as being macroeconomics will be identified and explained.

Secondly, a diagrammatic representation or model of the economy which can be used as a basis for analysis will be developed.

Thirdly, it will be shown how the level of economic activity can be measured and presented in national accounts.

115

Fourthly, the question of how the economy works will be considered. This will necessitate a study of macroeconomic analysis involving consideration of alternative theoretical views about how the economy behaves.

Problems of macroeconomics

There are a number of problem areas associated with the study of the national economy. Many of these relate to aspects of microeconomics already considered. In identifying these macro problems comparison will be made with the equivalent microproblem.

Total resource usage

This concerns the extent to which the economy is making use of the total resources at its disposal. The comparable microeconomic problem is the allocation of resources among different activities (mainly achieved through the market mechanism). The resources, or factors of production, are land, labour and capital. Measures of total resource usage are usually based on these factors, for example, the total level of employment; the amount of capacity (capital) utilisation. It is obviously difficult to measure the extent to which land, plant, machinery and buildings are being used, therefore the resource most frequently measured is labour. For this reason the state of the economy is often defined in terms of the numbers unemployed. Full employment is considered to be desirable whilst high unemployment is considered undesirable. Most of the theoretical models of the economy take unemployment as the most significant bench mark of economic health, and many policy discussions are on the subject of unemployment — both its level and structural composition. Unemployment will be considered further in Chapter 7.

Overall price level

Whereas microeconomics is concerned with the structure of relative prices between all products on the market, macroeconomics is concerned with the overall price level, often defined in terms of the level of inflation. Inflation is defined as the rate of increase in the general price level. It is measured by

116

taking a typical 'basket of goods' and measuring the increase in price over a given period. Thus it is a measure of average price increase. As the basket of goods represents the consumption of an 'average family' it can be seen that the inflation rate is only a crude average. This is one reason why inflation is considered to be such a problem. Given that the rate is an average, it can mask wide variations, with some items increasing much more than, and some items much less than, the rate of inflation. The price information which buyers and sellers receive becomes confused. As seen in Chapter 3 this can be a problem, because there must be perfect information on which to make rational decisions if the market is to function properly. Since inflation undermines the fundamental operation of the market system by interfering with the flow of information, it can be seen that a government which believes in the efficiency of market forces would consider the control of inflation as a priority.

A related problem is one of unfairness as inflation may affect certain groups of people disproportionately. For example the average family will not include pensioners, single parents and others who may spend more of their income on items such as food, energy and transport, all of which may have risen faster than the average rate of inflation.

Distribution of income

Whereas microeconomics is mainly concerned with the distribution of income between different occupations and industries, macroeconomics is concerned with the distribution between the large income classes. Two of the most important are wages and profits. One of the main reasons why the distribution between these two classes is so important is that profits are theoretically one of the main sources of funds for industry. Firms making profits are able to plough them back into the business and expand. A government anxious to make the market economy operate more effectively would be keen to ensure that profit levels were high enough for firms to reinvest. The higher the level of wages in the economy as a whole, then generally speaking the lower will be the level of profit and investment.

It is assumed that firms do in fact use high profits for reinvestment purposes. However this may not be the case as high profits may be used for other purposes including:

1. higher dividends to shareholders
2. mergers and takeovers
3. overseas investment
4. property speculation
5. higher cash reserves.

The problem of distribution of income between wages and profits is of course highly influenced by politics.

Broad allocation of resources

The allocation of limited resources among all the competing uses is a microeconomic problem. At the macrolevel resources are allocated between two broad areas of usage, namely:

1. consumption goods, and
2. capital (or investment) goods.

Consumption goods are directly used by consumers and contribute to the current standard of living. Capital goods include plant, machinery, factory buildings and infrastructure, and represent an investment for the future in that the benefits to consumers occur later. This fits the general principle of investment, that is giving up something now in exchange for something greater in the future. Individuals have to make decisions of this kind, for example deciding whether to have a holiday, or save for a deposit on a house. Firms also have to decide whether to reinvest profits in new plant or provide the owners (shareholders) with a higher standard of living. Similarly the country as a whole has to decide the proportion of its resources that should be used to boost current consumption and the proportion that should be invested for greater benefit in the future. In a market economy it may be difficult to co-ordinate such decisions. Governments may attempt to achieve their decided objectives through taxation and public expenditure. Countries need to make these decisions continually, but sometimes a significant event may put the issue into sharp focus. An example was the discovery of North Sea oil in the 1970s.

Growth of productive capacity

Most politicians and economists advocate economic growth. This is the capacity of the economy to produce more and therefore

118

increase standards of living. It relates closely to the last problem in that the key to growth would appear to be investment. If more resources are used to build up the capital stock of the economy, the standard of living will be higher in the future even if there is some reduction now.

However there is an argument against growth *per se*. It includes the associated problems of environmental pollution, the depletion of natural resources, and the long term issues first identified in Chapter 1. It is also argued that not all growth contributes to a higher standard of living. Growth through defence spending is often quoted as an example of this. This question of growth will reappear in Chapter 7, when considering long term policy measures.

Effect of international trade

The UK has an open economy (as stated in Chapter 5). Approximately one-third of production is exported, and one-third of what is used is imported. Therefore the UK is more dependent on trade than countries such as the USA and France which are more self-sufficient. The international trade position can have a substantial impact on aspects of the domestic economy such as employment and prices.

The main problem areas of macroeconomics have now been identified. Each of these will subsequently re-appear. In particular the issue of unemployment is frequently taken as the bench mark of economic health in the economy as a whole.

Modelling the economy

As already seen, the use of diagrams to illustrate economic concepts (for example, the microeconomic process and the market model) can be helpful. Such diagrammatic models are used as a basis for analysis and explanation. To facilitate the study of macroeconomics use is similarly made of a model. This is usually referred to as the **circular flow of income**.

In building up a model of the whole economy it must first be remembered that the UK has a market economy. This emphasises yet again that micro and macro can be thought of as two ways of looking at the same topic. Whereas microeconomics studies individual markets or groups of markets, macroeconomics studies markets at an aggregate level. In other words instead of examining buyers and sellers of a particular product, buyers and sellers as a whole are considered, that is, as major economic roles or groups within the whole economy.

In macroeconomics these roles are:

1. Buyers who represent the demand side of the economy, and are called **households**.
2. Sellers who represent the supply side of the economy, and are called **firms**.

They are shown in Fig. 6.1.

Fig. 6.1   Buyers and sellers in the national economy

In Fig. 6.1, the box 'F' represents firms as a whole, and the box 'H' represents households as a whole. The relationships between 'F' and 'H', (that is, between all firms on the one hand, and all households on the other) will now be considered.

In a market economy, there are three sets of market relationships between firms and households — two of these are direct, and one is indirect.

The two direct relationships are:

1. Members of households sell their labour services to firms in exchange for income (Y). This occurs through the **labour market**.
2. Firms sell their products to households in exchange for consumption expenditure (C). This occurs through the **goods market**.

In addition, an indirect relationship between firms and households exists. Households may not spend all their income, but may undertake some savings (S). Similarly, firms may need more money than they receive directly from households in the form of consumption expenditure. For example they may require funds for investment (I) in plant and machinery. The answer is that firms pay households for the use of that part of their income which they do not wish to spend at the present time. Firms and households are 'introduced' for this purpose through the intermediary of financial institutions such as banks or the Stock Exchange, who collect householders' savings and advance them

120

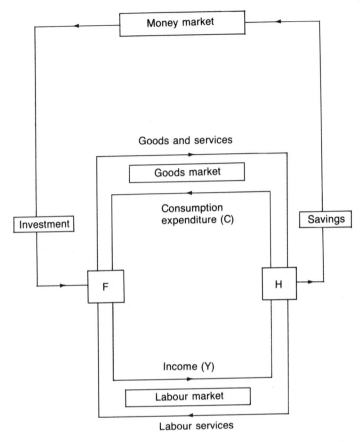

Fig. 6.2 The private sector of a market economy

to firms. These financial institutions are collectively known as the **money market** or **capital market** and represent a third, albeit indirect, relationship between firms and households.

These three market relationships are illustrated diagrammatically in Fig. 6.2.

Figure 6.2 illustrates the market relationships between firms and households and represents the **private sector** of the economy. However to show a more complete picture of the economy two other sectors must be taken into account:

1. the public sector
2. the international trade sector.

The public sector

This covers the activities of public bodies such as central and local government. These activities are shown on the diagram by allowing for taxation (T) as a leakage out of the main flow in the same way as savings, and by allowing for government expenditure (G) as an injection into the main flow, in the same way as investment. However it should be noted that G could exceed T. In these circumstances the government may borrow households' savings to meet the deficit. Thus the government may also enter the money market to raise money, normally by selling gilt edge stock, or bonds, as they are usually called.

The international trade sector

This covers the transactions which occur between residents or organisations in the UK, and those outside the UK. They are shown on the diagram by a leakage of imports (M) from the main flow, and an injection of exports (X) into the main flow. A great deal of international trade is financed through financial institutions, thus the international sector is also involved in the money market.

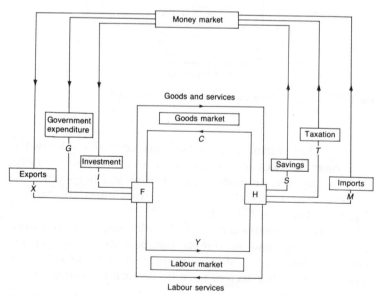

Fig. 6.3 The national economy with private, public, and international trade sectors

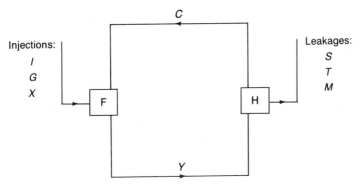

Fig. 6.4   Circular flow of income

The whole economy consisting of the private, public, and international sectors is shown in Fig. 6.3. Normally this model is simplified to show only the flows of monetary variables, as illustrated in Fig. 6.4. This diagram or model is normally referred to as the circular flow of income and is used as a basis for macroeconomic analysis.

The national accounts

The circular flow of income shows the main components of the economy. Since it is of value to be able to measure the size of the economy, a system of national income accounting exists. A variety of terms are used to define and measure the size of the economy. These include National Income, Gross or Net National Product, Gross or Net Domestic Product. Each of these measures the size of the economy. However they will differ slightly because the items included vary.

In principle, the size of the economy is measured by totalling the economic activity. As might be expected measurements of this kind are difficult to make. To overcome this difficulty attempts are made to break into the circular flow of income at various points, see Fig. 6.5.

As Fig. 6.5 shows, there are three points at which total activity can be measured:

1.   by production
2.   by income
3.   by expenditure.

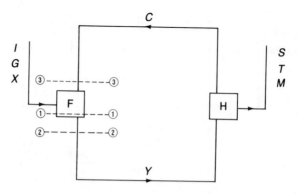

Fig. 6.5 Measuring the size of the economy

By production

This totals the value of production of all firms, classified by industry. An allowance is made for the fact that many firms produce intermediate goods. This was previously explained when considering the vertical dimensions of an industry. To avoid double counting of production only the *value added* for each firm is included. Thus the contribution made by the brick manufacturer to national product is the value of the bricks produced less the value of the inputs.

By income

This totals the various incomes in the economy. The main categories of income are obtained from:

1. employment
2. self employment
3. profits
4. rent.

Initially the profit figure is usually measured gross, but an allowance is made for depreciation (a figure set aside for replacing capital equipment which has worn out) to give a net figure.

By expenditure

Broadly this includes the various categories of aggregate demand as shown on the circular flow of income diagram. It includes:

124

1. consumption expenditure
2. investment by firms
3. public expenditure
4. exports.

Various adjustments are made to allow for depreciation.

Theoretically each of these three measures should be identical. However differences occur in practice due to the various methods of statistical collection and the adjustments which are made. There is therefore considerable debate about whether these sets of statistics are reliable.

Macroeconomic analysis

The problems of macroeconomics have now been identified and the way in which the economy as a whole is modelled and measured has also been explained. Now for the controversial part — how does the economy actually work? If the market economy is left to operate on its own, will it behave well or will it require a measure of public intervention to modify or replace it? The answers to these questions are of great importance and are the subject of considerable debate. This is to be expected given the three schools of economic thought previously identified. The remainder of this chapter will consider some of the theories which seek to explain how the market economy as a whole operates. In the next chapter consideration will be given to the public policy measures which flow from these theories.

To facilitate the analysis, reference is made to the circular flow of income (see Fig. 6.4). This shows the various components of the economy. The section relating to national accounts explained that the expenditure flowing into firms should equal the volume of production, which in turn should equal income. If this is taken a stage further, it can be said that this also reflects the amount of economic activity, and hence the amount of employment available in the economy. In macroeconomic analysis the total expenditure $(C + I + G + X)$ is usually referred to as **aggregate demand**. It is aggregate demand that determines the level of employment. Any changes in the level of aggregate demand will lead to a change in the level of employment at least in the short term, because as previously mentioned labour is the resource which can be varied most easily. Thus the level of Y in the circular flow model is considered to be indicative of the level of

125

employment in the short term. Changes in the level of Y lead to changes in the level of employment.

When analysing how the market economy would operate if left to itself two fundamental questions need to be asked.

1. *Will there be a tendency for the economy to be in equilibrium?* The idea of equilibrium has already been encountered in the context of a balanced supply and demand in a market. Now the question to be asked is whether the economy as a whole will be in equilibrium, that is, will all markets be in equilibrium simultaneously? In the context of the circular flow model, equilibrium occurs when leakages $(S + T + M)$ equal injections $(I + G + X)$.

2. *What will be the level of activity in the economy?* This question can be rephrased to ask what will be the level of employment? Although the economy may be in equilibrium, it cannot be assumed that this will be at a level of full employment.

Therefore it is necessary to know whether a market economy will be stable (that is, in equilibrium) and also whether it will make full use of all the resources (that is, give full employment). As a starting point, use can be made of a numerical example which depicts a simple private sector market economy. In this example it is assumed that the ideal position of equilibrium and full employment exists. An imbalance will then be introduced into the system. If the market economy operates as predicted by market theory it should correct itself, regaining equilibrium and full employment. The various schools of thought disagree on this point. Monetarists tend to argue that this occurs, whereas Keynesians and Radicals tend to argue that imbalances are not corrected. The numerical example will be developed in Figs. 6.6, 6.7 and 6.8.

1. Start from a position of equilibrium at full employment with $Y = 1000$, as shown in Fig. 6.6.
2. An imbalance can now be introduced by assuming that households decide to save twenty percent of their incomes. This leads to a reduction in C and hence Y, which as seen results in a reduction in employment in the short term. Income is now 800. Assuming that those households still in work will continue to save twenty percent of their income, S is now 160 (twenty percent

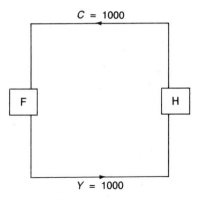

Fig. 6.6   Full employment equilibrium

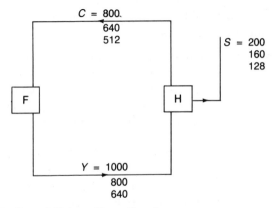

Fig. 6.7   De-stabilising effect of savings

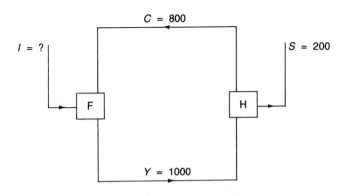

Fig. 6.8   Stabilising effect of investment?

of 800) and C is 640. This appears to result in a downward spiral in C, Y and hence employment as shown in Fig. 6.7.

3. However savings are deposited in banks or other money market institutions (see Fig. 6.2). Firms may borrow these funds for investment purposes, but this raises a problem in that it is not known how much of S will be borrowed by firms as I. See Fig 6.8.

It must be recognised that there are different theoretical answers to questions such as these. Supporters of the free market argue that adjustments take place to ensure that equilibrium is quickly regained in the event of an imbalance. Critics argue that imbalances are not necessarily corrected and may deteriorate. During the twentieth century there have been three broad periods when a particular view has strongly influenced the thinking of UK economic policy makers.

1. The **neo-classical** view predominated until the late 1930s. This consisted of support for the free market with as little public intervention as possible. It was believed that a market economy is generally self-regulating giving equilibrium and full employment if left to operate on its own.

2. The **Keynesian** view dominated from the Second World War until the middle/late 1970s. It was believed that there were severe problems with the free market in that it was not self-regulating and would not give equilibrium and full employment automatically. It was therefore believed that there was a need for substantial public intervention. This resulted in the growth of the mixed economy with a large public sector.

3. The **Monetarist** view has dominated since the mid to late 1970s. This may be seen as the re-establishment of the neo-classical position (in fact the purest kind of Monetarists are referred to as New Classicists). There is still steadfast support for the free market, although some of the views of neo-classicism have been updated.

Many of the current topics debated in both the economics profession and politics divide between Keynesian/Monetarist views, although there is also a significant if minority Radical view. In order to further an understanding of macroeconomic analysis,

128

the views embodied in the three periods above will be examined with reference made to the three macromarkets (that is, labour, goods, and money) described earlier in the chapter.

The neo-classical view

With reference to Fig. 6.8, it will be remembered that there remained the unanswered question of what proportion of S would be taken up as investment (I) by firms and returned to the circular flow. The neo-classical view is that all savings will be invested, thus leakages will always equal injections, and the equilibrium will be maintained. This is explained in terms of the *money market*. If S represents the supply of loanable funds, and I represents the demand for loanable funds, then the price of loanable funds (that is, the rate of interest, r) will balance the market as shown in Fig. 6.9. It is believed that if the market rate of interest fluctuates freely, it will enable S and I to equalise thus ensuring equilibrium.

Another neo-classical approach to equilibrium concerns the analysis of the *goods market*. This is formulated in terms of Say's

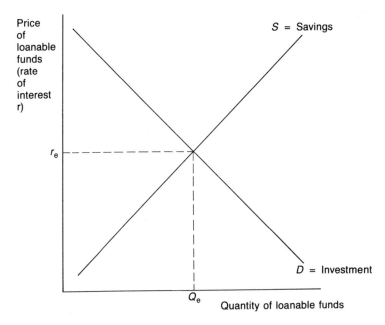

Fig. 6.9 Neo-classical view of the money market

Law, that is, 'supply creates its own demand'. This means that when goods are supplied, people are paid to produce them. This gives the overall spending power to buy all the goods back. Hence the goods market will always be in equilibrium because there is always enough income to buy the available goods. Here there is no possibility of insufficient aggregate demand to buy the goods produced.

This explains the neo-classical argument in favour of equilibrium, but does not fully justify the belief that full employment is the normal situation in a free market economy. For this it is necessary to discuss the neo-classical view of the *labour market*. Here the same simple market argument is used in that labour, like any other commodity, has a price or wage at which supply (SL) and demand (DL) will be equalised. This is shown in Fig. 6.10.

In a free labour market as shown in Fig. 6.10 the equilibrium wage (W_e) will ensure employment of (Q_e). This is defined as full employment in that all people prepared to offer themselves for work at the wage of W_e would be employed. In this situation there is only one explanation for unemployment — wages are above the equilibrium at, say, W_1. At W_1, SL exceeds DL

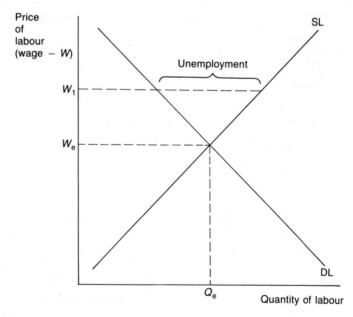

Fig. 6.10   Neo-classical view of the labour market

130

resulting in an excess supply of labour, that is, unemployment. Thus unemployment is explained in terms of wages being excessive, or to use a common political phrase — 'workers are pricing themselves out of jobs'.

The reason why wages are at W_1, rather than W_e, is usually explained in terms of the imperfections in the labour market which prevent wages from falling to the equilibrium. The imperfection most frequently cited is collective bargaining between trade unions and employers. In addition it is claimed that the minimum wage rates laid down by wages councils force firms to pay above the market rate. It is further suggested that high social benefits undermine the desire to work. These matters are obviously of great importance particularly when decisions are made regarding policy. They will be discussed further in Chapter 7, when considering changes in the labour market since the 1980s.

The neo-classical analysis of the labour market is enduring. The modern Monetarist analysis is similar and can be seen in policies which are directed at making the labour market operate as freely as possible.

To summarise, the neo-classical view believes that provided money, goods, and labour markets are allowed to operate freely and without imperfections there will be a tendency towards equilibrium and full employment. The free market economy is thus self-regulating.

The Keynesian view

This view has its origin in the work of John Maynard Keynes who was an economist writing in the 1930s at the time of the economic depression. Keynes was highly critical of the neo-classical view in many fundamental respects. The main conclusion of the Keynesian view is that the free market economy is not self-regulating, and does not guarantee equilibrium and full employment. In fact it is argued that the market economy could be unstable, and even if equilibrium is eventually established, it may be at a point below full employment. In other words whereas neo-classicists argue that there is a tendency to full employment as there is always sufficient aggregate demand in the economy, Keynesians believe there is a real possibility of there being insufficient demand. Keynes believed that the slump of the 1930s was the result not of a passing phase of market imperfection which could be easily corrected, but of the economy having settled into a stable period of deficient aggregate demand and unemployment. For this reason, demand management policy (see Chapter 7) designed to ensure sufficient aggregate demand for full employment, has been used for much of the post-war period. The basis of Keynes's arguments will now be examined, and in particular the neo-classical view of the money and labour markets will be re-appraised.

The neo-classicists ascribed an important role to the rate of interest, claiming that it balanced savings (that is, the supply of) with investment (that is, the demand for) loanable funds (see Fig. 6.9). This view was rejected by Keynes who believed that the rate of interest did not have such a dominating effect.

With regard to savings, these were identified as the residue from income after expenditure on food, shelter and entertainment. The main influence on savings therefore was income. This view was based on the assumption that people would not reduce their consumption in order to take advantage of higher interest rates.

With regard to investment, this was identified as being a long term proposition. Consequently investment was not heavily influenced by short term changes in the rate of interest. Decisions on investment were believed to be mainly influenced by business confidence and expectations of future demand for products.

Since the market for loanable funds would not be balanced by the price there was not necessarily any mechanism for making savings and investment equal. Leakages could therefore exceed injections in the circular flow, and there could be deficient aggregate demand, and persistent unemployment. Indeed this was the problem which Keynes identified in the 1930s, that is, money which was being saved was not being taken up by firms as investment because there was insufficient confidence in the economic future.

This is not to say that the rate of interest does not have an important role in the money market as a whole. It has an important effect on whether wealth is held in the form of money or some other kind of financial or tangible asset. It will also affect the firm's costs, and the cost of mortgages. However its direct effect on the level of investment is more limited.

The Keynesian analysis of the labour market is also substantially different from the neo-classical analysis. In Fig. 6.10 it was seen that unemployment is the result of wages which are fixed above the equilibrium (W_e) at, say, W_1. The neo-classical remedy for restoring full employment would be to reduce wages from W_1

to W_e. As labour was cheaper this would encourage firms to employ more workers. The Keynesian view is that reducing wages has two effects which operate in opposite directions:

1. Wage cuts would indeed reduce the costs of labour and encourage individual firms to employ more workers.

However

2. Wage cuts would also reduce the amount of spending power in the economy as a whole. Aggregate demand would reduce and firms would employ fewer new workers and even lay off existing workers.

There are therefore two effects of wage cuts. On one hand they tend to increase employment but on the other hand they tend to reduce it. Consideration needs to be given to which effect is the stronger. Consideration also needs to be given to whether more people employed at a lower wage will outweigh fewer people employed at a higher wage. The Keynesian argument is that the second effect is stronger, with wage cuts leading to a reduction in employment rather than a reduction in unemployment. The reasons why this second effect is stronger than the first are:

1. The effect is felt first. Firms generally face a reduction in demand before individual firms benefit from lower costs which encourage more employment.
2. The above is accentuated by the **multiplier effect**. This term is used to describe the spillover effect which occurs when there is a change in economic conditions. It is best explained using the example of an urban area. If a factory closes in a town this may result in the loss of, say, 1,000 jobs, and £10 million of income. However the losses are not confined to this. The people who have lost their income will spend less money on local services, such as shops and leisure facilities. This will reduce income still further. The factory itself will stop buying components or other services, which adds another twist to the downward spiral. The ultimate effect on the local economy of a factory closure would extend beyond the initial loss. Of course the multiplier effect can also work in the opposite (positive) direction. A new factory will lead to wealth over and above the employment actually

created. If these mechanisms are applied to the national economy including the effect of wage cuts on employment, it can be argued that lower wages reduce spending power. If the spillover or multiplier effects are also taken into account this will result in a significant drop in aggregate demand.

It is therefore argued that the net effect of wage cuts will be a reduction in the level of employment rather than a restoration of full employment. The overall conclusion of the Keynesian view is that the market economy is not self-regulating, and does not tend towards full employment and equilibrium. Furthermore, attempts to remove imperfections in the labour market by allowing wages to be reduced will do more harm than good. Since the market cannot be relied upon to give the desired result strong public intervention is needed particularly to maintain sufficient levels of aggregate demand to ensure full employment.

This strategy was adopted in the post-war period resulting in an increase in public expenditure and in the size of the public sector. The market played a reduced role in the economy, and it was widely believed that the problem of unemployment had been resolved. However doubts emerged in the 1970s and in due course some of the earlier ideas regarding the economy were re-established by the Monetarists.

The Monetarist view

This view largely restates the neo-classical view. There is an important philosophical basis to Monetarism, namely that the free market is the best way of running the economy, and that the growth of public expenditure and the public sector should be reversed. Monetarism became known initially for its explanation of inflation (to be discussed in Chapter 7). However its support for a range of free market ideas soon became apparent.

As far as the labour market is concerned there is little difference between the views of the neo-classicists and those of the Monetarists. Both groups have a strong belief that excessively high wage levels are the main cause of unemployment and that full employment can be achieved by the removal of the imperfections in the labour market which prevent wages from falling to the market equilibrium.

However an important objective for Monetarists was to

counteract some of the Keynesian views, especially those which justified increased public spending and demand management policies generally.

As previously mentioned the multiplier effect forms part of Keynesian thinking. It has been used, together with increased public expenditure to stimulate aggregate demand and employment. However Monetarists have argued that the multiplier effect has less significance. If this is so, then the justification for public expenditure is reduced. This argument is based on a theory of consumption which claims that people have a perception of long term or **permanent income**. Spending patterns are believed to remain constant over a period of time. Therefore if people lost their jobs, as in the earlier example of the factory closure, this would not result in a large negative multiplier effect because spending would be maintained by, say, relying on savings until further employment was found. Similarly improved circumstances will not result in a large positive multiplier effect because people will be cautious about increasing their expenditure in the short term. One of the weaknesses of this argument is that no account appears to be taken of the reduction in demand by the firm in the earlier example which closes the factory.

In Chapter 7 consideration will be given to more general criticisms of demand management policies.

Summary

This chapter has considered the economy as a whole. The macroeconomic method was used mainly but since this is in the context of the market economy microeconomic methods are still important. Indeed the neo-classical and Monetarist arguments make great use of standard market theory. Having identified problems of macroeconomics, developed a diagrammatic model, and shown how to measure the size of the economy and present it in national accounts, it was possible to analyse how the economy works. It was seen that there are a number of theoretical views regarding this, which basically divide between those who believe the free market economy, if left to itself and with imperfections removed, will give full employment equilibrium, and those who believe that the free market may be unstable and not give full employment, requiring instead a large measure of public intervention to give a mixed economy. The free market view as advocated by neo-classicists prevailed until the late 1930s. It was replaced by the Keynesian view, which supported the mixed economy. This view was generally accepted for much of the post-war period, until challenged by a modern free market view known as Monetarism. This has gained wide acceptance in both political and academic circles. Some of the alternative theoretical arguments have been discussed in this chapter although it has been restricted to the main argument relating to full employment, without considering questions such as inflation. This will be studied in the following chapter, together with consideration of the implications of alternative policies.

Tutorial questions

1. What are the implications of reducing the proportion of the nation's resources expended on investment?
2. Is the only reason for unemployment that wages are too high in some sectors of the economy?
3. Explain how the decision to open a new vehicle manufacturing plant in a town would lead to an increase in prosperity?

7

Policy issues

Introduction

It has been a constant theme in this book that the UK economy operates mainly through the use of the market system although there are substantial areas of public intervention. In the previous chapter it was seen that there are *two* conventional theoretical approaches to solving the problems of the economy:

1. *To improve the economy by increasing public intervention.* Advocates of this approach believe that the free market is a defective mechanism which will tend to result in unemployment, wasted resources, and damaging long term effects such as 'de-industrialisation'. The solution therefore is seen to be a mixed economy with a substantial public sector.
2. *To improve the economy by allowing the free market to operate more efficiently than in the past.* The solution would be public policy measures to remove impediments or imperfections which prevent the market from working in accordance with market theory, as discussed in Chapter 3.

Both of these approaches have been used by governments. The first approach (that is, Keynesian) was used for most of the post war period by both Labour and Conservative governments until 1979. The Conservative government elected at that time then utilised Monetarism. The year 1979 is often regarded as the beginning of Monetarist policy, but it can be argued that similar policies were introduced under the previous Labour government. This suggests that there had been a general rejection of Keynesian policies, largely because it was believed that they led to inflation.

This chapter will firstly consider policy objectives for the economy as a whole. Governments generally have targets in respect of these objectives. The nature of post-war economic policy will then be examined, including the instruments of policy which were used to achieve the objectives of Keynesian demand management. The associated problems of demand management will also be considered leading to the beginning of the Monetarist period in the late 1970s. Finally, the UK economy into the 1990s will be examined.

While many of the principles explained in this book will remain valid for the foreseeable future, it must be pointed out that ideas on policy issues are liable to change. Therefore it is suggested that the reader keeps closely in touch with developments in the economy. The financial pages of quality newspapers provide the most up to date and accessible information.

Objectives of macroeconomic policy

These correspond closely to the problems of macroeconomics discussed in Chapter 6, and include the following.

Full employment

This is used as the main indicator of total resource usage as well as being a social and political objective.

Stable prices

This is the absence of inflation. The presence of inflation has the detrimental effect of distorting the price mechanism. It is also considered unfair to those on fixed incomes. Furthermore, inflation makes UK goods more expensive and therefore less competitive with imported goods.

Distribution of income

This refers to the division of income between wages and profits. It is often argued that profits are the main source of re-investment in the economy, and that a sufficient proportion of national income should be distributed as profits to encourage this re-investment. However this should be tempered by the need for fairness in the distribution of income.

A suitable allocation of resources

In a macro context this allocation is between consumption goods (which improve current standards of living) and capital goods (which improve future standards of living).

Economic growth

The ability of the economy to produce more as time passes is considered to be the key to higher standards of living and consequently this tends to be a policy objective of all governments.

Healthy balance of payments

This is the ability of Britain to 'pay its way' in the world by exporting at least as many goods as it imports. Balance of payments problems can have a detrimental effect on the internal domestic economy as will be seen later in the chapter.

Post-war economic policy

During the post-war period when Keynesian influence was strong, a number of **instruments of policy** were used to attain the objectives outlined above. The predominant objective was full employment and it was believed that the key to this was to ensure sufficient aggregate demand. Consequently these measures came to be known as **demand management** policy instruments. They included:

1. fiscal policy
2. monetary policy
3. incomes policy
4. exchange rate policy
5. announcements.

Fiscal policy

This is basically budgetary policy. It is indicated on the circular flow diagram (Fig. 6.4) as a leakage T, and injection G. If G exceeds T there is a budget deficit. This has an expansionary effect on the economy, which is accentuated by the multiplier as described in Chapter 6. If expansionary fiscal policy is used over a number of years, public spending and the size of the public sector tends to grow.

Monetary policy

This type of policy is less interventionist since it operates in a more anonymous way through financial markets. It concerns the availability and price of money and credit. The availability of money is called the money supply (Ms) and the price is the rate of interest (r). The policy of controlling Ms was scarcely used in the Keynesian period, although control was exercised over certain types of credit such as hire purchase. In general, monetary policy was regarded as a support to fiscal policy.

Since the late 1970s monetary policy has become more widely used, especially as many believe there is a link between the total Ms and the rate of inflation. Since the late 1980s the role of interest rates has received a great deal of attention, and this will be considered later in the chapter.

Incomes policy

This attempted to intervene directly in the process of setting prices and incomes either by the use of legislation, or simply by government exhortation. Incomes policy has been tried by many governments, with the objective of relating pay increases to productivity increases. By relating pay to productivity no inflationary pressure is generated. Incomes policy often entails the setting of a pay norm. However it suffers from the major drawback that in an economy where incomes are determined by a mixture of market forces and collective bargaining, direct intervention 'goes against the grain'. Despite past failures, many believe an incomes policy is the only way to control inflation without high unemployment.

Exchange rate policy

This is designed to control the balance of payments and to correct deficits. The exchange rate is the value of the pound against other currencies, and it determines the relative prices of UK and overseas goods. If the pound reduces in value (that is, devaluation) then UK goods will be cheaper, encouraging exports, and overseas goods will be more expensive, discouraging imports. Imports can also be restricted by the use of import controls, which may reduce imports either by increasing their price, or by physically limiting the amount of imports entering the country. An area of discussion has been whether the exchange rate should be fixed or floating. The advantage of the latter is that the value of the pound automatically changes in accordance with market forces and therefore requires no further attention. However the disadvantage of a floating rate is that it is more liable to attract currency speculation. Exchange rate policy is increasingly seen as being closely linked to interest rate policy, with both having an important impact on domestic inflation and unemployment as well as on the balance of payments. This will be considered later in the chapter.

Announcements

It could be argued that this is not really an instrument of policy. However announcements are useful in that they affect the psychology of economic actors. Announcements can be thought of as optimistic statements made by politicians which attempt to influence behaviour. For example, a statement that inflation is being reduced and that investment is rising may encourage people to behave in a certain way thus making it a self-fulfilling prophecy.

Problems of demand management

As previously mentioned, demand management gave rise to a number of problems. These led to demand management becoming less popular, and certainly since 1979 the government has used alternative policies. The problems of demand management will now be considered.

The nature of unemployment

Demand management assumes that unemployment is essentially the result of demand deficiency, that is, lack of aggregate demand. However there are other causes of unemployment.

Unemployables
This refers to those people who are unable or unwilling to work for some reason.

Frictional unemployment

This is temporary unemployment due to workers being between jobs or temporarily laid-off.

Structural unemployment

This is a more serious kind of unemployment which arises when there is a mismatch of supply and demand in the labour market. Two common types of structural unemployment are:

1. *Regional unemployment*, where there may be plenty of workers available in certain places, but insufficient firms to employ them.
2. *Inappropriate skills*, where workers are unemployed because they do not have the skills which local employers require.

The main feature of these categories of unemployment is that traditional demand management cannot reduce them. Modern Keynesians argue that public expenditure may solve the problem of structural unemployment, but such expenditure would need to be more carefully directed than in the past. For example expenditure on education and training, regional policy and infrastructure has been suggested.

Technical problems of 'fine tuning'

During the Keynesian period attempts were made to tune the economy to keep it exactly at the level of full employment. This proved extremely difficult to achieve as conditions were constantly changing and the information and data on which policy makers based their decisions was already out of date. Attempts to fine tune the economy led to continual changes in policies which left firms and consumers confused, and reduced their confidence to act. This form of demand management was discredited and is no longer advocated. It is now recognised that the information on which policy is based is inaccurate and out of date, and must be treated with caution.

Deficit financing

Demand management in the UK involved a strong fiscal policy with high levels of public spending, and substantial budget deficits. These deficits were financed using one of three methods.

Borrowing

Money is borrowed by selling gilt edged stock or bonds through the money market (as shown in Fig. 6.3). As previously mentioned, the government competes for the same funds as firms in the private sector. Critics argue that there is a danger of increasing interest rates and 'crowding out' private firms.

'Printing' money

The government expands the amount of credit in the system to pay for its own expenditure. This action has the possible danger of causing inflationary pressure.

Asset sales

This has been used in the privatisation programme since the early 1980s. It has been criticised for, among other reasons, reducing government debt by a once for all sale of irreplaceable assets at low prices.

It can be seen therefore that each method of deficit financing has associated problems.

Balance of payments problems

These problems occur because certain implications arise when attempting to operate the economy at full employment. Full employment gives high income which leads to high spending power and aggregate demand. If UK firms cannot increase supply quickly enough (and full employment implies there will be few labour resources to draw on) then one consequence will be higher levels of imports being drawn in, causing a balance of payments deficit. To counteract this it may be necessary to reduce activity in the economy and relieve the pressure on imports. This was common in the 1950s.

Over time 'import penetration' has continued and more manufactured goods (both consumer and capital goods) are now imported than exported. This represents a substantial change in the traditional role of the UK as a strong manufacturing producer and exporter. Consideration will be given later in the chapter to the problems of the UK balance of payments, particularly the ability of UK industry to increase supply in response to increased demand. The components of the balance of payments, particularly the current account and capital flows, will also be examined.

Inflation problems

Inflation has been seen as one of the main consequences of demand management attempts to secure full employment. This problem is similar to the problem of balance of payments in that when there is full employment and high aggregate demand firms may be unable to quickly increase their supply to meet this demand. The result is that in addition to increasing imports, much of this spending power may be dissipated in inflation. This inflation is due to excess demand, and is often called 'demand pull' inflation. An alternative source of inflation occurs through increased costs of production. These cost pressures include wages rising faster than productivity, increases in world commodity prices, or a fall in the value of the pound. This type is known as 'cost push' inflation.

It has been seen that inflation causes problems in the operation of the price mechanism. This is particularly acute when contracts are made and prices are fixed for a period in advance, for example when bargaining for wages in the coming year. In such cases the anticipated level of inflation will form part of the bargaining process. If these allowances for inflation are agreed as part of the settlement, inflation will inevitably occur.

At one time it was believed that inflation could be 'traded off' against unemployment. If unemployment was high it could be reduced by increasing the rate of inflation. This has proved to be incorrect. If inflation is increased economic actors (consumers and firms) may temporarily think that they *specifically* are better off and so they will increase activity thus leading to more expenditure, employment and output. However after a while it is realised that there is actually a *general* inflation in progress. Therefore they are no better off and will revert to previous behaviour. Thus the introduction of inflation has at best only reduced unemployment temporarily. The problem with trying to use inflation to reduce unemployment is that although the benefits are temporary, the higher level of inflation remains because people have adjusted their behaviour to a new level of inflationary expectations.

Policies to counteract inflation vary between controlling the money supply, cutting government expenditure and introducing incomes policies. The first two policies are regarded as Monetarist remedies and may lead to increased levels of unemployment. Incomes policies are associated with Keynesians. Despite past failures these policies still command support because they are considered preferable to high unemployment.

Summary of problems of demand management

In a market economy, these problems are mainly concerned with attempts to balance supply and demand at an aggregate or macro level. With reference to the circular flow of income diagram (see Fig. 6.4), it can be seen that the aggregate demand in the economy is comprised of the following categories:

1. consumption (C)
2. investment (I)
3. government expenditure (G)
4. exports (X)

while aggregate supply is the total production of firms within the box 'F'.

Whenever demand in a category exceeds supply there is a problem, usually manifested as a balance of payments deficit and/or inflation.

Excess demand in the consumption category is probably the most common. This may occur due to a boost in incomes through, say, reductions in taxation and/or lower interest rates which encourage increased borrowing. If supply can be increased sufficiently to meet the extra demand then all will be well. However supply may well lag demand, since supply tends to be inelastic relative to demand. In such a situation people will not be able to use their increased spending power on consumption with UK firms. Instead, this spending power may:

1. be spent on imports of foreign goods, causing a balance of payments deficit and/or
2. be dissipated into rising prices. This may be inflation of a general nature, or it may be concentrated into specific areas such as the housing market.

Similar arguments apply to the other categories of aggregate demand. Excess demand for investment goods leads to imports of, and/or increases in prices of, plant, machinery and building products. Excess demand for exports which cannot be met by UK firms will probably result in a loss of business to overseas competitors with possible balance of payments problems in the future. Increased government expenditure could lead to higher

145

levels of imports, but it is more likely to cause inflationary pressure due to higher borrowing competing interest rates upwards.

The problems of demand management defined above were particularly associated with the post-war era of Keynesian policy. However it is possible that similar problems will continue even though Monetarism has been the dominant philosophy since 1979. The next task is to examine the state of the UK economy into the 1990s in the light of policy possibilities.

The UK economy and policy into the 1990s

In the past, economic policy has often been studied in terms of macro measures (dealing with the economy as a whole), and micro measures (dealing with parts of the economy such as industries, markets and firms). For example, the first part of this chapter was mainly concerned with the objectives of macroeconomic policy. This macro/micro distinction has become less useful in the 1980s because the main argument centres around the use or otherwise of market forces, as stated in the introduction to this chapter. In fact as emphasised in Chapter 1 microeconomics and macroeconomics are really two ways of looking at the same sorts of problems.

In studying economic policy into the 1990s a useful distinction can be drawn between those policies which have *short term objectives* such as stabilising the economy, and those which have *long term objectives* such as improving the efficiency of the economy. This short/long term distinction is a useful starting point, but should not be over-emphasised since short term changes may have long term implications.

Before considering each of these policies in turn the broad changes in direction of policy should be outlined. As mentioned in the introduction to this chapter, the period since the late 1970s has seen the replacement of Keynesianism by Monetarism as the dominating philosophy. This has entailed a move away from a mixed economy with a large public sector to one which is much more market orientated and with a smaller public sector. The main aim of policy remains an efficient economy, but attempts to achieve this have been through pursuing different objectives. Under Monetarism the *two main objectives* have been:

1. *The elimination of inflation*, based on the belief that for the market economy to operate effectively, the

146

conditions for perfect competition must be present as far as possible (this was explained in Chapter 3). The major problem with inflation is that it distorts the price mechanism and undermines the knowledge of the market by both producers and consumers. This reduces their ability to make rational decisions. Inflation must therefore be eliminated if the economy is to prosper. This is a departure from the Keynesian philosophy which believed that market imperfections could be solved by public intervention, and that full employment should be the priority objective.

2. *The revival of the market economy*, based on the belief that this is the most efficient way to organise economic activity. This involves a number of measures designed to make the market operate more effectively. Many of these measures have long term significance which change the basis on which the economy is run.

In addition to changes in objectives there have also been *changes in the mechanisms used* to control the economy. A range of policy instruments outlined earlier in the chapter were used in the Keynesian period. However many of these, especially expansionary fiscal policies and incomes policies, are not compatible with Monetarism since they involve more intervention in the market. The main policy on exchange rates has been to allow the value of the pound to float. This leaves monetary policy as the only active measure substantially used. In the early 1980s efforts were made to control the quantity of money in circulation (that is, the money supply), but towards the end of the 1980s the interest rate (that is, the price of money) emerged as the primary instrument of control under Monetarism.

The short term and long term aspects of policy can now be considered.

Short term policy measures

As mentioned above, of the objectives of policy discussed earlier in the chapter, the elimination of inflation has been the primary Monetarist target since 1979, replacing the earlier Keynesian priority of full employment. Also as mentioned above, the rate of interest has emerged as the primary instrument of economic policy.

However the objective of short term economic policy remains

essentially the same, that is to have economic resources working as fully and effectively as possible, (for example full employment), without causing inflationary pressure, balance of payments difficulties, or problems for industry. This has always been a difficult balancing act. In the 1950s and 1960s the main problem was that attempts to achieve full employment tended to cause balance of payments problems, while in the 1970s inflation emerged as a significant problem. It has also been argued that the growth of public intervention during the Keynesian mixed economy period has led to problems for industry such as inefficiency, overmanning and the pre-emption of resources by the public sector. In the 1980s unemployment increased substantially while inflation appeared to be brought under control. The balance of payments remained healthy during much of the 1980s although some believe that this was mainly due to revenues generated by North Sea oil.

Towards the end of the 1980s it appeared that unemployment, although still high, may have passed its peak. However some detected signs of inflation and balance of payments pressures reappearing. On the industrial front, or supply side, many believed that there had been significant improvements in the productivity and performance of industry, particularly in manufacturing. This will be further examined later under long term policy measures.

To understand these trends it must be realised that the economy is a complicated set of mechanisms with a complex web of inter-relationships between the many economic variables. It has been emphasised at various points in this book that there is considerable disagreement between economists and policy makers on the nature of these relationships. Just as the earlier part of this chapter considered short term policy in the post-war period from the point of view of Keynesianism as the dominant philosophy of the time, so policy into the 1990s will initially be analysed from the point of view of Monetarism.

As previously mentioned, the main instrument of short term control to have emerged in the late 1980s was the rate of interest. The way forward is to examine the way in which interest rates affect the economy. Their effect on the components of aggregate demand (as depicted in the circular flow of income model — see Fig. 6.4) will be examined. This will encompass consideration of wider issues such as effects on the balance of payments, inflation and industry.

Interest rates and consumption

This is related to the effect of interest rates on savings. In simple terms the amount a consumer saves will not be spent. The inclination to save will therefore affect consumption. However the willingness and ability of consumers to borrow in order to finance consumption is also important. In conventional economic theory it is expected that low interest rates (that is low price of money) would encourage consumption (especially with borrowed money) while high interest rates would have the opposite effect.

If this is correct, low interest rates which lead to high borrowing could have certain adverse effects:

1. A high demand for consumer goods which may not be met by UK industry. This may lead to an increase in imports and/or inflationary pressure.
2. The ability to borrow more may have a similar effect to raising income. This may tend to increase expenditure on and hence demand for housing. Since the supply of housing relative to demand is inelastic (see Chapter 3 including Fig. 3.9), prices will increase. The macro effect of such a situation is a booming housing market which could have adverse consequences such as inflationary pressure; deterring first time buyers from entering the housing market; preventing the mobility of labour due to different levels of housing costs in different parts of the country.

Alternatively, high borrowing and consumption may have a beneficial effect on the economy if UK industry (the supply side of the economy) is able to increase production to meet demand. However, it should be noted that increasing demand through lower interest rates (or through other measures such as tax cuts) is easier and takes effect more quickly than trying to increase the supply through measures designed to increase productivity and output.

The effect of interest rates on consumption, as predicted by economic theory, has been explained above. It is now necessary to consider whether this applies to the UK. For example if there is a borrowing-induced consumption boom which results in increased imports, inflationary pressure, and booming house prices, is this boom likely to be curbed by higher interest rates? Economic theory suggests that high interest rates mean a high price of borrowing. This will lead to less demand for borrowing and consequently less consumption. However certain changes may have occurred since the 1970s which may have made this mechanism ineffective.

1. Many people tended to reduce their savings in the 1970s because high inflation was constantly eroding them. This encouraged spending instead.

2. High inflation resulted in high **nominal** rates of interest (the **real** rates were relatively low after inflation had been deducted). It would seem that people have become accustomed to high nominal rates.

3. It is possible that people may not respond with perfect knowledge to rates of interest, and are prepared to pay higher rates provided they can afford the repayments.

4. The availability of credit has greatly expanded in terms of both quantity and source. For example housing finance was once dominated by building societies who lent under strict guidelines. There is now a plethora of institutions not only willing to lend but whose conditions are more relaxed.

5. Even if high interest rates could curb house price rises and inflationary pressures, it is possible that UK consumers have developed a taste for foreign goods which would be difficult to reverse.

If the above points represent a long term or permanent change in the behaviour of UK consumers, then higher interest rates may not solve the problem. However, Monetarists disagree with this analysis and believe that the economy can only maintain a certain level of borrowing (that is, there is an upper limit to the amount of borrowing which will take place). Therefore if the rate of interest (the price of money and credit) were to rise high enough, borrowing would slow down and savings would begin to increase. This would reduce the excessive consumption which had resulted in high levels of imports and inflationary pressure. The Monetarists have therefore continued their support for the market mechanism, by saying that all will be well when the correct price of money and credit (the rate of interest) is found. Even if this is true it would appear that the increase in interest rates necessary to curb consumption is greater than previously thought.

Interest rates and investment

In theory lower interest rates should lead to more investment and vice versa. This is because the rate of interest is the price firms pay to borrow money for investment purposes. If the cost of borrowing is cheaper more investment will become profitable. If interest rates rise the cost is higher and less investment becomes profitable. By the same analysis interest rates affect the other costs of the firm. For example, if firms need overdraft facilities to maintain liquidity (see Chapter 4) high interest rates increase costs and low rates reduce them.

The link between the rate of interest and the level of investment is not clear. The Keynesian argument (explained in Chapter 6) that investment is primarily a matter of long term confidence is widely accepted. Monetarists argue similarly along the lines that confidence in the market economy is the path to high investment and output.

Even if the rate of interest does affect investment, it would only affect the *demand* for investment. If the rate of interest fell the cost of borrowing for each firm would fall and the incentive to invest would increase. However if every firm tried to do this the macro effect would be problems on the supply side. Industries producing investment goods (including much of the construction industry together with manufacturers of machine tools and commercial vehicles) would be unable to meet the demand. There would be long delays, increased prices (such as rapidly rising tender prices for construction contracts) and any benefit obtained from lower interest rates could easily be nullified.

It would seem that a policy of raising or lowering interest rates would have limited effect on investment, although it could have considerable effect on the other costs of firms and hence the performance of industry.

Interest rates and government expenditure

If interest rates rise it will cost government more to borrow from the money markets to finance its expenditure (see Chapter 6 including Fig. 6.3). This problem is often put the other way round by Monetarists. That is, a high level of government borrowing and expenditure tends to compete with the private sector for funds. The effects are that not only is the private sector starved

151

of funds (or 'crowded out'), but also the rates of interest are competed upwards. Monetarists further argue that a high level of government borrowing and expenditure was mainly responsible for increasing inflation in the post-war period. It can therefore be argued that rather than interest rates affecting government expenditure, it is a question of government expenditure affecting interest rates. This is one reason why the Monetarist government since 1979 has reduced government borrowing and expenditure.

Keynesians do not agree that government expenditure necessarily leads to higher interest rates and inflation. They argue that the right kind of government expenditure (such as investment in infrastructure) will have a beneficial multiplier effect (see Chapter 6) which will boost the economy. Furthermore, it is argued that there is no guarantee that funds not borrowed and spent by the public sector will be utilised by the private sector.

Interest rates and exports

It has already been seen that interest rates affect consumption and hence imports. To understand the effect of interest rates on exports it is appropriate to widen the discussion into consideration of the balance of payments in general. This will add to what has already been considered in Chapter 6 and earlier in this chapter.

The terms imports and exports cover a variety of items including tangible or visible goods, and intangible or invisible services such as tourism, banking, shipping and insurance. Visible and invisible trade, together with net income from abroad on investments, form the **current account** of the balance of payments. When a country is said to have a balance of payments problem it often means a persistent deficit on the current account. In the case of the UK this has generally meant a high level of imports, not only of consumer goods as already explained, but also of investment or capital goods such as plant and machinery.

The balance of payments must balance. This is necessary because anything bought from abroad has to be paid for in the currency of the supplying country (Dollars, Deutschmarks, Francs, or whatever), and anything bought from the UK must be paid for in Sterling. If the UK has a current account deficit, overseas currencies must be obtained in order to pay for the extra imported goods. These funds can be obtained from a variety of sources:

1. Reserves held by the Bank of England may be used.
2. Borrowing from overseas financial institutions or the International Monetary Fund (IMF) may take place.
3. Overseas firms may invest capital funds in the UK through new factories or offices
4. Overseas residents may save in the UK by placing funds with financial institutions in the money market.

Funds obtained from each of these sources would have the same accounting effect of making the balance of payments account balance, but not all are equally desirable. If the financing of deficits is by the inflows of long term capital investment funds, this may be desirable because it promotes economic growth and employment in the UK. For this reason Monetarists often argue that the balance of payments problems which have emerged since the late 1980s are not such a problem. However if the capital flows are short term investments in financial assets, this 'hot money' may simply be seeking a quick return and is just as likely to be withdrawn with no long term benefit to the UK economy. Keynesians tend to argue that because of the nature of the City as a financial centre, the UK gets a high proportion of 'hot money' rather than long term capital investment.

It has been seen how interest rates affect consumption and imports. Interest rates also have an effect on exports, defined as flows of money into the economy. Visible exports are affected differently from the financial flow type of exports. To explain this the effects of increased interest rates will be examined. If interest rates in the UK rise this makes it an attractive location for short term funds. Money may be placed in government bonds, in bank accounts or in any other interest bearing financial asset. It was mentioned earlier in this chapter (under exchange rate policy) that the rate of interest affects the exchange rate which in turn affects the balance of payments and the domestic economy. In the context of this discussion, when rises in interest rates induce flows of 'hot money' into the UK, the exchange rate (or value of the pound) tends to increase. This is because overseas residents have to exchange their currencies for Sterling, thus increasing the demand for Sterling on the foreign exchange markets, which in turn increases the value of the pound. The effect of this on exports is unfavourable because a higher value of the pound means that the prices of UK goods increases and exporters find it more difficult to sell their goods abroad.

This is a double blow to the balance of payments. A higher exchange rate means not only more expensive UK goods, but cheaper overseas goods which encourage even more imports. However there is some benefit because since the UK imports so many raw materials, food and consumer goods, the lower the price of these imports, the lower is inflationary pressure in the economy. Since the main policy objective of the government since 1979 has been the elimination of inflation, interest rates have been increased whenever it was considered necessary. This has reduced inflationary pressure through the mechanism of higher exchange rates and lower prices of imported goods. However the disadvantage has been higher prices of UK goods leading to fewer export sales and the consequent factory closures and higher unemployment in UK industry. Monetarists argue that this has been beneficial in that it has enforced more competition and made UK industry ultimately more efficient. However critics argue that efficient as well as inefficient firms have been forced out of business by excessively high exchange rates especially in the early 1980s. This issue will be taken up again under long term policy measures.

Summarising the effects of short term policy measures

This is not easy. The elimination of inflation has been the prime Monetarist objective since 1979, based on the belief that for a market economy to work effectively, in something like the manner predicted by market theory, stable prices together with the better knowledge and more rational decision making which results, are essential. The fiscal aim of the government has been to achieve a broadly balanced budget (see description of fiscal policy earlier in this chapter). The main policy instrument used has been monetary policy particularly the rate of interest. The effect of the interest rate on the various components of the economy has been examined. During the 1980s the government frequently found itself increasing interest rates. This may have been to increase the value of the pound and reduce inflationary pressure. Alternatively, it may have been to try to stem the expansion of borrowing and consumption, and reduce the expansion of imports and relieve the pressure on inflationary items such as house prices. Critics of the government argue that sole reliance on high interest rates to control inflation and the level of imports has a detrimental effect on industry because it

154

leads to exporting difficulties, higher costs and probably less investment. This results in loss of output, and rising unemployment. The long term effect on industry of short term measures such as high interest rates is of course contentious and needs to be examined.

Long term policy measures

The distinction between short term and long term policy measures is by no means straightforward. The previous examination of short term measures revealed a number of long term effects. For example, Monetarists believe that the essential reason for short term use of interest rates to control inflation is also in the best long term interests of the economy.

In the long term, the majority of economists and policy makers advocate economic growth (first explained in Chapter 6) as the main objective. Economic growth entails the ability of the economy to increase production and it is believed that here lies the key to higher standards of living for consumers (and the re-election of the government for another term of office!). Growth is measured by increases in the size of the National Product (see 'The national accounts' in Chapter 6).

Before considering how growth evolves, a note of caution must be added. The pursuit of growth does not receive universal support. Many argue that increases in National Product do not always add directly to the standard of living for consumers, with spending on armaments often quoted as an example. Furthermore, many point to the risks of environmental pollution, urban congestion, and the depletion of natural resources. Monetarists argue that market forces will control matters such as the discovery and exploitation of resources, although others express doubt about this. It was argued in Chapter 1 that the market being primarily a short term mechanism, does not easily take account of long term factors.

Notwithstanding these reservations, economic growth has undoubtedly been the main long term objective of governments. The overall growth rate is measured in the national accounts by use of statistics such as the Gross Domestic Product (GDP). However it is the means by which growth is achieved which presents the problem. The requirement is for the more efficient use of more and better quality resources.

Ultimately economic growth is dependent on industry's ability to perform more effectively. It is often referred to as the **supply side** problem.

At the beginning of this chapter it was shown that two approaches to economic policy, including the achievement of growth, have been used. These approaches were based on alternative theoretical views of the economy. Until 1979 the Keynesian mixed economy view prevailed. This entailed a high degree of public intervention in the market, including measures to improve the supply side through policies such as public ownership and financial support to industry. Since 1979 the policy has been more market orientated. This will now be examined further.

As previously mentioned, the two main policy objectives of the Monetarist government since 1979 have been the elimination of inflation and the revival of the market economy. The latter concerns the long term objective of improving the supply side of the economy. It is characterised by measures which are designed to *make the market work better*. An important aim of this has been to change the broad distribution of income in the economy. As mentioned in Chapter 6 and in the first part of this chapter, the main division of total income is between wages for labour, and profit for capital. Monetarists believe that profit is the main source of investment, and is vital if the economy is to grow. Measures to improve the profitability of firms have therefore been a priority since 1979. A convenient way of examining the policies which have been adopted to try to improve the effectiveness of the market uses the context of the three macro markets identified in Chapter 6, under 'Modelling the economy'. These are the *labour market, goods market and capital market*. Measures which have been introduced will be examined under these headings. Some criticisms will be considered later.

Changes in the labour market

There have been widespread changes, many designed to 'free' the labour market. Monetarists believe that the problem of the post-war labour market was that there was too much emphasis on collective bargaining rather than on the individual contract between employer and employee. This is claimed to have had the effect of suppressing profits through:

1. raising wages above the market equilibrium, causing high costs to the firm and unemployment (as explained in Chapter 6 — 'The neo-classical view'); and
2. enforcing restrictive labour practices which reduced productivity growth and increased costs (discussed in the context of the individual firm in Chapter 4 — 'Choose appropriate production methods').

A number of policy measures have been introduced to influence the labour market. These vary in effect. Some are aimed at the individual; some at collective relationships; some at wider aspects of the labour market such as the mobility of labour. In short the government has attempted to make the labour market as close as possible to the model depicted by market theory (see Chapter 3), and to alleviate the problems of rising wages and static productivity mentioned above.

Among the policy measures are:

1. Changes in the tax system including cuts in income tax designed to act as an incentive to work harder.
2. Changes which encourage mobility of labour in terms of location and skill. Thus the government claims to have made it easier to change location (due to the expansion of home ownership), and to improve skills by education and retraining opportunities.
3. Encouragement of self employment which is regarded as an incentive to work and an aid to mobility of labour.
4. Reduction in the powers of wages councils and other bodies which may have set minimum wages (possibly above the market equilibrium) in certain industries.
5. A major shift in emphasis away from collective bargaining, particularly in matters affecting productivity. Legislation has been introduced which has changed the balance of power between employers and workers (including trade unions).
6. Pay settlements in the public sector which have been more in line with market forces of supply and demand rather than comparability with the private sector.

Changes in the goods market

The most significant change has been the transfer of activity from the public to the private sector, a process normally called **privatisation**. There are two aspects to privatisation:

1. deregulation
2. change of ownership.

Deregulation

This means that particular economic activities are no longer restricted by anything other than market forces of supply and demand. For example, fares on public transport may no longer be fixed; public sector organisations may be allowed to borrow capital anywhere in the market instead of being subject to strict controls.

Change of ownership

This applies where ownership changes from the public to the private sector.

Most privatisations since the beginning of the 1980s have involved both these aspects, but they need not go together. It is quite possible to deregulate public sector firms or industries and make them subject to market forces without selling them to the private sector. Indeed in many cases deregulation has preceded sale.

A number of parts of the economy have been subject to privatisation including the following.

1. Public utilities such as gas and telephones which are natural monopolies (see Chapter 3 — 'Technological barriers').
2. Other public corporations which may previously have been nationalised for various reasons, such as industrial rationalisation. Examples include Jaguar and the National Freight Corporation.
3. Services within otherwise public organisations. These services have been sub-contracted out to the private sector. Examples include the cleaning and catering services in hospitals and schools.

The main reason for privatisation, according to Monetarists, is that the benefits of the market system (see Chapter 3) will be more readily attainable. These include wider consumer choice and efficiency in the allocation and use of resources.

In addition to privatisation, changes have been encouraged in the private sector. For most of the post-war period there has been a competition policy, or anti-monopolies policy, to encourage competition in industry and prevent the harmful effects of monopoly such as increased prices. This has continued, under the auspices of the Office of Fair Trading, and the Monopolies and Mergers Commission. There has also been the stated philosophy of encouraging the growth of small businesses, this being an extension of the self employment policy previously mentioned.

Changes in the capital market

These too have been substantial, and have included:

1. The abolition of exchange controls allowing funds to flow freely in and out of the country.
2. Abolition of controls on credit such as hire purchase and bank lending.
3. Encouraging wider share ownership, partly through making it easier for small investors to buy shares through the privatisation issues.
4. Allowing building societies to have a much wider role. Whereas before they could only lend out in mortgages what they had received in savings, they are now able to borrow from the money markets and lend more widely. They now compete with banks on the provision of a wide range of financial services.
5. Ensuring international competition in the Stock Exchange, and making the City even more of a financial centre. This process was known as the 'Big Bang'. The main aim of changes in the capital market has been to open the market to more competition and to ensure that capital will be available to firms and individuals who require it.

Criticisms

The changes in the three macro markets have now been considered. As expected, many of the arguments used by the government to justify these long term policy measures have been contested. Among the criticisms are the following:

1. There is some doubt about the basic premise that

increased profitability of firms results in investment and growth (see Chapter 6 — 'Distribution of income').

2. Collective bargaining should not be discouraged because if operated effectively it makes for greater co-operation in industry.

3. There is some doubt that tax cuts increase incentives significantly. It is possible to argue that lower tax rates give a higher income which means that *less* work is required to maintain current standards of living.

4. In theory, home ownership gives an asset which makes it easier to move to a different part of the country. In practice, the widely different levels of house prices could prevent mobility, since movement from cheaper to more expensive areas would not be possible, and movement the other way may not occur through fear of being unable to move back if required.

5. The training programmes introduced have been insufficiently financed and of poor quality.

6. Reducing the powers of wages councils removes protection from low-paid workers who cannot defend themselves. This is unjust.

7. There is some doubt whether there has been a fundamental change in the labour market. Wage pressures may be reduced while inflation is under control, but they could easily increase as soon as inflation reappears. This is accentuated by the shortages of especially skilled or 'core' workers in certain locations. Such workers found little difficulty in obtaining wage rises throughout the 1980s and what has possibly emerged is a two-tier labour market of core and peripheral workers (a concept introduced in Chapter 4).

8. There is some doubt about whether privatisation has really achieved the benefits of better consumer choice and more efficiency. Some critics argue that privatisation is completely misguided. Others argue that deregulation may help to achieve the benefits of competition, but that change of ownership is undesirable. This is because change from public to private ownership in itself does nothing to aid efficiency, and that it is in any case unfair because of the amount of taxpayers' money which has been invested in public corporations. This is particularly relevant where shares are offered at low prices designed to ensure sale.

9. Where services are contracted out and the most competitive tender secures the contract, this may suppress the wages of people operating the services, which is unfair. In such circumstances the quality of the service might also suffer.

10. There may be some moral or political objection to allowing control of public monopoly utilities to be in private hands.

11. While much has been done to force competition in the public sector, little has been done in the private sector. Critics argue that the government has been too ready to assume that any firm in the private sector is self evidently competitive and efficient. This ignores the monopoly power of multi-national companies.

12. The relaxation of exchange controls has encouraged speculative dealings in currencies which have led to rapid inflows and outflows of 'hot money' which destabilise the UK economy.

13. The general relaxation of controls in capital markets has greatly increased the ease of obtaining finance. This expanded consumer borrowing, leading to higher imports, a house price boom and inflationary pressure. Subsequently, very high real interest rates were required to 'cool' the economy.

This has been a long list of criticisms to set beside the arguments in favour of the government's long term economic policy. In the end the overriding debate centres on whether the encouragement of market forces will achieve the objectives. Since the Monetarist government believes they will, they advocate policies which match. Critics do not have the same belief in the market and advocate alternatives. These range from adjustments to the market of various Keynesian persuasions through to more radical transformation of the economy which relegates the market to a minor role.

Summary

Approaches to economic policy vary according to the view held on the value of market forces in organising economic activity. This difference was highlighted at the beginning of this chapter. Indeed it has been stressed throughout the book. Firstly consideration was given to the economic policy as practised in the post-war period up until the late 1970s. This was principally Keynesian demand management, and its study included the objectives of macroeconomic policy; the instruments of policy; and finally the problems encountered in operating demand management. The main problems to emerge were the apparent incompatability between full employment on the one hand and stable prices and a healthy balance of payments on the other. The 1980s witnessed a break from the past with the emphasis on market forces as embodied in the Monetarist philosophy. A wide range of short term and long term economic policies were considered along with some criticisms. There is wide disagreement on whether the policies since 1979 have improved the supply side of the economy as the government has claimed. The conclusion to be drawn is that the type of policy advocated depends mainly on one's view of the working of the economy, and that this is subject to social and political beliefs as well as economic. The reader was advised of this at the beginning of the book. The reader is also reminded that ideas on policy are subject to change and that efforts should be made to keep up to date.

Finally, many policies affect the built environment although they have not been particularly drawn out in this chapter. In recent years increasing attention has been paid to the inner cities as well as to the continuing problem of regional imbalance. Consequently policies on land use and economic development in these locations have been debated and advocated. To a large extent they fit into the general debate on policy as discussed in this chapter. They will be considered separately in various applications in Part 3.

Tutorial questions

1. What can be done to make incomes policies more successful than in the past?
2. Could full employment ever become the first priority objective of government once again?
3. Do high interest rates have a significant effect on consumption expenditure?
4. To what extent have labour market policies since 1979 affected the costs of firms?

Part 3

Applications of economic principles to the development of the built environment

Introduction to Part 3

This final part examines some specific areas of economic decision making related to the development of the built environment. Some of these areas will be considered for the first time, whereas others, first introduced in Part 1, will receive further consideration in the light of the knowledge gained from studying economic principles in Part 2. In all instances reference will be made where appropriate to the principles of economics studied in Part 2. The reader is encouraged to make use of the Carbury case study material introduced in Part 1.

The general five stage framework for developing the built environment was introduced in Part 1, that is:

1. identification of urban and building need
2. decision to build
3. design of buildings
4. construction of buildings
5. occupation and use of buildings.

Whilst this framework is still useful, it will become apparent when considering the various applications in Part 3, that the stages have permeable boundaries, and that the same economic principles may be applied to a number of stages. For example, the objectives of the firm, studied in detail in Chapter 4, appear to have most relevance when considering construction firms in stage 4. However it is equally true that most clients are also firms. Indeed, a growing number of clients are in the business of providing buildings for others and are 'producing' a product for the market like any other firm. It can therefore be seen that the economic principles appropriate to the firm are just as relevant at stage 2 — the decision to build.

Nevertheless, many of the 14 applications to be discussed are particularly related to one or other of the stages. For example Applications A, B, C, D and E relate to stage 1; F, G and H relate to stage 2; I relates to stage 3; J, K, L and M relate to stage 4; N relates to stage 5.

The applications can be briefly summarised as follows:

Application A considers the allocation of land uses, starting with the use of market forces, and progressing to examine the need for public intervention.

Application B highlights the particular characteristics of land, some of which were identified in Application A. Land values will receive some consideration.

Application C continues the land use theme, placing particular emphasis on the problems associated with inner cities and their regeneration. The regional aspect of this problem is also examined.

Applications D and E consider two specific areas of urban need, namely housing and transport, which were first introduced in Chapter 3.

Application F re-examines the reasons why clients build, and focuses particularly on the emergence of the professional client, that is, one who provides buildings for others to occupy and use.

Application G considers the way in which the client's team is organised to meet the objectives. In particular, the role of the builder and the method of engagement will be examined.

Application H considers the ways in which a client assesses the viability and feasibility of a particular project. In many cases, this involves regarding a building as a long term investment asset.

Application I considers the economics of design, particularly the need to ensure that the design develops in accordance with the objectives of the client.

Application J considers the construction industry as an economic force. The various resources which the industry requires are examined.

Application K considers in general terms the control of costs during the construction phase, including the liquidity or cash flow problem. This is examined from the point of view of both client and contractor.

Application L considers the strategy of the construction firm towards its present and potential future markets. This includes an examination of the expansion of the firm over time and its inclination to become a developer.

Application M considers the nature and development of production methods in building, and the way in which these compare to other industries. The importance of productivity is emphasised.

Application N considers the economic factors related to the life of the building.

Application A

Markets for land uses

Introduction

The allocation of land to the various possible uses is a fundamental problem in the first stage of developing the built environment, that is, the identification of urban and building need. As already discussed, decisions on the allocation of resources in the UK economy are usually based on market forces which are amended or replaced by public intervention where appropriate. This application will firstly consider the way in which market forces should ideally work in the allocation of land uses. Secondly, it will show how the operation of the market in practice differs from the theoretical model. This will highlight the need for public intervention to ensure the suitable development of land. At the same time it must be ensured that the development permitted will be sufficiently profitable to encourage clients and developers to use the land available. Thus it becomes clear that the allocation of land has to balance the public interest as a whole, and the private interest of individuals and organisations such as clients and developers.

To understand the question of land allocation, the specific problems of the market and the resulting need for public intervention will be examined. Following this, some solutions to the land allocation problem will be considered. These range from the use of traditional planning procedures to partnership schemes. In the next application an examination of the special features relating to land will be undertaken, and in the following application inner city land use will be considered.

The market in theory and practice

The market model was explained in detail in Chapter 3 and shown diagrammatically in Fig. 3.4. The essence of this theory is that the supply of and demand for land (or anything else) should balance at an equilibrium point, and that this should occur in a perfectly competitive market thus ensuring that members of society, that is, consumers, get the best possible deal. The operation of the free market ensures consumer sovereignty, and the efficient allocation and use of resources.

The general problems of this theory were also discussed in Chapter 3, together with the specific problems related to markets in the built environment. The most notable feature of such markets was the inelastic supply of land relative to demand. This was shown diagrammatically in Fig. 3.8. It was shown that land is inelastic in supply partly because of its quantitative physical limitations, and partly because of the time taken to bring land into use. There is little that can be done about the former problem, but solutions to the latter could include faster construction methods or streamlined planning procedures. These will be considered later.

In the event of the market situation shown in Fig. 3.8 occurring, the smooth market adjustments of price and quantity shown in Fig. 3.4 will not take place. Instead there are two possibilities:

1. Adjustment will take place in an extreme fashion along the *price axis*. An example was shown in Fig. 3.9 where an increase in demand for housing, and hence housing land, was met, not by a smooth and modest price adjustment, but by *escalating prices*.
2. If escalating prices are insufficient to 'balance' the market, or where no market price exists, a reaction may occur along the *quantity axis*. This may take the form of *overcrowding* and dilution of quality. The example given in Chapter 3 was road congestion.

The practical problem of land allocation

Given that the theory and practice of the market for land allocation do not coincide, there appears to be a need for public intervention to modify market forces. Suggestions as to the extent of such intervention will vary according to the schools of thought, ranging from minimal planning through to nationalisation of all development land. In this latter case all development could be carried out by public sector bodies, taking it completely outside the scope of market forces. However if it is assumed that at least a proportion of development is carried out by the private sector, *the essential practical problem of land allocation becomes balancing the public and the private interest.*

The public interest

This seeks to achieve an allocation of land use and development which results in the type, quantity and quality of buildings, infrastructure and open space which society requires. Of course the public interest is not always easy to determine. These decisions are normally entrusted to elected bodies and officers at central and local government level. However this does not give a definitive answer since conflict could occur between central and local government.

The private interest

This seeks to achieve the objectives of the client or developer, first considered in Part 1. This will be re-examined in application F. If the client's objective is to build for social gain there should be little difference between public and private interests. However if the objective is to build for financial gain these interests may be distinctly different.

The balance between public and private interests may be difficult to achieve, but various solutions are possible. Before discussing these solutions, the specific problems of a free market in land allocation will be considered.

Problems of a market for land uses

Many of the problems which occur in markets concerned with the allocation of land uses are similar to the problems of markets generally. Many of these problems were discussed in Chapter 3, particularly market imperfections. In addition reference was also made to other problems which included distribution (or fairness) and externalities. These will now be considered.

Market imperfections

An imperfection prevents a market from behaving perfectly in accordance with market theory. In practical terms this means that smooth price and quantity adjustments in the market are not likely. As already seen, the results could be escalating prices, and/or congestion and dilution of quality.

The special features of land as a resource including its imperfections will be further examined in the next application, but some of these will be mentioned here.

1. Land is inelastic in supply both in terms of its fixed quantity and immobility as to change of use.
2. There may be a temptation to hold land speculatively rather than develop it, in the expectation that its value will increase further.
3. Each parcel of land or site forms part of a particular environment. Successful development may depend on the simultaneous development of a number of sites. For example, a private client would be unlikely to develop a single site in a derelict area of an inner city if the remainder of the area is left unimproved.

Distribution issues

This concerns the effort to ensure a fair distribution of land uses, where all the needs of the members of society are met as far as possible. In a free market for land uses, demand may be such that the price may be so expensive that even modest housing could be outside the range of some people. Other consequences of a free market and high price of land include the lack of provision of open space, and the lack of amenities and services such as leisure, education and health in convenient or central locations.

Externalities

It was first mentioned in Chapter 1 that markets and market prices may not take account of all the social costs which are generated by some economic activities conducted through the market. Externalities can be thought of as a *divergence between private and social costs*. The magnitude of such externalities can be measured in terms of the resources which are required to be expended in nullifying their effects. A conventional analysis of externalities will follow using the example from Chapter 1 of a chemical plant discharging its waste into the river. The effect of this can be shown as in Fig. A.1.

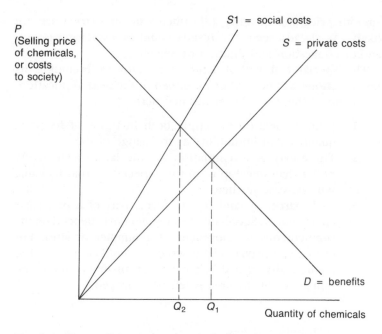

Fig. A.1 Externalities and a chemical plant

In Fig. A.1 the quantity axis measures the quantity of chemicals produced; the price axis measures the price at which chemicals are sold and the costs imposed on society; the demand curve D measures how much chemical would be bought at different prices and can therefore be regarded as a measure of the benefits expected. It is therefore equivalent to **social benefits**; the supply curve S measures how much the chemical firm would be willing to supply at different prices. This is mainly dependent on the costs of production and so the supply curve is a measure of the firm's **private costs**; the curve S_1 shows the total costs to society, that is **social costs**, generated by chemical production, including the cost of pollution. Thus as production increases, so the divergence between private and social cost increases. In conventional economic analysis the objective should be not to ban chemical production because this loses too much in benefits. Instead the target should be to reduce production from Q_1, which is the amount the chemical firm would choose to produce under market forces (since it balances demand with private costs), to Q_2, the amount which balances demand with social costs. This might be achieved by legal compulsions or financial penalties such as additional taxes per unit of production.

The above analysis, which accepts the possibility of some pollution, is not universally supported. It does not take account of the distribution of costs and benefits. It may be that society as a whole benefits from chemical production, but the costs may be incurred disproportionately by those living near the plant. A similar argument applies to a major project such as a new airport. This may be of benefit to a region of the country, but the costs in terms of noise and disruption will be borne by a smaller number of people living near the airport.

There is also the question of long term environmental damage which is not easily accounted for by the market. Therefore many argue that the way to solve the problems caused by externalities is to enforce safer production methods even if this results in a loss of benefits to society in the short term.

When developing the built environment there are clearly some projects which are potentially capable of generating large social costs or externalities. However there are a number of more commonplace examples which also generate externalities in that they impose costs which have to be borne by someone other than the client, developer or builder. Some examples are:

1. Increasing the population density in an area, for example by converting houses which were originally intended for a single family into several flats. This can put pressure on the existing road space causing traffic congestion and parking problems. It can also put pressure on services and infrastructure such as health care and sewerage, necessitating more provision and higher maintenance costs.

2. A housing development or new factory located near an existing school may mean that extra precautions must be taken by the community to ensure the safety of the children in the light of the hazards caused by the additional traffic.

3. The design of some buildings or the materials used could have a detrimental effect on the community in that people find them unattractive and inconvenient. This may affect the way in which they go about their daily lives. It has also been argued that poor design and/or planning may

cause increased levels of vandalism and other social problems.

Of course externalities are not always undesirable. Many generate social benefits or positive externalities. Just as poor building design may cause social problems, so good building design can reduce them. New infrastructure can generate positive social benefits, a point raised at the beginning of Part 1 in connection with a new transport system. Indeed one of the solutions to the public/private interest conflict when developing the built environment is to encourage private developers to include provision of positive externalities in their proposed schemes. The solutions will now be considered.

Solutions to the land allocation problem

It has been established that the main practical problem of land allocation is to ensure a balance between the public and private interests. It has been shown that since a free market in land uses would cause problems, there is a need for public intervention. Reference to this was first made in Part 1 where it was shown that local authorities generally zone land into various uses. Beyond this basic zoning, local authorities vary in their attitude to intervention. This will depend to some extent on political control. A Conservative controlled council would probably be influenced by Monetarism and allow market forces as much scope as possible. A Labour controlled council may be more radically minded and advocate a wider range of public intervention measures. Some Labour councils or 'hung' or balanced councils may adopt a more Keynesian approach of using public intervention but in the hope that the private sector will play a large role in development. Some of these options will be described.

Traditional town planning

This is sometimes referred to as **negative planning**, negative in the sense that the local authority makes no positive suggestion to the private developer, but simply accepts or rejects a proposed scheme. Of course the developer is not completely uninformed since each site will have a designated use; there may be well known functional or aesthetic design requirements applicable to

174

a locality; an informal discussion with planning officers prior to submission of proposals may be possible.

Local authorities differ in their use of traditional planning procedures with some having a reputation for being 'anti-developer' and some being 'pro-developer'. Whilst they have a duty to act in the interest of those whom they represent, there is growing evidence that central government (Monetarist) policy since the beginning of the 1980s has had the effect of reducing the power of councils to decide matters locally. This is because of the planning appeals procedure. A developer whose application is refused permission at local level can appeal to the appropriate central government department such as the Department of the Environment, or the Welsh Office. The number of such appeals succeeding has increased since the early 1980s.

Replacing the market

There has always been some public sector development outside the scope of market forces. This includes development in connection with the provision of infrastructure, health care, education, sports facilities, cultural facilities, managed open space, public transport. Again local authorities vary in their involvement in these areas. Some will make high provision while others will leave the provision of sports facilities and so on to the private sector.

Some local authorities may wish to go well beyond this provision and be directly involved in the industrial and economic development of their area by building industrial estates and providing financial support to existing or new industry.

In common with other areas of economic activity, central government has required since the beginning of the 1980s that such provision is increasingly met by the private sector, if at all.

Partnerships

During the post-war period there has been some tendency for the private and public sectors to work together. This is sometimes described as an aspect of **positive planning**, positive in the sense that the local authority influences more directly the kind of development which takes place. Since the latter part of the 1980s it has taken on new forms.

The basic principle of partnership is that if conflict exists between private and public interests a solution is to internalise the conflict by a suitable partnership arrangement. In the externalities example discussed earlier, it would mean a merger of interests between the chemical firm and the local authority, who between them would decide on the socially optimum level of production.

On a practical level it must mean that there is some benefit for both the private developer and the public interest. There are certain advantages which a private developer would hope to achieve:

1. That the approvals process, for example the obtaining of planning permission, will be achieved with the minimum of problems and in the minimum amount of time.
2. That the local authority will help by assembling the land required for the proposed scheme, possibly by its use of compulsory purchase powers. This may be necessary in larger schemes where the developer has not been able to acquire all the necessary land by market purchase.
3. That the public sector may have made some contribution to the required infrastructure by not only obtaining the land, but perhaps also by clearing it and putting in roads and other services. This may be a substantial attraction to private developers.

The main advantages for the public sector are:

1. That the community should get the sort of development that it needs.
2. That public money should not be put at risk in some uncertain venture. The risk bearing will be left to the private developer.

Partnerships may take many forms:

1. They may be of a limited **planning gain** type where planning permission is granted in exchange for an undertaking from the developer to fulfil a community need. For example permission for a new office development may be granted on the understanding that the developer also provides a civic theatre, or a public park, or a new link road.
2. They may be more extensive and formalised, say for the building of a new shopping precinct. The local authority's compulsory purchase powers may well be required, as

176

the developer may be unable to assemble the extensive land required. In addition to the town acquiring a new facility, the local authority may also receive a portion of the rental income, plus of course additional income from rates.

3. Many 'partnerships for urban renewal' are now being formed in some of the older areas of our cities. These will be mentioned again in Application C, and when considering the market strategy of construction firms in Application L.

Summary

This application considered the problems of the allocation of land to various uses. In the UK economy most allocation decisions are left to market forces. Consideration was therefore given to the economic theory of land allocation through the market, and the problems that arise in practice, in particular the potential conflict between the public interest of the community and the private interest of clients. The specific problems of the market for land uses, such as imperfections, distribution issues and externalities were discussed. Finally, some solutions to the problem of land allocation were considered. These included traditional town planning, the replacement of the market with more public intervention, and the use of partnerships between the private and public sectors.

Tutorial questions

1. Is the conversion of large houses into smaller flats a reasonable solution to a housing shortage?
2. Should a factory causing air pollution be closed down?
3. Discuss cases you are familiar with where local authorities and private developers work together.

Application B

Special features of land

Introduction

Obviously land is a fundamental resource or factor of production in developing the built environment. In fact, as discussed, the allocation of the available land between competing uses is the first stage in the framework for developing the built environment. Economic analyses of land often start from the premise that land is a factor of production as described in Chapter 1, and that this determines both its use and value.

However because land is inelastic in supply, as previously discussed, certain other features become important. Of particular interest is the effect that public actions such as planning decisions or infrastructure provision can have on the value of a particular piece of land. The result of this is that the future value of land may be uncertain. In this event land could become the subject of speculation. This might result in land being hoarded rather than made available for development. It might also mean that the price paid for the land is the critical factor which determines whether a particular project may be viable or not. For these reasons it is not possible in a modern context to treat land purely as a factor of production in the traditional sense, although this is a useful starting point.

The traditional view of the economic purpose of land

Land is a factor of production and as such attracts a payment for its use. The payment made for the use of land is called **rent**, just as payment for the use of the factor labour is called **wage**, and payment for the use of the factor capital is called **interest**. The demand for land and hence its price should be a reflection of the demand for the product which is made on the land. There is no

178

demand for land itself. Instead demand for land is a *derived demand*, that is derived from the demand for the product or service produced on the land. Therefore the rent paid for the land and hence its value depends on the value of whatever is produced on the land. The land value is passive and should not in itself significantly affect the product.

The above explains how the rental price for hiring the use of land evolves. But of course land might also be bought and sold, and therefore it has a capital value. This can be calculated as a sum of all the rents accruable to the land in its present use.

A further aspect which affects land values is that of **location**. Values tend to fall as distance from the centre of the town increases. Thus house prices in the suburbs are lower to compensate for the cost and time of travelling to work in the centre. There is clearly some truth in this, partly supported by the fact that road or rail services which improve connections with the centre often lead to higher house prices in the locations affected. However, the theory that land values are affected by the distance from the centre needs modification in the light of inner city decay which is evident.

An alternative view

Land is an active rather than the passive influence described above in developing the built environment. The value of land cannot easily be based on the value of what is produced on the land. In fact it is possible that the value of the land will determine the value or price of the product rather than vice versa.

Because land is inelastic in supply it has scarcity value. Also, as discussed in Part 1, the value of land may largely be determined by public decisions, thus leading to **publicly created land values**. The two major ways in which public actions affect land values are as follows.

Planning decisions

If an area of land is re-designated for residential rather than agricultural use, this will increase its value substantially.

Infrastructure provision

The provision of new roads and other services can increase the value of a site and make it more attractive to a developer. On a larger scale it is recognised that major infrastructure provision can have a great impact on land values through encouraging development. Examples include the development along the London–South Wales M4 corridor; development around the M25; rising house prices in areas where rail services have been improved.

Public influence on land values is substantial but uncertain. For example, there may be pressure for new housing on green field land, but it is not known whether the local authority will agree to this, or if so on which particular sites. Uncertainty of this kind may lead to speculation as to the value of the land. Therefore land becomes desirable in its own right not just as a resource which is useful only if it is farmed or built upon, but also as a potentially profitable **commodity**. In fact if land is a speculative commodity it may be profitable to withhold it from development. This could make the shortage more acute and increase values further.

In many ways land is an ideal commodity for speculation not only because it is inherently short in supply, but also because once acquired it does not incur any costs to maintain in its current condition. By contrast, other resources do incur costs to maintain. For example labour has to be fed and trained, capital has to be repaired, maintained and updated.

When land is acquired for speculative reasons, the normal supply and demand market conditions tend to break down. For example, if prices rise, then rather than the normal response of a reduction in demand, it is quite likely that the stocks of land held will be increased in the expectation of even greater price rises and hence capital gains. Conversely if prices fall, then instead of demand for land increasing, speculators may find it less attractive to acquire land because of falling capital values.

In summary, the alternative view to land being a resource or factor of production is the view of land being a speculative commodity.

The power of land ownership

This power was recognised in the nineteenth century by economists who developed the original idea of **economic rent**. This was defined as the difference between:

180

1. the amount paid for a factor or resource, and
2. the amount necessary to keep that factor or resource in its present use.

Thus for maximum rent, 1 should be high, and 2 should be low. On these criteria land fits the bill well for the following reasons:

1. Since land is inelastic in supply it can command a high price when demand is high.
2. The costs of keeping land intact (as opposed to the buildings which may be situated on it) are low.

Thus the price of land could easily include a large element of economic rent. In a wider sense economic rent can accrue to any of the factors — land, labour and capital. These correspond with the three main income classes. It has already been seen that labour and capital each require a certain level of expenditure to keep them intact:

1. Labour requires food, clothing, shelter, training and the ability and resources to reproduce itself.
2. Capital requires maintenance and an allowance to replace parts which wear out, that is, a depreciation allowance.

By contrast land requires very little to keep it intact.

The implications of this could be far reaching. Given that the economy is capable of creating a certain amount of wealth, then the question of how this wealth is distributed is of great importance. Labour and capital at least require a certain amount of wealth expended on them to keep them intact as has been seen. Beyond this the rest of the wealth created by the economy is a surplus. Alternatively it can be seen as the amount available for economic rent. The argument used in the nineteenth century was that because land was in short supply, land owners could extract a very high level of economic rent for its use. Thus land owners were extracting a high proportion of the economy's surplus wealth relative to labour or capital. The danger of this was that the surplus earned by capital was squeezed which meant that investment in the economy would also be squeezed. This was based on the assumption that land owners would spend their income on high living, whereas capitalists would reinvest their profits for the long term benefit of the economy.

Relating this to the study of the firm in Chapter 4, it was seen that firms need to make a certain surplus or profit to survive, and that this needs to be increased to allow for funds to be available for new investment and growth. Where landowners are able to extract a high rent this puts pressure on the firm's profits. In the formula profit = revenue − costs, high rents for land increase the firm's costs and squeeze profits.

The question must now be asked whether this nineteenth-century analysis is relevant today. Clearly the same distinct income classes of land, labour and capital do not apply. Land is no longer exclusively owned by the aristocratic class of land owners. Firms themselves may own a great deal of land. But this does not mean that the power of land ownership is irrelevant. It is probably the case that the conditions which enabled land to attract a high surplus or economic rent in the past are still present, in that certain types of land are still inelastic in supply and can therefore command a high price relative to the cost of keeping it intact. Whereas the argument applied to all land including agricultural land in the nineteenth century, today it is more appropriate to land which can be built on or which might receive permission to be built on.

In a modern context, the example of housebuilding could serve. House prices may increase significantly in some locations but this does not mean that the builder's profits would have risen commensurately. This is because most of the house price increase would have been the result of increased prices paid for the land on which the houses are built. Thus in the formula profit = revenue − costs, high prices of houses (revenue) would be offset by a higher price of land (costs) and so the profit level may be unchanged. In a competitive market the profit margin would be relatively small with the land owner extracting a large surplus. Builders might be able to increase their profits if they were able to buy their land at advantageous prices, before it had increased in value, rather than by buying land at the current market rate together with other resources such as labour and materials. It can be seen that high profitability of builders may not be due to any great proficiency in building, but more due to effective buying and selling of land, and collecting the surplus or economic rent accruing to land ownership.

Publicly created land values

This is an issue because, as previously mentioned, land values are affected by public decisions on planning matters or infrastructure provision. The value of a piece of land may be affected if:

1. A planning decision changes its permitted use.
2. Some change in infrastructure changes the attractiveness of that piece of land to a purchaser.

It is possible that the public decision in question could affect the land value positively or negatively. This whole issue is known as the **compensation/betterment** problem.

If a public decision increases the value of land then the question of betterment arises, whereas if a public decision reduces the value of land then the question of compensation, or worsenment arises.

In the majority of cases a public decision is likely to increase value. Examples include, allowing houses to be built on a piece of land previously designated for agricultural use, or building a new motorway which improves accessibility. However such decisions can have the opposite effect. For example, if a motorway is built a mile away from a house the property will probably increase in value, but if the motorway is built fifty yards away, it is more likely to reduce in value.

Where public decisions increase land values, the question arises of whether these publicly created land values should be regarded as a windfall gain to the land owner, or whether all or part of this gain should be recouped by the public through taxation or some other means. Windfall gains are often seen as being contradictory to the normal methods of reward in a market economy. Such rewards include payment for labour services, or profit for entrepreneurial risk undertaken in running a business.

The question of land taxation has proved to be a controversial issue over the years. The problem can be broken up into a number of areas:

1. Should land be taxed, especially publicly created land values?
2. If so, what method of taxation should be used? Should the tax be levied on land only after it is developed; should it be levied on all land regardless of when it was developed; or should it be levied on all land including land which is currently undeveloped?
3. At what rate should the tax be levied? For example what proportion of publicly created land value should be recouped by the public?

Public policy on this issue has tended to fluctuate over the years with Labour governments generally seeking a more interventionist approach than Conservative governments. Some attempts have been made to tax publicly-created land values (or betterment). This has applied to:

1. betterment created by planning decisions, and to
2. profits on new developments.

The problem with this type of taxation is that there is no incentive to develop land. In fact it could be argued that there is an incentive to do nothing. If for example a Labour government were to introduce a tax on new developments, land owners might feel inclined to hoard their land until a Conservative government is returned, in the hope that the tax might be abolished or at least reduced. Post-war experience appears to support this argument. For example Labour's Betterment Levy of the 1960s was later abolished, while the Development Land Tax of the 1970s was reduced.

So the system appears to have encouraged the hoarding of land in the hope that it will increase in value further. Alternative ways of dealing with this problem have been suggested.

Site value tax

Given that every piece of land has a designated use, tax should be levied on it in accordance with that use whether it is built upon or not. This should discourage the hoarding of land, increase the supply of land for development, and hopefully lead to lower prices.

Public ownership

Public ownership or nationalisation of land represents the ultimate control over land. In this system land as a resource would effectively be removed from the influence of market forces and instead be administered. Land could then be released to developers or builders who required it, at an administered price.

Summary

As mentioned, the land question has been one of the most consistently controversial issues since the nineteenth century at least. The system of taxing new developments only appears to encourage the speculative hoarding of land. Some say that this system should be retained because it is supported with a well-established planning and legal framework which would be difficult to change. Some argue for an increase in the rate of tax to make it more equitable. Others argue that the whole basis of the present system must be changed and that the main objective of a land policy must be to increase the supply of land for development. For this reason site value taxation has many supporters as does public ownership. Non-radicals are more likely to support the site value tax because it retains a more significant role for market forces, and also because they fear there may be bureaucratic problems with administered land. Radicals are more likely to argue that the only way of guaranteeing land supply, ending speculation, and enabling builders to concentrate on building and developers to concentrate on providing usable space, is to take development land outside the scope of market forces.

Whether existing systems prevail or new systems are introduced, there will be losers. It is quite likely that the land question will continue to be the problem it has always been.

Tutorial questions

1. What is the justification for taxing publicly-created land values?
2. Discuss the importance of land acquisition to the housebuilder.
3. How does monopoly power of land ownership affect the efficiency of the economy?

Application C

The inner cities

Introduction

Traditionally a great deal of attention has been paid to disadvantaged parts of the country. This usually took the form of studying economic activity on a **regional** basis to explain the varying levels of wealth, employment and other indicators of economic health. Studies were made of declining industries such as coal mining, shipbuilding, and textiles and the effect of this decline on certain regions of the country. However in recent years attention has focused on more concentrated areas, particularly the older run-down parts of our urban areas. This recognises the variations which occur within regions. Deprived areas can be found within otherwise prosperous regions, for example, parts of London in the overall prosperous South East of England. By the same token regions which have been considered deprived have always had some areas of wealth and prosperity.

The subject of the inner cities has become increasingly popular since the mid-1980s, with great interest shown by politicians, economists and industrialists (including builders). Terms such as 'urban renewal' and 'urban regeneration' are very much to the fore. Firms have recognised the inner cities as places where they can fulfil their objectives of making a profit in a way which also has public appeal.

This application will consider the inner city question, starting with an examination of the nature of the problem. This will include aspects of wealth and employment, together with aspects of the built environment such as urban dereliction. Solutions can then be considered. In common with many other economic activities, the question of the relative roles of market forces (the private sector) and public intervention becomes the main issue. It would appear that market forces alone cannot solve major problems of urban decay. The various degrees of public intervention will be examined. Many of these solutions have been

186

tried in various parts of the UK. There appear to have been a number of success stories where certain cities have had a revival of fortune. It is not always easy to say exactly why. It is probably the case that each area has its own range of economic, social and political characteristics and may respond to different stimulii.

The nature of the inner city problem

When a once prosperous city declines, the visible signs often include:

1. redundant factories and warehouses
2. decaying infrastructure
3. high unemployment
4. derelict land
5. poor services
6. low income per capita
7. poor housing.

The reason why a city begins to decline can probably be identified as being the result of either:

1. the permanent decline of an industry, or
2. the relocation of an industry out of the city, perhaps to green-field sites which may be in the same region or in a different part of the country or even in a different country.

In both cases, once a decline begins the negative multiplier effect (first described in Chapter 6) begins to take effect. For example, a factory closure will result in the direct loss of a certain number of jobs and a certain amount of income. The people who have lost their jobs will spend less on local goods and services and shops will suffer a loss of business. Similarly the factory will no longer purchase local services. The total effect of a factory closure including all the knock on or spillover effects can be significant. The result is a lower level of demand and a lower level of services. This is probably the main feature of inner city decline. It is a difficult process to reverse.

The permanent decline of an industry

This has affected many of the older industrial cities of Britain. These cities may previously have depended heavily on one particular industry or at least on a very limited range of industries. When demand for the product of the industry reduces, perhaps because of obsolescence or cheaper foreign goods, such regions are severely affected. The loss is sometimes of such magnitude that it cannot easily be replaced. In addition the workforce may have had skills specific to that industry and these skills may not be easily adaptable. In many cases a port or dock area, complete with a full range of services, may have grown up to export the product of the industry. In such circumstances the decline of the industry affects the docks areas severely. Examples of cities which have been affected in this way include Merseyside which has declined as a textile exporting port, and Cardiff as a coal exporting port. Many inland ports, linked to the sea by river or canal, once important for their import and/or export activities, have now been superseded by ports on the coast which can accommodate large containerised ships more easily.

Some of these obsolete dock areas, including the largest of all, London, have become the subject of great interest in the field of inner city revival.

The relocation of an industry

This can occur for a number of reasons. Often it is related to the suitability of premises, and transportation to the market. Inner city sites may be restricted with little room for expansion and the rebuilding of factories to modern standards would probably be difficult and expensive. Furthermore the inner city location was probably originally suitable because of its proximity to the main means of transportation — the waterways, or railways. These were the means by which resources were brought in, and finished products transported to their markets.

A green field site can offer a number of advantages — increased floor space; room for expansion; the opportunity to rent flexible factory space on industrial estates built by a professional developer (this reduces the need for manufacturers to have capital tied up in property). In addition such industrial estates are often located close to good road links, including motorways. Many firms prefer to transport their goods to the market by road.

Imperfections in the land market affecting inner city revival

Before considering some solutions, brief mention will be made of some of the problems of land as they affect the inner cities. Reference should also be made to Applications A and B.

Land hoarding

This speculative element to land was discussed in Application B. Derelict land may appear to be worth very little. However since the costs of holding land are so low, it may be retained until it increases in value. If an inner city revival seems a likely prospect, the owners of the land will not wish to sell until land values have reached their full potential.

Atomised land ownership

It has already been seen how the negative multiplier effect can reinforce the inner city problem. To reverse this process, it would be useful if advantage could be taken of a positive multiplier effect. Thus once redevelopment has begun, this process would be mutually reinforcing. However a problem arises in that in a competitive land market there are numerous land owners. Individual owners would probably be unwilling to redevelop their land for fear that other landowners might not follow suit. In such circumstances a single redeveloped site may be a 'white elephant'.

The imperfections mentioned above highlight the need for public intervention. This can be a starting point for considering solutions to the inner city problem.

Solutions to the inner city problem

It has been seen that there are imperfections in the market which make widescale revival of an area difficult without some public intervention. The negative multiplier effect is difficult to reverse. In other words it is difficult to set in motion the virtuous circle of the positive multiplier effect.

As may be expected, suggestions for solving the inner city problem are diverse. They range from seeking a solution by the use of market forces alone (without public money), through to circumventing the market and the private sector, and solving the problem entirely through public provision. In reality most solutions seem to have used a mixed approach with a role for both private and public sectors. In particular a number of partnership arrangements have emerged, the main principles of these being described in Application A.

Whatever approach is adopted there are a number of fundamental questions to be tackled:

1. Who will have control over the way the inner city is developed? Will control be left to the market, or will public bodies decide?
2. Who will finance the development? Will private developers provide the money, or will the public sector also make a contribution?

A market approach tends to assume that the main problems lie with obstacles to the free working of the market. Therefore if all obstacles could be removed the market would assert itself and the problem would be solved. Some perceive that the main obstacle to the market is the planning system because it interferes with the market for development by discouraging clients from building.

With this in mind the government introduced **Enterprise Zones** in the early 1980s. This measure sought to encourage development in particular inner city areas by the relaxation of planning controls and by some tax concessions. Very little public money was involved. Enterprise Zones did not prove to be very effective but they did highlight one particular problem of selective public intervention. The object of offering tax concessions is to encourage *new* development and new employment. However there is the risk that such concessions can draw resources away from a neighbouring area which may be almost as disadvantaged but which does not enjoy the benefit of having Enterprise Zone status. The area selected for this type of support must therefore be carefully chosen.

In the mid-1980s an approach was introduced which involved higher public expenditure. **Urban Development Corporations (UDCs)** were set up, the first being in London Docklands, with other examples in Merseyside and Cardiff Bay. Although public funding of the UDCs is limited, their aim is to act as a catalyst and set in motion a positive multiplier effect. The main items on which the public money should be spent are:

1. the assembly of sites, possibly using compulsory purchase powers
2. the clearance of derelict structures from the sites
3. the provision of infrastructure, particularly new road and transport schemes.

190

By preparing sites in this way the UDCs are creating their own betterment (see Application B). The profits made on the sale of these sites to private developers can then be used to purchase more land, thus setting up a rolling programme of site preparation.

The compulsory purchase powers of UDCs were mentioned. Related to these are planning powers. In the areas of their jurisdiction the UDCs often have superior planning powers to the elected local councils. The government's intention is that UDCs should take planning decisions on more 'commercial' criteria than might be the case with local authorities.

The success of UDCs has not yet been proven. Certainly the public money spent in London Docklands has been multiplied many times, but some argue that this is due to the unique location of the area near to the City of London. The multiplier effect in Merseyside has been much smaller.

Apart from land assembly and preparation, and the provision of infrastructure, there are other possible public actions which can be taken to solve the inner city problem. A traditional method of trying to induce a positive multiplier effect is through more widespread public spending. One way of doing this would be to instigate public development programmes such as administrative buildings, sports centres and so on. An example was the building of a new headquarters for South Glamorgan County Council opened in 1988 in the heart of the Cardiff Bay development area. The intention is that the building and those working in it will attract supporting services, and lead to a positive multiplier effect in the area generally.

Another possible solution was suggested in Application B, where a system of land taxation based on site values was discussed. Such a tax may be introduced to ensure that all suitable land would be brought into development rather than held back for speculative gain.

Summary

There has certainly been some success in reviving many of the inner city areas. Exactly why this has happened is not clear. It is possible to argue that either market forces or public intervention or both have been the main motivators. It is probably the case that a different set of conditions apply to each different area. London Docklands differs from Merseyside which differs from

Tyneside which differs from Cardiff and so on.

What is undeniable is that interest in the inner cities has grown, and these areas now attract attention from developers, builders, building societies and banks, as well as organisations such as the CBI. Many firms have divisions specifically concerned with the inner cities, with titles which include the terms 'urban renewal' or 'urban regeneration'. There is disagreement on why these firms have become involved. It could be to improve their image; or to take advantage of profitable opportunities; or to satisfy a genuine desire to make a contribution to the rebuilding of a community. Alternatively it could be a combination of these reasons. In many cases partnerships or joint ventures between private firms and local authorities have been set up.

The last decade of the twentieth century could witness great changes in British cities.

Tutorial questions

1. To what extent should market forces be relied upon to revive the inner cities of Britain?
2. Is manufacturing industry likely to return to the inner cities in the late twentieth century?
3. Why might builders be interested in undertaking projects in the inner cities?

Application D

The housing market

Introduction

The housing market has a high profile. The number of people who have a direct stake in this market has increased. In consequence the housing market has grown from being simply a means of acquiring somewhere to live to being of great economic, social and political significance. Housing is no longer only to be enjoyed, but is seen as an area where money can be made and in which wealth is tied up. As governments have increasingly recognised houseowners as an interest group, the housing market has become politically significant.

In this application the characteristics of the housing market will be examined including general factors which influence demand and supply. The change in attitudes outlined above will also be examined. Consideration will then be given to the imbalances in the market including those which cause rapidly rising house prices from time to time. These rises are sometimes followed by falls in real or even in money terms. Finally the relationship of the housing market to, and its interaction with, other markets will be considered.

Characteristics of the housing market

Brief mention was made of the housing market in Chapter 3 when it was shown that inelastic supply relative to demand is a significant feature of this market (see Fig. 3.8). The result of this is escalating prices in the face of increased demand (see Fig. 3.9). Further study of the market model as it applies to housing will follow.

The term *housing market* requires examination. Although referred to as an entity, the housing market does not exist in a unified form. It can be sub-divided in a number of ways, and has various characteristics.

1. The housing market is geographically based. One set of housing market circumstances cannot be applied to the UK as a whole. There will be regional variations in demand, supply and price. In some areas of the country there may be high demand and rapidly rising prices, while in other areas demand may be sluggish and prices static. Within regions or even within individual towns there may be considerable variations in market conditions.

2. The term housing market normally refers to the private owner-occupation market. However it should be remembered that there also exists a public sector renting market and a private sector renting market. The latter, although commonly found in Western Europe, is much less common in Britain, although there have been possible signs of a revival in this market since the late 1980s. Public sector, normally local authority, provision of housing declined rapidly in the 1980s with very little new building and sales of the existing housing stock. The result has been a growth in the number of people who acquire housing through private purchase.

3. A considerable variety of product exists within the housing market. For example supply consists of both new and older property, and property of differing sizes and standards of quality. This is reflected in variations in price. There are also large price differences between similar houses depending on their location. The most common explanation for this is the variations in the value of the land on which the houses are built.

4. Adjustments in the housing market do not occur as depicted in the market model. The forces of supply and demand in the housing market interact to give a price and quantity, as in Fig. 3.1. However market adjustments do not occur smoothly as in Fig. 3.6. It has already been seen that due to inelasticity of supply, the adjustments more closely resemble those shown in Fig. 3.9. It can be seen that the market is dominated by changes in demand. The supply of housing consists of new and second-hand properties. The quantity of housing is reflected in the number of transactions in the housing market, that is people selling and/or buying property. Price and quantity may not change simultaneously in response to changes in demand. An increase in demand will be reflected first

194

in an increase in transactions (quantity). This will be followed by an increase in prices. Similarly a reduction in demand will first be reflected in a reduction in the number of transactions which take place. Prices will then stabilise or even fall, at least in real terms.

General factors influencing demand and supply

In Chapter 3 it was stated that:

1. the general factors which affect the demand for any product are price, incomes, tastes and the prices of substitute and complementary products.
2. the general factors which affect the supply of any product are price, and the costs of production as determined by technology, price and availability of resources and levels of taxation.

These general factors are also applicable to housing, but in a modified form. When considering demand for housing, the dominating influence, other than price, is considered to be *incomes*. Changes in income result in changes in demand for housing. It should be noted that changes in income may occur through both direct and indirect means.

1. Increases in wages and salaries represent a direct increase in incomes and are likely to stimulate demand for a higher standard of housing from individuals. This will lead to an increase in the number of transactions in the housing market.
2. Indirect increases can have an identical effect on incomes as direct increases in wages and salaries. For example a reduction in the level of income tax effectively increases incomes and can increase demand for housing. Cuts in interest rates enable people to take out larger loans and so effectively increases income. Conversely an increase in interest rates has the effect of cutting incomes, and reducing the demand for housing.

Tastes for housing includes matters such as preferences for new or older housing, the location of the property, or even the preference of whether to buy or to rent. However consumers do not make these decisions on a totally independent basis. Their tastes may be influenced by the attitude of lenders who may be

195

unwilling to finance the purchase of a property of unusual design or construction.

Price of alternatives would include matters such as the cost of renting. As previously mentioned rented accommodation has become less of an option.

As already mentioned, the *supply of housing* tends to be inelastic. Supply consists mainly of existing properties with new properties being a relatively small percentage of the total housing stock. In general, the inclination to move is the main determinant of supply. The supply of new property is mainly influenced by the availability and price of building land (discussed in previous applications). It is also influenced by technological possibilities such as high productivity building methods (to be discussed in Application M).

Changing attitudes to the housing market

It was stated in the introduction to this application that the housing market has increased in economic, social and political significance. Some of the changes in attitudes which have led to this will now be considered.

The most important change in attitude is that many people no longer regard their property merely as somewhere to live and enjoy. In other words, property is no longer regarded as a purely consumption good, but to some extent as an investment good. People now expect to make a financial return on their property. An expectation has grown that there is no better investment than 'bricks and mortar'. A number of consequences of this attitude can be identified.

1. Historically people moved only when necessary, for example due to a change of employment, a growing family and so on. However some people now move for financial reasons, for example to acquire a larger, more valuable house, whenever this becomes financially possible.

2. There is a tendency to borrow greater amounts than before. This may be due to both the desire to borrow more, and the willingness of lenders to lend more. The housing finance market was dominated by building societies. They operated strict guidelines which related not only to the type of person to whom they were willing

to lend, but also to the amount of the loan, normally based on a multiple of the income of the individual concerned. The finance market has now become more competitive with a wider range of institutions offering loans at greater multiples of income. People seem more willing to commit themselves to higher levels of borrowing to finance house purchase.

3. It appears that some people use the wealth tied up in their property to finance the purchase of consumer goods. Mortgage interest relief can be obtained on loans up to a certain amount taken out for house purchase. People may borrow the whole of this amount even though it may be more than they require for their property purchase, the balance being spent on consumer goods. Furthermore, after some time has elapsed, the amount outstanding on the mortgage may have fallen below the figure on which mortgage interest relief is allowed. It is therefore possible to take out a new mortgage to bring the loan up to the full amount on which this relief can be claimed. This releases the equity tied up in the house for the purchase of other goods.

Changes in housing market participants

The traditional image of the house purchaser is that of a family consisting of husband, wife and two or three children. This image has dominated the plans of builders supplying the market, with the usual house size having three of four bedrooms.

However there have been a number of changes which have necessitated the need for smaller units.

1. There are increasing numbers of elderly persons who are financially secure. They represent the first generation of more widespread home ownership and those retiring with a reasonable pension. There has consequently been a growth in the supply of properties specifically designed for elderly and retired people.

2. There are increasing numbers of single person households. This may be the result of young people leaving the family home to live on their own, higher divorce rates and so on. The first-time-buyers market has consequently changed from being predominantly that of

young couples looking for a home in which to raise a family, to being orientated towards the single person.

In view of this increase in single person households, there has been a growth in demand for smaller houses and flats. In many cases larger houses have been converted into smaller units to meet this demand.

3. Inheritances are beginning to have an effect on the housing market. Elderly people, who form part of the first generation where home ownership was more common, are leaving property to their heirs. Such inheritances are often used either to enter the housing market for the first time or to buy a larger property.

The importance of first-time buyers in the housing market has been mentioned. Indeed it can be argued that they underpin the whole market. When first-time buyers enter the market this enables previous first-time buyers to sell and move to a larger, more expensive property. The owners of this property will, in turn, probably move to a more expensive house. It can be seen therefore that first-time buyers set in motion a whole chain of property transactions. For this reason, the housing market tends to slow if the number of first time buyers decreases, or if they have less finance available for property purchase.

Certain changes can adversely affect people buying property and in particular first-time buyers. In the short term, an increase in mortgage interest rates effectively reduces the amount which can be borrowed. An important change to the law made in 1988 was the abolition of multiple mortgage interest relief on a property. Before this change, people purchasing a property jointly could each claim mortage interest relief. This concession was granted to groups of single people or unmarried couples who could claim multiple interest relief on a property. Since the concession was withdrawn, only *one* multiple of mortgage interest relief is allowed per property, regardless of the number of purchasers.

The effect of mortgage interest relief is generally controversial. The original intention was to encourage individuals to buy their first home. However mortgage interest relief has the effect of increasing incomes, which leads to an increase in demand. Since the supply of housing is inelastic, prices will increase, as shown in Fig. 3.9. Many people advocate the phasing out of mortgage interest relief on the economic grounds that since it simply leads to an increase in property prices, it has little real benefit. Indeed if it encourages a speculative housing market it can even have inflationary and other destabilising effects (see Chapter 7). The political problems which might be encountered if this action were taken would, however, be substantial given the very large number of people with mortgages.

Changes in housing market participation could occur in the future if the tendency to work from home increases. Technological advances now make it possible for people to work from computer terminals or micro-computers in their homes. If this pattern becomes common the effect on the housing market could be substantial. There would be less need to travel to work and the location of workplaces (often concentrated in centres of cities) would be less of a contributory factor in increasing house prices nearer the centre. Matters such as the concentrated central location of workplaces cause imbalances in the housing market and will be considered next.

Imbalances in the housing market

It has been argued that the housing market does not adjust easily as shown in the simple market model described in Chapter 3. It was shown at the end of Chapter 3 that the inelastic supply of land mainly determines the development of the built environment. It was argued that the result of inelastic land supply may be escalating prices and/or dilution of quality due to overcrowding. In the case of housing this latter point would express itself as urban sprawl and pressure to build on green-field sites. This suggests that the housing market does not necessarily tend towards a stable equilibrium, indeed it is generally out of balance. An effect of this is that house prices generally will either be rising faster than the average rate of inflation, or falling in real terms.

In general, people appear to believe that rising property prices are inevitable. However, whilst general price falls in money terms have been unusual in the past, price falls in real terms certainly have taken place. This occurs when house prices either stabilise or increase in money terms by less than the rate of inflation. In such circumstances, this represents a fall in house prices in real terms. In times of low inflation falling prices in real terms could soon express themselves as falls in money terms.

Consideration will now be given to some of the factors which cause house prices to increase rapidly. Some have been mentioned earlier. If these factors are reversed house prices could fall in real or even in money terms. Some factors which cause prices to rise will affect the housing market generally. Other factors have more localised effects. Sometimes these localised effects may be related to increased economic activity in a particular area, and sometimes these may be due to a 'ripple effect' from other areas. Thus what happens in London is said to have a ripple effect elsewhere, the size of the effect being proportional to the accessibility to London.

Some factors which affect the housing market will now be considered.

1. The dominating influence of a commercial centre. People working in a large commercial centre may wish to buy property which is close to their workplace but may find prices too expensive. Consequently they buy cheaper property further away from the centre. This has the effect of gradually increasing prices in a wide commuter belt round the centre.

2. Infrastructure improvements such as new road links and rail electrification can improve accessibility to a commercial centre, and increase house prices in a wider commuter area.

3. Increased economic activity, either in an established commercial centre or in a less well established area, often leads to an increase in the number of workers. In the face of inelastic supply, property prices would be forced up. There has been a tendency for some firms to relocate. This creates new centres of activity. For example there has been a growth in the number of firms offering financial services in areas outside the traditional financial centre of London.

4. The supply of land for housebuilding purposes may remain inelastic due to planning policies such as the protection of green-field sites. Local authorities may also be reluctant to allow the widescale conversion of larger properties into smaller units because of the pressure this could put on services and infrastructure.

5. There has been a decline in the availability of rented accommodation in both the private and public sectors, as previously mentioned. This results in more pressure on the market for owner-occupied properties.

200

6. There has been greater competition amongst financial institutions offering finance. Finance has not only become more widely available, but the multiple of income which can be borrowed has also increased.

7. As previously mentioned, mortgage interest relief has maintained a high demand for housing. Since the supply is inelastic, prices have also been high. However the abolition of multiple interest relief has reduced the pressure on the housing market to some extent.

8. A rapid increase in salary levels might easily be reflected in escalating property prices. For example, during 1985−87 many people employed in the London financial services industries earned very high salaries. It has been suggested that this had an effect on the London property market. Of course the subsequent loss of confidence in the financial markets which occurred in October 1987 was reflected in a decrease in demand and in prices which rose less rapidly, or even fell in some cases.

9. If a degree of monopoly (see Chapter 3) exists among housebuilders, this could affect the supply of new housing. If housebuilding firms become larger, or form consortia, such firms could exercise greater control over the market. However as new housing represents only a small proportion of the total housing market, this effect may be limited overall, although it could be significant in certain areas where a great deal of new building takes place.

10. It can be seen from the above that the housing market is imperfect, with lack of knowledge being of particular importance. It has been claimed that in the absence of sufficient knowledge on the part of buyers, agents acting for the sellers of property are able to persuade buyers that the market is very active and may even be able to secure higher prices.

The above points are some of the influences which tend to cause imbalances in the housing market. They often result in increased prices, although some of these influences could also have the reverse effect.

Interaction between the housing and other markets

Housing finance market

Historically a problem of imbalance existed between the housing and housing finance markets. The provision of finance for housing was dominated by building societies who were restricted in the amount that they could lend. Only the amount that savers had deposited with them could be lent to borrowers. Inevitably times of peak demand for finance rarely coincided with times of peak availability. The housing finance market was characterised by 'feast or famine' situations.

The above problem has been partly alleviated for the following reasons:

1. There is now greater competition from other financial institutions for the provision of housing finance, as mentioned earlier.
2. A review of the law now permits an expanded role for building societies. They are able to offer a wider range of financial services, in competition with banks. They are also able to borrow finance from the money markets which enables them to increase the amount they can lend for mortgages, since they are no longer restricted to the amount that they can attract from savers.

Labour market

This matter becomes of importance when the difference in the price of housing in one part of the country compared to another becomes very great, since this affects the mobility of labour. It is not uncommon to find high unemployment in one area whilst labour shortages exist in another. It is a matter of debate whether new economic activities should be encouraged to locate in areas of high unemployment rather than excess labour being encouraged to seek employment in prosperous areas. Government policy has often sought to encourage the former solution since communities are retained and extra strain is not placed on expanding areas of the country.

However if the alternative solution of excess labour moving to other areas is encouraged, the probable high cost of housing in such areas could make this relocation impossible. The problem could be further exacerbated by a lack of rented accommodation at prices which can be afforded.

Summary

The housing market consists of more than simply finding somewhere to live. It has great importance as a market for personal investment. It is also of great political significance given the number of owner-occupiers in Britain. The importance of interest rates to the UK economy were explained in Chapter 7. Clearly interest rates also have a profound effect on the housing market, particularly in the way they affect demand through changes in income.

Hence there is a link between the state of the housing market and the state of the economy generally. When the economy is doing well, or is perceived to be doing well, this often leads to a boom in the housing market. This may of course be a speculative boom, since the housing market, like the land market, is prone to speculation. Consequently confidence in the housing market can quicky disappear resulting in a reduction in the number of transactions. This may be followed by static or even falling prices, both of which represent a cut in the real price of housing. In such circumstances, personal wealth is eroded, perhaps to the point where the value of a house may be less than the amount owed on the mortgage. Failure to meet mortgage repayments could lead to re-possession and if this became widespread the political consequences of a speculative housing market could be far-reaching.

Tutorial questions

1. For what reasons do people decide to move house?
2. Explain the relationship between the price of land and the housing market generally.
3. Discuss likely future changes in the housing market of your own area.

Application E

Transportation

Introduction

Transportation was identified in Part 1 as one of the supporting services, or infrastructure, necessary if a collection of buildings is to function as an urban area. In this application the purposes of transport will be examined together with the means of transport used in the UK. The economic problems associated with transport, first identified under the heading of roads in Chapter 3, will then be examined. The problems of transport in a market economy will be discussed together with some possible solutions.

Purposes of transport

Transportation is necessary for economic, social and political reasons. The primary purpose of transport is to enable people to get to work to earn a livelihood for themselves and their families, and to contribute to the wealth of society. The distance that many people are prepared to travel to work and the time that this takes has increased over the years. Before the Industrial Revolution people worked at home, but since then most people have travelled to work. The term commuter has evolved to describe those who travel some considerable distance to their place of work. In more recent years, there has been a reversal of the trend with a tendency for increased numbers of people to work from home. There has been an increase in the number of people employed at home on a casual basis in a variety of manufacturing industries. This type of casual employment has always existed in the clothes manufacturing industry, and it is believed that it has become more widespread. In addition, the invention of the microchip has opened up the possibility of more people working from home, through the use of computers. This possibility was mentioned in Application D when it was suggested that increased working from home could have an impact on the housing market.

These above trends notwithstanding, it is likely that the majority of people will continue to travel to work. One particular difficulty which occurs for the transportation system is the **peak loading problem** at the beginning and end of each working day. The transport system must have the capacity to accommodate maximum loads even though this capacity is only required for limited parts of the day. A similar problem is faced by other public utilities which cannot store production. In the same way that transport cannot be produced continuously and stored until required, electricity is generated as required, telephone calls are connected on demand, and so on.

In addition to transporting people to and from their place of work, the system is also required to transport resources and finished products. Firms not only need to obtain resources but must also be able to transport their finished products to their markets.

Transport is also used for the purposes of leisure as most people enjoy social and recreational pursuits outside their homes. This could include days spent visiting the coast or countryside, visiting friends or relatives, or perhaps visiting theatres, pubs and restaurants.

The above purposes or functions of transport may appear to be predominantly economic, but social and political factors are also important. For example, a transport system which is subsidised may allow those people who are less well off to take advantage of work and leisure opportunities which would otherwise be out of their reach financially. If people in general become aware of the importance of transport and the problems which arise when the system is inadequate, central and local government may see the political significance of investment in transportation systems. This reaches national significance with major projects such as the Channel Tunnel, although the route of a by-pass is of equal importance to a smaller community.

Means of transport

There are various ways of classifying the means of transport. For example transport can be undertaken either individually or collectively. Although transport undertaken collectively is described as 'public transport' it can be financed either through public provision, or privately through the market. Methods of classification include:

1. *The degree of technical sophistication.* Journeys may be undertaken on foot, on horseback, by cycle, motorcar, train and plane. Each additional degree of sophistication opens up wider geographical travel possibilities. Sometimes it has social implications. For example, it has been suggested that prior to the invention of the bicycle, most people found marriage partners within their own village. The bicycle enabled an increasing number of people to travel regularly outside their own immediate area.

2. *Method of provision.* Transport can be provided through either the market or public expenditure. Most types of transport require some public support. Collective public transport is often directly subsidised, whilst the private car requires road space, normally provided by the public sector.

The economic problem of transport

In the UK economy problems can be analysed in terms of how the market performs. A brief examination of roads was undertaken in Chapter 3. This showed that the supply of road space is inelastic relative to demand (see Fig. 3.8). However because no direct price is paid for road use, or more accurately, payments are not commensurate with the amount of usage, price adjustment is not possible. This inability of price to adjust is a market failure.

It was also shown in Chapter 3 that because prices cannot adjust pressure is put on quantity. In practical terms this results in congested roads and dilution in the quality of travel. This congestion is the price paid by society as a whole and is therefore an externality as described in Application A and illustrated in Fig. A.1. As the amount of activity (number of road journeys) increases, the social costs imposed through traffic fumes, noise and congestion rise. Conversely, the provision of improved infrastructure in the form of new roads eases congestion and generates positive externalities.

Another problem with the market approach to transport is that of possible unfairness. If market forces result in high prices, usage may fall and services could eventually be withdrawn on the grounds that they are uneconomic. This has been a problem with certain aspects of public transport notably rural bus services. Such services can rarely make a profit and normally require a public subsidy to keep them operational as they are seen as a social benefit. In the absence of such provision it is likely that many of the people using the transport would be isolated since few would have alternative private transport.

A further problem related to transport concerns the peak loading problem mentioned earlier. The demand for transport at peak times is inelastic because people generally travel to and from work at similar times. This is particularly the case if most workplaces are in the centre of the city. If car parking is limited and congestion caused by the convergence of too many cars is severe, people have no option but to use public transport to travel to work. In such circumstances the only realistic alternative solution would be rail travel. However by its nature this has the disadvantage of being a monopoly which leaves the commuter vulnerable to monopoly pricing. Some competition from buses and coaches may be feasible, but as already mentioned at peak times roads are heavily congested making movement difficult.

Solutions to the transport problem

The main problems of transport provision as outlined above can be summarised as the tendency to congestion particularly at peak times, and unfairness in that some people may be excluded from travel. In common with many other instances of economic problems in the UK, suggested solutions vary between those who advocate a greater role for the market, to those who advocate more public intervention. Some examples will be given.

Making markets work more effectively

These solutions might seek to reduce imperfections in the market and unfairness in transport provision. The major imperfection is that payment is not made in accordance with road usage. That is, there is no market price, say, per mile for the use of road space. Some kind of **road pricing** would therefore be useful, with the price charged per mile varying according to location and time of day. In other words price should be set according to demand. The implementation of such a scheme would be difficult. Tolls may be possible but these would have to relate to a particular length of road and the time taken to collect the toll money could easily cause congestion. Tolls exist in Britain for the use of certain bridges and tunnels. In Europe it is common to find tolls charged for the use of particular stretches of motorway. As an alternative to tolls, it may be possible to introduce an 'electronic tagging' device. Cars could be fitted with meters which come into use automatically whenever the car enters particular zones at particular times. Although the technology for such a system may exist, the problem of fitting meters to a large number of cars may make this solution impracticable at present.

Other kinds of market measures may also be applied to public transport. For example the deregulation of bus services has occurred in many towns. In theory deregulation should encourage wider competition and result in more services and lower fares. If these improvements encourage people to travel by bus rather than private car road congestion will be reduced. The lower fares would also allow more people on low incomes to travel. However in practice the experience of deregulation has been somewhat ambiguous. It is possible that privately owned bus operators have been eager to run services on profitable routes, but have been less willing to provide services on unprofitable routes. These unprofitable routes would still therefore require subsidising.

Although road building has traditionally been carried out by the public sector, the possibility of the private sector financing road building has received some consideration. For example, the Channel Tunnel is privately financed from the British side. Other suggestions have included a bridge over the River Thames, and fast lanes to be constructed alongside existing motorways. Tolls would be paid for the use of these roads.

It is of course possible for the public sector to increase the supply of road space. However experience seems to suggest that demand for road space is very flexible and that new road schemes seem to attract traffic. It would appear that people have a preference for private rather than public transport, and only use the latter when traffic congestion leaves them no alternative. Consequently the provision of more road space encourages a switch to the use of private vehicles until congestion recurs.

Public intervention

If the assumption that people prefer private transport is correct, road congestion is inevitable. People will use their cars until such time as congestion makes travelling unbearable. A solution to this problem is to make public transport more attractive. This might result in people preferring to use public rather than private transport. Some ways in which public transport could be made more attractive are:

1. lower fares
2. more frequent services
3. more reliable services
4. more comfortable buses or trains
5. greater attention to security especially at night.

Whilst these improvements would cost a great deal, and in purely financial terms would probably be a loss maker, the social benefits or positive externalities generated may compensate. This option was introduced in Part 1 where a wider definition of the term *economic* was explained. In the past, a number of local authorities have operated inexpensive public transport systems but they have found it difficult to sustain these in the face of discouraging central government policies.

Where widescale public intervention in transport provision is not possible the opportunities for less ambitious approaches may still exist. It is possible to encourage the use of public transport through special season ticket offers, and park and ride schemes. On some routes it may be possible to provide a service through the use of smaller vehicles. Other measures might be taken to encourage the shared use of cars, particularly those entering city centres at peak times. In the USA special lanes are often reserved for 'car pools'. In Britain, insurance restrictions were lifted some years ago to allow payments to be made to the driver to enable the sharing of travel expenses.

Summary

Many of our urban areas are heavily congested with traffic. In many instances this congestion is not confined to the beginning and end of the day, but seems to continue for the whole of the working and shopping day. The social costs in terms of delays to the movement of people and goods, the stress and accidents are very great.

Whatever might be possible for long distance transport, it is difficult to envisage a private sector solution for travel in and out of the city. The only solution seems to be good public provision. To some limited extent city centre congestion may have been alleviated by out of town shopping centres with their large car parks.

Long distance travel is undertaken by people using both private and public transport. Subsidies to the latter have been steadily cut for a number of years. Transport of goods is increasingly by road with very large vehicles dominating some motorways. These large vehicles can cause congestion, mainly because of the heavy wear and tear that they impose on motorway surfaces. The resulting closure of motorway lanes for repairs leads to further delays and congestion. It is possible that this trend may be irreversible especially with firms favouring locations which are near road rather than rail links as described in Application C. It is difficult to be optimistic about the future of transportation in Britain.

Tutorial questions

1. Is the provision of transport purely an economic decision?
2. Discuss solutions to road congestion in a town you are familiar with.
3. What benefits might there be if a preference for public transport were to permanently increase?

Application F

Construction clients

Introduction

This application together with Applications G and H, are broadly concerned with the second stage of developing the built environment explained in Part 1, that is the decision to build. The client is the individual or organisation who initiates a construction project. This application will firstly define the role of clients in the construction industry, following which the functional purpose of construction projects will be examined to ascertain whether there is any difference between this and the economic purpose of clients in undertaking a project. It will be seen that many clients regard projects as investments. Therefore the nature of investment and construction projects as investments will then be discussed.

The role of clients

The client is the individual or organisation who initiates a construction project, and must be distinguished from the occupiers or users of the finished project. Whilst some clients build for their own use, increasingly projects are being undertaken by 'professional' clients whose business is to provide space for others. In addition there are public sector clients who provide buildings and infrastructure for social, community and wider economic needs. The term 'developer' has been used frequently in this book. Whilst the terms developer and client are interchangeable, the term developer is usually reserved for the professional commercial client.

In Part 1 an extensive list of potential clients was considered. It was seen that each type of client expected to gain some benefit from the project. The various benefits were described in outline — consumption, direct financial gain, indirect financial gain, social. These benefits will be further considered in this application, particularly the investment aspect of building.

From the material considered in previous applications, it is evident that the role of the client is multi-faceted and may be divided between several organisations. Aspects of the client's role include the following.

Identifying and implementing the need

This marketing function is the core role of the client. It includes the identification of a social need or of a market opportunity for profitable development. It also includes drawing up and implementing a plan of action to satisfy this need or opportunity.

Land assembly

This relates to the acquisiton of the necessary land and obtaining planning permission. This may prove difficult where a large site is involved, particularly where a number of existing uses may have to be bought out, or where the site is environmentally sensitive.

Finance

A construction project has to be financed in both the short and long term. Land purchase and construction costs have to be financed in the short term until the building is complete and able to yield a return. This topic will be considered in more detail in Application K. If the building is sold on completion, as with speculative housebuilding, any profit is realised at that time, and long term finance is not required. However if the building is retained in order to yield a return over a period of time or at some time in the future, long term finance is necessary. This situation is similar to a householder taking out a mortgage over a period of, say, twenty years to finance the purchase of a property. Long term finance will be considered in Application N.

Management

This aspect applies when the client retains ownership of the building on completion. In this case, the client aims to maximise the benefit which can be derived from the building. This includes negotiating the terms of leases and arranging maintenance programmes. These were considered in Part 1 under the fifth stage

212

of developing the built environment — occupation and use of buildings, and will also be considered further in Application N.

These various aspects of the client's role may be embodied in one individual or organisation, or they may be divided between a number of individuals or organisations. The land assembly function of local authorities has already been discussed, particularly in Application C. To take another example, the marketing and finance roles may be separated in large commercial projects. A professional developer may conceive, plan and organise the project, while an insurance company or pension fund may deal with the financial aspects of the project.

The functional purposes of construction projects

In order to understand why clients build, it is first appropriate to examine the economic purposes of construction projects. This question has already been discussed to some extent both in Part 1 and in previous applications. In a way, the purpose of all construction projects is ultimately to satisfy the needs of people. These needs may be satisfied directly or indirectly, privately or publicly. A three way classification is sometimes adopted.

Consumption

Some buildings satisfy peoples' needs directly and privately. This is the usual meaning of consumption, with a consumption good being something which satisfies a need. Most household goods are consumption goods because they add directly to the consumer's personal standard of living. However the meaning of consumption can be extended beyond the individual to the family group or any other individuals who have been invited to share in this consumption. This type of consumption is distinguished from that which is provided and used collectively. The best example of buildings which are used for consumption purposes is that of housing. The primary purpose of a home is that it should provide shelter, comfort and enjoyment. In this sense a home is a consumption good, although as seen in Application D, many people also see their home as an investment.

Factor of production

Many buildings are required not for their own sake, but because they enclose space within which some other productive activity takes place. These buildings are factors of production, and are categorised as capital, as discussed earlier in Chapter 1. Such buildings include factories, offices and shops — the places where goods and services which people need are produced and sold. The demand for such buildings is indirect or derived, that is derived from the demand for the good or service which is produced in the building. It is similar to the traditional view of land values outlined in Application B, where the demand for land, and hence its value, is derived from the demand for the product produced on the land. Buildings which are factors of production make an indirect contribution to consumption in that they are used to produce goods and services which are ultimately consumed. From the point of view of the firm using the building, it is regarded in the same way as a piece of machinery, that is as an investment good.

Social

Some buildings have a social purpose in that they are provided publicly to satisfy a wider community need. They may provide facilities for individuals to use or consume, such as sports centres, or they may provide facilities for collective consumption such as theatres. Some social buildings such as schools, colleges and hospitals can be categorised as social capital. They contribute to the training and 'maintaining' of the workforce, and thus have an economic purpose in addition to their social purpose. Many public construction projects provide infrastructure such as road and rail links, sewerage and water supplies, gas, electricity and the other services necessary for the efficient operation of the economy.

Why clients build

If all clients built for their own use, their reasons for building would correspond to the functional purposes of buildings outlined above. However this is not always the case. There are *two* reasons why clients build:

1. for their own use
2. for some other individual or organisation to use.

This is an amended framework to that used in Part 1 — the decision to build, where the four reasons given were:

1. consumption
2. direct financial
3. indirect financial
4. social.

Of these categories, 1, 3 and 4 correspond with the functional purposes of buildings. Building for consumption reasons occurs when people build for their own use. The only likely example would be people arranging for a house to be built to their own specification with their own use in mind. Since most people buy their house either from a builder, if new, or from an existing householder, if the house is second-hand, the instances of clients building for consumption are small.

Clients who build for indirect financial gain often regard the building as a factor of production as discussed previously. Such clients are usually firms who are motivated by profit. They expect the building to enhance their profits through increasing efficiency. In the context of the profit formula discussed in Chapter 4 (Profit = Revenue − Costs), the purpose of the building, be it factory, office or shop, is to increase productivity and hence reduce costs.

Clients who build for social benefit do so for non-market reasons. Whilst mainly comprising the public sector, these clients might also include charitable organisations and housing associations. It should be remembered that public sector clients, particularly nationalised industries, might also initiate projects which are market orientated.

Clients who build for direct financial gain are, broadly speaking, those clients who build for others to use. They are professional clients in that building is their business. The products they sell are buildings or space in buildings. In the context of the profit formula, Profit = Revenue − Costs, the income from selling or leasing the building adds to revenue. This category of client, that is those who build for others to use, has grown in importance. This growth will now be considered.

Changes in patterns of client behaviour

As previously identified, clients can be classified as those who build for their own use and those who build for others. There has always been an important role for the professional client for some types of building. For example in the commercial property field, including city centre office blocks, the developer, as the

215

professional client is usually called, has long had a substantial influence. Whilst there will probably always be the corporate client who requires a headquarters building which reflects the prestige and importance of the firm, the majority of firms generally lease their office space from developers.

In housebuilding, there have always been some individuals who have had houses built to their own specification. However this is an expensive option which is only available to a minority. There has also been a growth in the number of people constructing their own houses. Self-build may be an economic option depending on the value that is placed on the considerable time required. In spite of its possible advantages few people have either the time or confidence to undertake self-build. The majority of people therefore rely on homes which were designed and built by others. The main providers of housing have been local authorities in the public sector, and speculative housebuilders in the private sector. Other providers include charitable organisations such as housing associations. In recent years local authorities have built very few houses and consequently private housebuilders now provide most of the additions to the housing stock.

The housebuilding industry has changed and is now larger scale. Whereas housebuilding was once considered the preserve of smaller builders or specialist housebuilders, now most major construction firms are involved, mainly because housebuilding has proved profitable. There is also the recent tendency for builders to form consortia so that entire new villages or towns could be built. Of course such large scale building would pose many problems such as obtaining planning permission and land assembly.

In addition to the established fields of office and housebuilding, the role of the professional client or developer has expanded into the areas of industrial and retail space. Whereas a manufacturing firm would once have had a factory built to its own specifications, it is now more likely to lease factory space. Typically, this factory space would be on a new purpose-built industrial estate located close to road links. Alternatively, factory space has been created through the renovation of large redundant factories which have been divided into smaller units. The ability to lease space is particularly useful for smaller manufacturers, since they can decide on the amount of space that they require and equip it accordingly. If the business proves to be successful and needs to expand, this can usually be achieved quite easily through leasing extra space. The major advantages of leasing space are that the manufacturer is able to concentrate on producing goods and does not have capital tied up in property. In addition, leasing space is a quicker option for a manufacturer than arranging for the land acquisition, design and building of a factory.

Developers of industrial estates often specialise in this type of work. They provide the factory space together with the necessary infrastructure. They may also provide basic communal services such as office support with up-to-date technology which small manufacturers could not afford individually. In addition to industrial developers, other developers have emerged who specialise in out-of-town shopping centres and retail units. Other developers have concentrated on providing specialised housing such as sheltered accommodation for the elderly. As mentioned in Application D, the market for the provision of housing for the elderly has grown considerably in recent years.

Without doubt there has been an increase in the proportion of construction projects built by professional clients who build for direct financial gain. Their business is to provide buildings for other people to use. This has implications for the role of the builder, which will be discussed in Application G. It also has implications for the nature of buildings as investments. This application will now briefly summarise the nature of investment and construction projects as investments.

The nature of investment

Investment, as explained previously (for example in Chapter 6) involves giving up some benefit now in exchange for greater benefit in the future. Although this is often measured in financial terms, sometimes the benefits may be non-financial. For example consumption benefits are measured in terms of personal pleasure and enjoyment; social benefits are measured in terms of the creation of human capital, congestion-free roads and so on.

The term investment asset is used to describe any asset which is expected to yield a greater benefit in the future. These benefits may be received in two ways:

1. The benefits may be received over a period of time, thus providing an **income**. For example an office building may be leased over fifty years to provide an income for the investor, that is the owner of the building.

2. The benefits may be received as a lump sum at some time in the future, thus providing a **capital gain**. For example a property may be bought and resold later at a higher price to provide a capital gain for the investor.

Whilst most investments offer either one type of benefit or the other, some investments offer both. For example:

1. Company shares offer the possibility of dividends (income) and growth in value (capital gain).
2. Government stocks also offer both types of benefit, although the income is a fixed rate of interest.

In addition to the way in which benefit is received, there are other important features of investment assets. The benefits received may vary according to:

1. the size of the **return**
2. the degree of **risk**
3. the extent of **liquidity**

These features may be traded off against each other. For example, a high return can only be expected if the risk of losing the investment totally is also high. Conversely a low risk investment would yield a relatively low return. The liquidity of an investment asset, that is the ease with which it can be converted into cash, is an advantage, which is reflected in the lower return which can be expected.

Construction projects as investments

Construction projects can be investments in a number of ways, as described earlier in this application:

1. as a factor of production
2. as an investment asset for direct financial gain
3. as a social investment.

In the *first* instance the project could be a factory, office or shop which enables the client to operate the business more efficiently. The building is an investment asset in the same way as a machine.

In the *second* instance, the project is a pure investment asset as it has been undertaken for a purely financial gain. Some clients, including property developers, specialise in such investments. Other clients, such as insurance companies and pension funds, invest in a portfolio of assets including property. The portfolio may contain a wide range of assets, the choice made being based on the investor's attitude towards the balance between return, risk and liquidity as outlined above.

In the *third* instance, the project is regarded as a social investment and will be appraised on a wider range of criteria than purely financial. The project may seek to fulfil social and political as well as economic objectives. Such projects could include those concerned with the creation of human capital, leisure amenities and infrastructure.

The methods by which these various projects are appraised, before the decision to build is taken, will be considered in Application H — Feasibility of projects.

Summary

In this application consideration has been given to construction clients, that is those individuals or organisations initiating a construction project. Distinction was drawn between the client and the occupier and the various aspects of the client's role were explained. The functional purposes of construction projects were discussed. These included consumption, factor of production, and social. However the reasons why clients build cannot be explained simply in terms of functional purposes because many clients build, not for their own use, but to sell or lease to others. Such clients are professional clients in that they build for direct financial gain, the provision of space being their business. This application concluded with consideration of investment and the nature of construction projects as investments.

Tutorial questions

1. Do public sector clients always build for social reasons?
2. On the criteria of return, risk and liquidity, how does investment in property compare with other investment opportunities?
3. If a group of people wish to start up a firm, what decisions must be made regarding premises?

Application G

Fulfilling the client's objectives

Introduction

In Application F, the objectives of clients and developers were considered. This can be taken a stage further to examine how these objectives might be fulfilled. Whereas Application H will consider the financial implications of projects, this application will consider procedural matters including the way in which a client sets up a project team to best achieve the objectives. It will be seen that a major question which arises concerns when and on what basis the builder is employed. These issues are often referred to as the study of **tendering** methods, or as they have become known in recent years, **procurement** methods.

In the post-war period a method of contractor selection emerged which was based on **selective tendering**. This method became the norm and it is now often referred to as the *traditional system*. However, due to the problems associated with this system, alternative methods of fulfilling the client's objectives have been devised and used in many instances. In this application the traditional system will be examined, particularly from the point of view of establishing its economic rationale as a price competition. The problems associated with the traditional system will be considered followed by brief consideration of some of the alternatives.

Traditional tendering systems

As mentioned above the client is concerned with the procedural matters connected with a project. In particular decisions have to be taken regarding the following:

1. How should the *project team* be organised? For example what should be the hierarchy; who should be in charge; and who should be the client's main point of contact?

2. At what point and on what basis should the *builder* become involved? For example, should the builder be employed before design commences or after its completion? To what extent should the price be fixed in advance?

Under the traditional tendering system the answers to the above questions are as follows.

Project team

Initially, the client normally appoints the architect as the leader of the design team. The architect is responsible for the design of the building and the supervision of the project on behalf of the client. Other consultants such as the quantity surveyor, structural engineer and services engineer may also be employed, but the architect will normally be the channel through which the client's wishes are made known. Therefore the architect, and the architect's organisation have a wide range of both design and management responsibilities.

Builder

With the traditional system the builder is normally selected after the design has been completed. The design would include drawings and in most cases a bill of quantities, which is an itemised list of all the resources required to produce the building. The drawings, bill of quantities and form of contract (usually a set of standard clauses) will usually form the contract documents, which are the basis of the relationship between the client and the builder. For this reason a builder who undertakes a project for a client is often called a contractor.

The builder is selected through a process of tendering. A number of contractors are invited to tender for the project based on the contract documents. The contractor who offers the lowest price is usually awarded the contract. At one time tendering was *open* in that once the announcement had been made, any firm could tender for the contract. This system of tendering was commonly used for public sector projects where, in the interests of public accountability, it was necessary to ensure that the tendering system was seen to be fair and without favouritism when contracts were awarded. This open system was subsequently replaced by *selective* tendering whereby a limited number of builders, all of whom were believed to be capable of undertaking the project, were invited to tender.

At first sight, the tendering system appears odd in that it is not used in many other industries. The main difference is that the functions of design and production are kept separate. In manufacturing industry, a single firm conceives, designs, produces and markets a product. However when traditional tendering is used in the construction industry, the design is carried out by the design team, including the architect, quantity surveyor and engineer, while the construction is carried out by the contractor. These functions are sometimes studied separately, with design being referred to as a study of **the product**, while construction is referred to as a study of **the process**. In fact these two functions overlap and cannot be treated in isolation.

In spite of the apparent oddity of the tendering system, it has persisted. Its perceived advantage is that it is designed to ensure the *lowest possible price* for the client. As seen in Chapter 3, the two outcomes of a market are price and quantity. In the construction market the client represents demand and the builder represents supply. When supply and demand interact there are market outcomes of price and quantity (see Figs. 3.1 and 3.4). Under the tendering system the *quantity* is fully defined at the outset in terms of the product required — design, quality of materials, time allowed for construction, and so on. Since the quantity is defined, the variable to be decided is *price*. In economic terms, therefore, the traditional tendering system can be seen as a **pure price competition**. With the client's *exact* requirements defined, the next stage is to identify the builder who can offer the most competitive price in the market. Whilst this may seem straightforward, in the same way that market theory has practical difficulties, so problems can occur with the selective tendering process.

Problems of the traditional system

As explained above the rationale for using the traditional tendering system is that it establishes a price competition which ensures, with all aspects of the project being fully defined, that the client obtains the lowest price possible. It can be argued, however, that selective tendering does not necessarily result in the lowest price. This may occur for a variety of reasons, some connected with the organisation of the project team and some connected with the role of the builder.

Information flow and diversity of skills

In the tendering system the client normally appoints an architect, who advises on the appointment of other consultants and on the selection of contractor. From the client's point of view the ideal situation is to have one point of contact, through whom all information can be channelled. This contact should also be capable of handling the project so that the client's objectives are achieved. To meet these objectives, the building must fulfil the functional purpose required, and be constructed without exceeding the client's budget. Therefore the client's main point of contact needs to exercise a wide range of skills including design, economic and managerial. Since it is unlikely that one individual would possess all the necessary skills, it has been argued that the operation of the tendering system puts too great a burden on the architect. Although architectural organisations may possess many of the skills required, nevertheless by their nature many architectural practices are likely to be design orientated whereas the client's objectives are more likely to have an economic bias.

Design period

With the tendering system it is normally necessary for the design to be fully completed before tenders are invited from contractors. This enables the contractors to tender on an equal basis and ensures a fair price competition. The tender is usually based on a full set of drawings and a bill of quantities. The architect therefore has to complete the drawings, and the quantity surveyor has to produce a bill of quantities before tendering can take place. This introduces a certain amount of rigidity into the process, since although the contract price is established, the inevitable subsequent changes to the project can be very expensive. In addition the length of time spent producing the full design and contract documents can be considerable. Many clients who are eager to achieve a quick completion may find this undesirable.

Builder's knowledge

The builder has a great deal of practical knowledge relating to production methods, the economic buildability of particular design elements and so on. If the builder does not become involved in the process until a later stage, that is after the design

223

has been completed, the client is unable to benefit from this expertise, and as a result may not obtain the most cost effective solution to the building design problem.

Uncertainties

The extent to which uncertainties are a problem depends on the conditions of the contract as well as on the prevailing economic conditions. The main cause of uncertainty when determining a tender price is the likelihood of cost increases during the contract period. Whilst the anticipated rate of inflation may be used as a guide, the effects of inflation are often uneven, as seen in Chapters 6 and 7. Ideally an inflation level of zero should exist in order that the client can be sure of the price to be paid. In addition, the conditions of the contract are significant as they define whether the price is to be **firm** or **fluctuating**. If the price is firm, the contractor's tender must allow for possible inflation. The contractor therefore takes this risk and may overcompensate for inflation in the tender price. In these circumstances the price that the client has to pay is increased, although this will depend on the degree of monopoly which exists in the market (see Chapter 3). If the price is fluctuating the contractor should be able to recoup any increase in costs from the client. In this instance the client takes the risk. However if the contractor is not entirely satisfied with the methods of reclaiming the costs, some overcompensation may still be made in the tender price. From the above it can be seen that in an inflationary period the associated uncertainties may mean that the pure price competition of selective tendering may not necessarily result in the lowest price for the client.

Contract variations

Although the price should be decided at the outset, with the client aware of the cost commitment, this may not always be the case. It has already been seen that changes to the project can be expensive. These may occur because the client has a change of mind; or the architect changes a detail of the design; or the original solution was not the most practicable; and so on. It has also been seen that during an inflationary period a degree of uncertainty exists in the tendering process. An additional problem concerns contractual claims. When changes to the project are made their value has to be agreed. Sometimes this can be based on the rates for items of work priced by the contractor in the bill of quantities. Where this cannot be done, there may be some dispute over what is considered fair payment for additional work. Other claims may arise when the contractor believes that the work measured in the bill of quantities is an underestimate of the work actually to be carried out. It is sometimes alleged that if a contractor prices the bill tightly to win the contract, say in times of shortage of work, there might be a temptation to seek and pursue claims vigorously. In exceptional circumstances the contractor might even have to rely on a number of successful claims to make a profit on the contract. This situation is not only damaging to working relationships, but also the client inevitably pays more. Arguably contractors are in a more favourable position when negotiating claims since their negotiators are on site more frequently. By contrast, except on very large projects, it is unlikely that the client will have a claims negotiator, such as a quantity surveyor, permanently on site.

Alternative systems

Given the problems of the traditional tendering system outlined above, alternatives have been formulated. Some seek to improve the flow of information by restructuring the project team and possibly changing the leadership. Other systems use different criteria when selecting the builder. This is based on the belief that the pure price competition of selective tendering does not necessarily achieve the lowest price.

There are a wide variety of alternative tendering systems, (or procurement systems as they are sometimes called). Many have been in existence for a considerable time, in some cases since the nineteenth century, although they may have fallen into disuse. In addition to the possible discontent which surrounds the traditional tendering system used in Britain, more recently there has also been strong overseas influence. With the exception of Commonwealth countries, the traditional UK system has not been widely used abroad. In particular the normal bill of quantities has not been used in the same way in, say, the USA. In recent years there has been a substantial increase in the number of overseas clients, developers, architects and construction managers operating in Britain, and this has undoubtedly influenced the methods used.

225

There is some disagreement on the extent to which alternative systems will be used. Some believe that they will only be used for a minority of projects, and that the traditional selective tendering system will remain the most commonly used. Others argue that the advantages of alternative methods will eventually replace traditional tendering altogether. However most agree that some element of competition should be retained in order to achieve some of the benefits of market forces.

The following list briefly summarises some of the alternative systems which are available. It should be noted that there are many variations on a theme and alternatives which differ slightly might easily be devised to suit particular clients or particular projects. The systems are:

1. negotiated contracts
2. unified systems
3. separate contracts
4. management contracting
5. project management.

In some cases a different form of contract may be used while in other cases the contract documentation is similar to that which is used for the traditional tendering system.

Negotiated contract.

A contractor is selected at the outset so that advantage can be taken of the contractor's knowledge and expertise during the design stage. This should result in a more cost effective design and a cost saving to the client. A bill of quantities may still be prepared but the rates and tender price will be the subject of negotiation between the contractor and the client's representative, usually the quantity surveyor.

The main advantage of this system is that use is made of the builder's knowledge at an early stage. Supporters of this system also believe that although the initial tender price is likely to be higher than with traditional tendering, the price is more likely to reflect the amount that the client eventually pays. This is based on the belief that where good working relationships exist and fair prices are set, there is less likelihood of claims for extra work.

Unified systems

The main characteristic of these systems is that the client has a single contract for both the design and construction aspects of the project. The two most common types of unified system are **package deals** and **design and build**. These two terms are sometimes interchanged, with the latter term being in more recent usage. However there may be some differences between them which should be mentioned.

Package deals

This is the more established term. It is often used to refer to the more standardised type of building which is commonly used to provide modern industrial and retail space. In this case the *design* part of the contract is fairly established and standardised, which means that a building rather than a design is sought. If the client is a large specialist developer the package deal will be limited to designing and constructing the building. However if the client is smaller or less experienced, the package deal might be extended to cover services such as finding the site; obtaining planning permission; and arranging the finance.

The advantages of package deals include greater predictability of price. Since the design is relatively standardised there should be few, if any, claims once the substructure is complete. Furthermore there should be several existing examples of the builder's work in this field, which will enable the client to make an informed decision on whether the builder is capable of fulfilling the objectives.

Design and build

This term has evolved more recently to describe the situation where a client approaches an organisation, usually a builder, who undertakes to design and build a project to suit the client's requirements. This differs from the package deal in that the project frequently involves a more complicated and certainly non-standard building. This system might be used by a professional developer or by a client seeking a special one-off project. The builder may use in-house architects to design projects, or employ firms of architects. Alternatively some architectural practices have diversified into contracting and now offer their own design and build service. This has only been possible in recent years since the relaxation of the regulations which apply to members of professional institutes.

An element of competition can be maintained as several design and build contractors can be invited to submit outline designs and tenders. Alternatively the client might negotiate with a single contractor. A modified bill of quantities might be used — a contract sum analysis, which enables the cost of any changes to be calculated.

The main advantage of a design and build system is that there is a single line of responsibility. The blame for any errors which may occur cannot be passed from the architect to the contractor or vice versa. A unified approach should give better communications, greater speed and a reduced need for variations and extras. In addition, the cost of the project should be known earlier than with other systems.

Separate contracts

In this instance there is no general contractor. The architect designs the project and arranges separate contracts for each trade or section of work. This requires a high degree of skill from the client's team. Since the client's financial commitment is not known at an early stage, there is heavy dependence on the financial control skills of the quantity surveyor. This system is less suitable for projects where public accountability is involved, because the client carries a great deal of risk. However there is the possible advantage of speed since parallel working can be undertaken, that is, work can proceed on site while the design continues to be developed.

Management contracting

This term is used to describe not one but a range of systems which place emphasis on the managerial skills of the contractor. The idea is believed to have originated from the USA where the terms construction project management or construction management are used. In this case the contractor holds the position of a consultant, and is paid a fee by the client to manage the project. The contractor may be selected at the outset or there may be a preliminary tender. A contract is made between the client and the construction manager, and there are separate contracts between the client and the other contractors. These other contractors would have been selected through tendering for work packages.

In the UK, the term management contracting often refers to a different arrangement, which also emphasises management skills but retains the contracting role. The firm is awarded the contract for a fee which might either have been tendered for or negotiated. The construction work is divided into work packages for which other firms, including possibly subsidiaries of the management contractor, will submit tenders. However the client's contract is with the management contractor only. Those firms carrying out the work packages are in effect sub-contractors, with the management contractor having to ensure that the work is completed within the tender price. There seems to be scope for variation with this system.

The advantages claimed for management contracting include speed and efficiency. Since contracts for individual work packages can be made nearer the time when the work needs to be carried out rather than at main contract stage, the prices should be more competitive with less need to allow for uncertainties such as inflation. However it has been suggested that costs may be higher as both the management contractor and the work package contractors include management or preliminaries costs in their prices. Nevertheless it is widely accepted that some form of management contracting has an important role to play in large projects, especially those which require a fast completion.

Project management

Under this system the client's instructions are channelled through one individual who is a professional member of the design team. The project manager is the client's main representative and is responsible for the overall control of the project. The various consultants such as architect, quantity surveyor, engineer, and the contractor will all be responsible to the project manager. Clearly the project manager needs to possess a wide range of skills and must have a knowledge of all aspects of construction including design, cost and construction methods. The project manager might be from within the client's own organisation, and indeed this is quite likely if the client is a 'professional' client or developer as previously described. Alternatively, the project manager may be from a separate professional organisation, as firms such as architects and quantity surveyors may also offer this service. The project manager may be involved at the beginning of the design stage, to oversee design and construction, or possibly even earlier during the feasibility stage to assist in defining and developing the client's requirements. The selection of the building contractor under the project management system could be through the use of traditional tendering, or by negotiation.

The claimed advantages for project management include strong all round leadership of the client's team. The person appointed is likely to have a good knowledge of financial control, which should make the benefits of traditional tendering as a price competition more easily achievable. However the skills required of an effective project manager are numerous and it is likely that such people will be in short supply.

Summary

This application has considered the procedures which clients might adopt to achieve their objectives. The main problems concern the organisation of the team and in particular at what point and on what basis the builder should be involved in the project. A system of selective tendering became the normal procedure in the post-war UK construction industry. The main benefit of this system is that in theory all aspects of the project are defined except the price. If a number of contractors who are known to be capable of undertaking the job are invited to tender, the resulting pure price competition should guarantee the client the lowest possible price in the prevailing market conditions.

However, in the same way that market practice and theory differ, so the practice of tendering might not give the lowest price as predicted by theory. Problems can arise regarding the flow of information and diversity of skills; the length of design period; non-utilisation of the practical knowledge of builders; uncertainty in an inflationary period; and the possibility of a large number of claims for contractual variations leading to increased costs.

In view of the problems of traditional tendering, alternative systems have been developed, many of which still retain some element of competition. These alternatives are varied and some examples were given. There is no single ideal procedure which all clients will adopt. There are many people who would not consider any system other than selective tendering, and this might be particularly important where there is a question of public accountability. Whilst each client must decide what is most suitable for them, the indications are that increasing numbers of clients see the balance of advantages being with alternatives to traditional tendering.

Tutorial questions

1. Which methods of procurement suit the client whose main priority is speed of completion?
2. Who is best equipped to lead the client's team on a large commercial development?
3. How can the client ensure that the most competitive price is obtained for a building contract?

Application H

Feasibility of projects

Introduction

The previous two applications have considered the objectives of construction clients and the procedures they might adopt to achieve those objectives. As described in Application F, the client seeks to achieve some benefit from the project. Before deciding to proceed, an appraisal must be carried out to ascertain whether a proposed project will meet the objectives. This is known as investigating the **feasibility** of a project. Although not all clients seek a financial return, most of the techniques used to ascertain feasibility have a financial basis. The feasibility stage deals with cost investigation or control before deciding to proceed with the project.

All clients expect that the benefits from a project will exceed the costs. This is similar to the general objective of a firm shown in the formula:

profit = revenue − cost

In the case of a construction project, revenue is known as benefit and the formula becomes:

net benefit = benefit − cost.

Thus the 'profit' on a project is described as the net benefit.

At feasibility stage, the main task is to investigate the likely benefits and costs of a project. If the result shows a net benefit the project can proceed. If not, adjustments might be made to make the project feasible, or alternatively it might be abandoned.

As discussed in Application F, for most clients the concept of investment has a strong influence on the decision to build. For this reason the core of feasibility studies concerns investment appraisal. This application will continue from Application F by considering investment appraisal generally for both the private

232

and public sectors. Following this a brief outline of some of the specialist appraisal techniques applied to investment in construction projects will be given.

Investment appraisal

The general nature of investment has been discussed previously, particularly in Application F. It has been defined as the giving up of some benefit now in exchange for some greater benefit in the future. Whilst benefits are often measured in financial terms, they may also be social. The benefits may be received at some time in the future as a capital gain; or they may be spread over a period of time as a stream of income. Investment assets have various characteristics such as size of return; degree of risk; and extent of liquidity. These characteristics may be traded off against each other. Construction projects may be investments in that they could be:

1. factors of production
2. assets for direct financial gain
3. assets yielding social benefits.

Construction projects, like other investments are concerned with **time**. Time normally has to elapse before the investment shows a return. The full return may be spread over many years, that is throughout the economic life of the investment. This applies to many types of building. Even when buildings are sold immediately they are completed, such as houses, there may still be some time lag before the return on the investment can be realised. This is referred to as the cash flow or liquidity problem, first introduced in Chapter 4 and to be further examined in Application K.

The basis of investment appraisal is the **time value of money**. That is, money received or costs incurred *now* are normally worth more than money received or costs incurred *in the future*. There are two main reasons for this, namely:

1. uncertainties
2. the rate of interest.

Uncertainties

By their nature, the effects of uncertainties are difficult to measure. Inflation is the principal cause of the erosion of the value of money. It is difficult to predict in the relatively short term, and even more difficult to predict over the lifetime of a building. Other uncertainties can also make calculations carried out at the feasibility stage unreliable. The speculative value of land has already been discussed in Application B. Many property investments may go ahead on the assumption (possibly mistaken) that continuing rising land values will be reflected in rising rents and hence rising benefits.

The rate of interest

This covers the more standard aspect of investment appraisal. It is generally accepted that money received in the future is less valuable because if the same sum were put into a low-risk financial investment, such as a bank, it would grow to a greater sum in the future due to the accrued interest. The rate of interest therefore affects the difference in value between money now and money in the future. If an estimate can be made of the rate of interest, this effect of the time value of money can be calculated. This type of calculation forms the basis of many of the methods of investment appraisal.

Methods of investment appraisal

All methods of investment appraisal compare benefits (or receipts) with costs (or expenditure). During the life of any investment project there will be receipts and expenditures in each accounting period (say a year). A textbook example might show a large single expenditure at the start, offset by a flow of receipts during the lifetime of the project The initial expenditure represents the capital cost of the building or machine, whilst the receipts represent rents or contributions to production. In reality the situation is complicated by expenditures which occur other than at the initial stage. For example, expenditures might occur on maintenance, management, repayment of loans and so on throughout the investment period.

Some, though not all, methods of investment appraisal take account of the time value of money. Two methods will be outlined. The second takes the time value of money into account, whilst the first method does not.

234

Payback

This is a simple concept. Calculations are made to determine the length of time that would elapse before the amount originally invested is recouped. No account is taken of the time value of money, or of the eventual total return if the investment project runs its full course.

For example if a choice has to be made between two projects each of which costs £10 million, project A which will recoup this outlay after five years will be preferred to project B where the outlay will be recouped after ten years, even though the total return on project B after, say, twenty five years would be greater.

Payback has been criticised as a method of investment appraisal because it does not take account of the timing of expenditures or receipts. It does, however, have a number of uses.

1. If there is a wide choice of potential investment projects, payback can be used as a relatively simple method of drawing up a shortlist.
2. If the finance for the project has to be borrowed from an external source, the lender may consider the payback period to be of great importance.
3. Given the uncertainties which arise over time, a simple method of appraisal may be considered more sensible than an elaborate method. For example, speculative increases in the future value of investment assets (such as property built on land which has a steeply rising value) can make calculations which have been based on current information unreliable.
4. Some investment assets form an inherent part of a larger asset and cannot be sold alone. If the larger asset as a whole might be sold in the future, it is important that the smaller asset should have paid for itself. For example, some home improvements, such as double glazing, are expensive assets which are unlikely to add their full cost to the sale price of the house. The houseowner seeks to recoup the cost not only when the house is sold but also through savings made on reduced heating bills. The time taken to recoup the cost (the payback period) is an important factor when deciding whether to invest in double glazing, particularly if there is any prospect of a house move.

Discounted cash flow (DCF)

This represents the conventional approach to investment appraisal. The technique takes account of both the timing and pattern of receipts and expenditures. It also takes account of the rate of interest but makes no allowances for any uncertainties. The main principle of DCF is that all receipts and expenditures during the lifetime of the project are related back to the present day by a process known as **discounting**. This is the reverse of the more familiar **compounding**.

1. With *compounding*, a pound invested now will accrue interest and be worth more than a pound in the future.
2. With *discounting*, the approach is reversed. Calculations are carried out to determine the sum that needs to be invested now which, with accrued interest, will be worth a pound at some future point in time. In other words, how much is a pound received or spent at some point in the future worth in today's terms?

Investment appraisal using DCF puts all receipts and expenditures during the lifetime of a project on a common basis. That is, they are discounted back to the present day to give a **net present value**. Before the appraisal can be carried out, a discount rate has to be selected as the criterion rate of return. All the receipts and expenditures are then discounted back to the present day using discounting factors. These discounting factors are published as tables which show the factors for various rates of interest over varying numbers of years. Computer programmes can rapidly speed up these calculations. When the discount rate has been applied to all the receipts and expenditures, the net present value can be calculated. If this is positive, the project is feasible; if it is negative, the project is not feasible. Where a number of projects are compared, the one with the highest net present value should prove to be the most profitable.

The remaining decision that has to be made concerns the basis on which the discount rate is selected. The usual approach is to choose the cost of capital (such as the market rate of interest for long term finance). This gives a break-even target for the project. Alternatively an investor may seek a specific rate of return or profit, which can be applied to determine whether the project will meet the objectives. If a range of options are available, the project which will return the highest profit can be identified.

236

Investment appraisal and social projects

The majority of investment projects, including many kinds of construction, are carried out for financial reasons. Some projects represent factors of production which contribute to productivity; other projects are assets which are built for direct financial gain. However some projects are expected to yield a social benefit and, as previously mentioned in Application F, they are appraised on a wider range of criteria than purely financial. Social and political considerations are taken into account. Many public sector construction projects fall into this category including infrastructure and buildings connected with the creation of human capital.

Investment appraisal for social projects (broadly speaking those in the public sector) differs from that used for private sector projects because of the problems associated with the market system, discussed earlier in Chapter 3 and more particularly in Application A. Due to the problems of market imperfections, unfairness and externalities, appraisal on market criteria alone will not give the socially optimum result.

Attempts have been made to adapt private sector investment appraisal techniques to the public sector using methods such as **cost benefit analysis**. These methods consider *all* the costs and benefits associated with a project, both financial and non financial. Cost benefit analysis has been applied to a range of projects, especially large scale infrastructure. For example, a well known study was undertaken before construction of the Victoria Line of the London Underground. This study found that in financial terms the project would be unprofitable as the likely income from fares would not cover the costs of construction and operation. However when the benefits of reduced traffic congestion and faster journeys to work were taken into account, the construction of the Victoria Line was found to be socially profitable. Another study was undertaken to determine a site for an additional airport to serve London. In this study account had to be taken of the costs of noise pollution and environmental damage. A number of problems arise when using cost benefit analysis.

1. How widely should the costs and benefits be taken into consideration? It has to be decided, for example, how far from a proposed airport the effects of noise should be taken into account.

2. How should costs and benefits be valued? Items such as noise and congestion can be particularly problematical.
3. Should the discount rate be similar to that used for private sector projects? It is possible that the very long term nature of some public projects would make this unsuitable.
4. Account must be taken of social and political factors. One aspect concerns fairness in the distribution of costs and benefits. Whilst a proposed airport may benefit the country as a whole, the costs may be borne disproportionately by those people who will be living near it. Other factors may be more political. For example a government may decide there is an overriding need for, say, a Channel tunnel or a nuclear power station whatever the findings of cost benefit analyses based on economic criteria might be.

Whilst sophisticated cost benefit analysis techniques may be appropriate for major projects, simpler techniques may be used on a smaller scale. These might use 'rule of thumb' rather than highly sophisticated calculations. For example, when a planning authority considers a proposal from a developer, account will be taken of the wider impact of the development on the community. There may even be a notional 'planning balance sheet' which forms a basis for negotiation. If the planning authority feels that the proposed development does not generate sufficient benefits for the community, they may suggest that the developer provides some extra benefit, such as a public amenity, before planning permission is granted. This was discussed previously in Applications A and C.

It must be stressed however that investment appraisal decisions in the public sector are subject to various pressures. Indeed it has been argued that political objectives often determine which projects are actually carried out.

Developers' budgets

Much of the discussion relating to investment appraisal can be applied to any investment project, construction or otherwise. For example payback or DCF techniques might be used to appraise investment in any factor of production whether a building or machine. However techniques have also been developed which are specifically suitable for property investment, particularly investments undertaken for direct financial gain. These techniques assist valuations surveyors in the feasibility study of proposed commercial developments. A brief outline will be given.

A developer's budget defines the breakdown of costs which have to be covered by the income that is generated by the project. The concept of the budget was first introduced in Part 1. With any development the benefits have to equal or exceed the costs for the project to be feasible from an economic point of view. The sum of the benefits is known as the **Gross Development Value (GDV)** and represents the income which the client receives.

Gross development values

As previously mentioned, GDVs can take several forms.

1. *A lump sum from the sale of the project on completion*. Housebuilding projects are the most common example of this form of GDV. The developer undertakes market research to determine the likely selling price of the houses.

2. *Rents received over time*. These are common in commercial developments. Market research can determine likely rents, which then need to be capitalised, that is, converted into a lump sum figure. This can be calculated by discounting back to find a present-day value, as previously described.

3. *Speculative element*. This element must also be taken into account when calculating GDVs. The future resale value of a project may change very quickly if certain market conditions exist. If supply is inelastic, an increase in demand will result in rising land prices and a rise in the value of any property built on it. A downturn in demand wil have the reverse effect with falling values in the property market and lower GDVs. These possible changes in value are difficult to predict and represent one of the great uncertainties of property development.

Elements of the budget

There are a number of costs, including:

1. land

2. construction costs
3. professional charges
4. finance
5. profit.

The GDV has to equal or exceed the sum of these costs for the project to be economically feasible. Many of these costs can be described quite simply:

Professional charges relate to the fees connected with the design, construction and management of the property.

Finance refers to the cost of financing the project. This would normally be the cost of borrowing, that is, the rate of interest.

Profit will be a target figure selected by the developer, and which will depend on market conditions, that is, the extent of competition or monopoly which exists in the market. The profit target will also vary depending on the degree of risk. As discussed in Application F, the higher the risk the higher the return (or profit) which can be expected.

In addition to these costs two other possibilities need consideration.

1. If the developer owns the land its cost can form part of the budget and the amount available for building costs can be isolated.
2. If the developer does not own the land, the building costs must be estimated. These can be incorporated into the budget and the amount available for land purchase can be isolated.

This process of isolating one of the two remaining major costs is known as calculating the **residual**. The residual method of valuing property is one of the most common methods used by surveyors.

The cost of land is probably the most critical element of the developer's budget. A profitable development may well depend more than anything else on the ability to find a site at the right price.

Approximate estimating

Whilst approximate estimating is not a method of feasibility study

240

as such, estimates of the building costs for a project may be required at various stages, particularly during the design stage. Estimates are difficult to make at the feasibility stage because very little design information is available. However, as seen above, an estimate of the building costs may be necessary if a residual calculation is used to isolate the land costs.

There are many methods of approximate estimating, which will be considered in the more appropriate context of Application I — Cost control during design.

Summary

Before the decision to build is taken a client will undertake a feasibility study to determine whether the project will meet the required objectives. Feasibility studies are usually measured in financial terms but can be expanded to include non-financial social costs and benefits. Various feasibility study techniques can be applied to investment assets. Investment appraisal techniques, including payback and discounted cash flow, form part of this category. Since the data on which appraisals are based are liable to change because of inflation or speculation, there are great uncertainties with these techniques.

In addition to techniques which can be applied generally, other investment appraisal techniques have been developed which are particularly suitable for construction projects. A commercial client will usually draw up a developer's budget which can be used to determine the amount available for either land purchase or building costs.

The decision to proceed with a project can be taken if the feasibility study gives a positive result. The land cost will be known, and a budgeted amount will be available as the **cost limit**, that is the maximum sum available for building costs. The next task is to translate the cost limit into a design which meets the client's requirements. The control of costs during the design stage is the main economic function, and will be considered in the next application.

Tutorial questions

1. To what extent does inflation affect the property developer's calculations?

2. What needs to be considered when appraising a major infrastructure project such as the Channel Tunnel?
3. How significant are building costs in a client's overall project budget?

Application I

Cost control during design

Introduction

An important item which can be identified following the feasibility stage described in Application H concerns the **building costs**. These form a major element in the client's budget. The client seeks to achieve a profit or net benefit from the project, that is benefit or income must exceed costs. It is therefore important that the budgeted building costs are not exceeded.

The design team might consist of an architect, quantity surveyor, engineer and so on. Following the feasibility stage a set of requirements, known as the **client's brief**, will be taken into consideration before design is commenced. The brief will include an allowed sum for building costs and details of the scale and standard of building accommodation required. For example, the brief might require:

1. X thousand square metres of office space,
2. suitable for high quality commercial occupiers, and
3. with building costs not to exceed Y million pounds.

The design team develops the client's brief into a more detailed plan, designing a building that will meet the client's objectives within the cost allowed.

The skills of the quantity surveyor are extremely important at this stage, as advice must be given to the architect on the cost implications of various design solutions. The core skill required is **approximate estimating**. At various stages before the design is completed, estimates will need to be made of the building costs. Indeed some estimates may be required before serious design work is commenced. As mentioned in the last application, a preliminary estimate of building costs may be necessary for budget purposes. During the design stage some estimates will be made for general information to confirm that the design as a whole is

243

within budget. Other estimates will be more detailed to assist the architect with particular elements of the design.

This application will outline some of the skills required during the design stage to ensure that costs are not exceeded and that the required objectives of the client are met.

The nature of cost control

The purpose of cost control, like any other form of control, is to ensure that results comply with some plan. In the construction context, there are many stages of cost control, all of which seek to ensure that the cost falls within the client's budget. Cost control is therefore necessary:

1. at feasibility stage
2. at design stage
3. at tender stage, to ensure contractors' bids fall within budget
4. during construction stage
5. during the life of the building to ensure that its performance and generation of benefits continue to meet the client's objectives.

If cost control information reveals that actual costs have deviated from planned costs at any stage, remedial action should be taken if possible.

Cost control in building concerns *estimating* the cost and updating the estimate as more information becomes available. Estimating requires the **measurement of building work**, that is the quantification and description of building work. It can be carried out at varying levels of detail, the best known being that undertaken for the preparation of the bill of quantities. Whilst most forms of estimating require some measurement, not all require the level of detail necessary when preparing a bill of quantities.

Approaches to estimating

There are two main approaches to estimating, as follows:

1. Manipulation of existing data so that it can be used for the building which is the subject of the estimate.
2. Building up an estimate from first principles, a process normally requiring approximate measurement.

244

The choice of method will depend on a number of factors, which can be summarised as follows:

1. How advanced is design? This determines the amount of information available and the sophistication and accuracy of the estimate which will be possible.
2. How detailed a study is required? Irrespective of whether the information available would permit a detailed estimate, it is possible that only a very approximate estimate is required.
3. How much time is available? If an estimate is required quickly the degree of detail will be limited.
4. The type of project. The building costs will be studied more closely if the building is of an unusual design. A reasonably accurate estimate will be attained relatively easily for a building of more standardised design.
5. The technology available. With the use of computers, the calculations involved in the estimating process can be speeded up. However it should be noted that the skills of the surveyor or estimator are still vital.

Manipulation of data

The most common approach to approximate estimating uses *historical data*, that is cost data which has been collected from projects which have been completed. Some of this data is available in published form whilst some may be generated internally, that is, collected from previous projects carried out by the individual or organisation responsible for the current estimate.

The existing data is adapted so that it can be used for the proposed project. A building as similar as possible to the one being considered is selected. The data is then updated in a number of ways.

1. Updating the data for *price*. The general level of building costs changes over time, usually in the upward direction. Historical data is updated to the time when the proposed project will go to tender. Cost indices are published which assist with this task.
2. Updating the data for *location*. In addition to the cost differences which occur over time, variations also exist between locations. For example, building costs are usually higher in remote locations. Localised shortages of some materials and types of labour can also add to

245

building costs. The very large construction projects of the late 1980s and 1990s have made high demands for resources which may exacerbate the situation still further in some locations.

3. Updating the data for *quantity*. The size and shape of two buildings may vary even though they are constructed for a similar use. Such variations have cost implications and allowances are made usually by way of a proportional adjustment. These adjustments are more difficult to make at the early stages of design.

4. Updating the data for *quality*. Whilst two buildings may be broadly similar in terms of size and usage their quality may be very different. These differences may be of a general nature or affect certain respects only. For example, one building may need a more sophisticated heating and ventilating system than another because of its exposed location. The prospective occupiers that the building is designed to attract will also determine its general quality.

First principles estimating

This method of estimating is the usual method described in textbooks. The price of labour, materials, plant, profit and overheads are calculated and added together to give the rate for, say, a square metre of brickwork, which is used for the bill of quantities. These rates become the basis of the tender. The term estimating generally refers to this method. The aim is to achieve accurate figures for building costs, since the offer the contractor makes to the client under the traditional tendering system is based on them. As previously mentioned, approximate estimating is more likely to make use of the manipulation of historical data, although first principles estimating can also be used. In particular, approximate quantities might be used in the later stages of design. Broadly speaking, approximate quantities consist of the main items in the bill of quantities with the smaller items subsumed. First principles estimating is more time consuming but may be necessary in certain cases. The data used might be generated internally within the firm. Published information is also available in various price books although this is more suitable for full estimating carried out for tendering purposes.

Methods of approximate estimating

The approaches to estimating, that is the manipulation of existing data, or building up from first principles, have been considered. Consideration will now be given to the methods of carrying out approximate estimating. *Three* methods will be considered:

1. single price rates
2. elemental estimating
3. approximate quantities.

Each method may be used at a different stage of estimating.

Single price rates

These are usually the simplest methods. Single price rates can be used at an early stage of the design or where a detailed analysis is not required. A rough estimate of the *total cost* of the proposed building is expressed in terms of some convenient variable. These could include:

1. Cost per unit. This is the simplest form of expression where the cost is expressed in terms of a unit of usage. Examples include pounds per school place; pounds per bed for hospitals and so on.
2. Costs per cubic metre. The total cost is divided by the volume of the building and expressed as pounds per cubic metre.
3. Cost per unit of floor area. The total cost is divided by the superficial floor area and expressed in pounds per square metre. This is a common method of expression which is considered to be more useful because the income generated by a building is also often measured in square metres. For example, rents for office and retail space are charged in pounds per square metre. In addition the format of pounds per square metre can be used subsequently in the more detailed methods of estimating described later.

Elemental estimating

As the design is developed, more information becomes available and a more detailed estimate is possible. The proposed building is analysed into functional elements, the principal of which could be:

1. substructure
2. superstructure
3. internal finishes
4. fittings and furnishings
5. services
6. external works.

Many of these elements can be sub-divided if additional detail is required. For example, superstructure can be sub-divided into frame, external walls, roof, and so on. Each element is priced separately and expressed as pounds per square metre of floor area.

The cost information obtained from this elemental breakdown forms the basis on which the elements of a building can be planned in advance of design. This will be considered further under 'cost planning'.

Approximate quantities

This method utilises the first principles approach to estimating. Whilst it is more accurate than the other methods, it is more time consuming and greater information is required. For this reason the method is mainly used either at the later stages of design or where particular accuracy or detail is required. As previously mentioned, the data used in the measurement of approximate quantities is often generated internally within the firm carrying out the estimate. Published price information is more commonly used in full estimating carried out for tendering purposes.

Approximate quantities are usually measured by taking a major item and deriving a rate for it. For example, the overall area of an external wall will be measured and a rate applied to it. The rate will include all the subsidiary items which would normally be measured separately in a full bill of quantities.

Cost planning

This is a more ambitious variation of preliminary approximate estimating described above. Rather than estimating a cost, the objective is to provide data which can be used to ensure that the design is developed to fall within the budget cost or cost limit laid down by the client. In other words the quantity surveyor provides the architect with cost information on various design solutions. The elemental format described above is utilised, as many designs are developed in this way. The architect is thus in possession of cost information for each element.

Cost plans can be carried out at various stages of the design process. Initially they will be preliminary, based on the first sketch plans. As additional information becomes available they will become more accurate. The essential feature however is that the cost of each element of the building is allocated *in advance* of design.

Cost planning may be carried out using the approximate quantities method in the later stages of design, but it is more likely to be based on historical data. A **cost analysis** of a past project will therefore be selected. This detailed cost breakdown of a project will be selected to be as similar as possible to the proposed project. Each element of the data will be adjusted in the four ways mentioned earlier, that is for price, location, quantity and quality. The cost plan for the proposed project can then be finalised. It will be used by the architect as a guide in the preparation of working drawings.

The importance of the early stages of the cost planning process should be emphasised. At an early stage all options are open and good cost advice can make real savings and lead to better value for money in design. As the design is developed more items are firm and the scope for cost savings is reduced. This principle can also be applied to the construction stage. If costs increase during the construction of one element, it is difficult to make savings elsewhere without reducing either the scale or quality of the building.

Cost checking

This represents the final stage of the design process before the preparation of the contract documents including the bill of quantities. As the design develops it must be ensured that it falls within the cost plan. The working drawings for each element are checked for cost and if necessary remedial action can be taken. Adjustments to elements of the design can in fact be made at any time up until tender stage. However, as previously stated, increased costs which are the result of changes made at a late stage are more difficult to claw back elsewhere. Changes which are made during the construction stage will usually result in the client paying more.

The main objective of cost checking is to confirm that the design is proceeding according to plan.

Summary

This application has given an overview of the largely technical process of controlling costs during the design stage. The economic importance of ensuring that the project costs are kept within budget must be emphasised. The building cost forms a major part of the client's calculation and must be adhered to, if the client's objectives are to be met. The design team has the task of designing a building which meets the client's objectives *and* keeps within the cost allowed. If this is not possible, the client must be advised quickly so that a decision can be made on which course of action to follow. Options might include the following:

1. Retain the building originally envisaged for meeting objectives and allow higher building costs, which might be offset elsewhere in the budget.
2. Adhere to the budgeted building costs and trim the scale and/or quality of the building accordingly.
3. Abandon the project. If this is necessary the decision should be made as soon as possible to avoid abortive work and expense.

Some of the skills employed by, say, quantity surveyors in cost control have been outlined. Of particular importance are the techniques of estimating, using either the manipulation of existing (historical) data, or building up of estimates from first principles. The distinction was drawn between approximate estimating and cost planning, the latter technique being more ambitious. It was stressed that cost planning will be more effective if particular attention is paid at the earlier stages of design, as it is here that all options are open and more substantial savings can be made. As the design (and construction) stages develop the scope for cost savings diminish. Changes which are made later are more likely to add to costs and may jeopardise the achievement of the objectives of the client.

Tutorial questions

1. Why is measurement the basis of estimating?
2. What factors determine the choice of approximate estimating technique used?
3. Are the aims of cost planning realistically achievable?

Application J

The construction industry as a whole

Introduction

Part 2 of this book focused to a large extent on aspects of the microeconomic process including markets and firms. Much of the material in Part 3 has used similar themes, for example, the profitability of projects from the point of view of clients. However, as shown in Chapter 5, it is possible to study an industry as a whole. The term industry is used to describe a collection of firms, and their microeconomic processes, whose operations have some commonality. In Chapter 5 the permeable nature of the boundaries of an industry were explained, and Fig. 5.1 gave a simplified diagrammatic representation of the construction industry. This application will examine certain issues which are applicable to the construction industry as a whole. Subsequent applications will revert to the microeconomic approach to firms and construction projects.

One of the issues to be considered concerns the relationship between the construction industry and the UK economy. Examinations of the workload and structure of the industry will be undertaken, including a study of the reasons why these may change. The resources used in construction will also be considered. Since land has already been discussed in detail in Application B, this application will consider other resources including materials and components. In addition the characteristics of the labour market, studied previously in Chapter 4, will be applied to the construction industry. It should however be noted that the concept of the industry as a whole is rather abstract. The study of individual firms, projects and sectors of the industry is necessary if a clearer and more complete picture is to be obtained.

The construction industry and the economy

The construction industry is the name given to the large collection of firms responsible for producing construction work. As mentioned in Chapter 5, this collection of firms is very loose indeed. Whilst this statement might apply to most industries, nevertheless the study of various industries and sectors, and the assessment of their contribution to the economy, can prove valuable. It was shown in Chapter 5 that industries contribute to the economy in terms of:

1. output
2. employment
3. exports.

The contribution of the construction industry to these three aspects of the economy will be considered.

Output

The output of the construction industry may be classified in a number of ways, including:

1. private and public sector work
2. housing and non-housing work
3. new work and repair and maintenance
4. the proportion of work carried out by large firms and small firms.

Various statistics are collected relating to construction output. The construction industry makes a large contribution to the economy in both quantitative and qualitative terms. In quantitative terms, construction represents one of the largest single industries, and accounts for approximately ten percent of Gross Domestic Product over a period of time. In qualitative terms, the most important feature of construction output is its contribution to investment in the economy. Investment goods are those which improve the efficiency of production and include, in addition to plant and machinery, buildings such as factories, offices and shops. Public investment is very often construction orientated, to provide infrastructure, schools and hospitals. If the economy is to be efficient it is essential that the construction industry should be able to deliver output effectively.

Employment

Due to both its size and contribution to output, the construction industry employs a large number of people. Its importance as an employer is further emphasised because the production methods used are often more labour intensive than, say, in manufacturing industry. Production methods will be examined in Application M, where it will be seen that although mechanisation has been introduced into the construction industry, it is used much less extensively than in manufacturing industry.

One of the consequences of labour intensive production is that if the level of output changes, the level of employment is affected disproportionately. There is a relatively strong multiplier effect and the expansion of construction work by, say, a public sector programme, is often advocated by Keynesians as a good method of increasing employment. In other words, the number of jobs created per million pounds of public expenditure would be greater if the money is spent in construction than in manufacturing.

Exports

Traditionally the construction industry has not been considered a significant exporter, or importer. Building materials often have a high weight/value ratio and are normally produced in the country of usage. In Britain's case an exception has been the need to import timber.

Certain changes have however taken place over more recent years. UK construction firms have undertaken contracts overseas, especially the massive construction programmes of the 1970s in the oil-wealthy countries of the Middle East. However such contracts do not make a very large contribution to the balance of payments because the contract sum is mainly spent on local labour and materials.

A more significant development has been the growth in imports, partly of traditional materials such as cement, but more importantly of components. As will be seen in Application M, building methods now utilise a higher proportion of manufactured components, and less traditional materials. Considerable quantities of these components are imported, with the result that the construction industry now has a balance of payments deficit with the rest of the world. There has also been

254

an increase in the number of overseas developers and consultants, such as architects and construction managers, operating in the UK. In addition there are signs that overseas contractors will also enter the UK market. At the present time this is limited, but the trend may continue, particularly in the context of the single European market projected for 1992.

Construction workload

As already mentioned, the output of the construction industry needs to be maintained to enable the economy to prosper. Construction provides much of the nation's investment and is therefore vital for continued growth. In this section the changes which affect the level and pattern of the workload over a period of time, will be considered.

The two most important changes which have occurred are:

1. demographic changes
2. public policy changes.

Demographic changes

These changes have had a particular affect on housebuilding. The main demographic changes, described in Application D, have resulted in a lower demand for the three or four bedroomed family house and a higher demand for smaller units. This has evolved because of increased numbers of:

1. financially secure elderly persons
2. single person households.

The overall effect is a higher demand for numbers of housing units. In particular the demand for purpose-built units for retired people has become an established market of considerable size.

Public policy changes

These were described in Chapter 7. The major policy objectives since 1979 have been the elimination of inflation and the revival of the market economy. To achieve these objectives various short and long term policy measures have been adopted. The main short term policy instrument has been the use of the rate of interest, while long term measures have sought to strengthen the market to make it operate more effectively. The most significant effect of this policy for the construction industry has been the great reduction in public sector work. Cuts in public spending have occurred across the board but particularly in housing where local authority housebuilding has virtually ceased. A much higher proportion of the construction workload is now in the private sector. As in many other cases there is disagreement on whether this situation is desirable.

Those who *approve* of the reduction in public sector demand claim that the industry can plan its workload with more certainty because it is no longer subjected to changes in public sector spending and hence demand. During much of the post-war period of Keynesian demand management (see Chapter 7) governments were accused of using the construction industry as a regulator. Thus whenever the government wanted to increase spending it would increase demand for construction work, or vice versa. The resulting fluctuating demand on the industry was destabilising.

Those who *disapprove* of the reduction in public sector demand claim that the problems of fluctuating demand in the Keynesian period were exaggerated. Although demand for new orders fluctuated, actual output fluctuated much less due to the varying length of contracts. Furthermore the cycles of fluctuating demand in the public sector were reasonably predictable. In the private sector, whilst high and rising demand might well be sustained for some years, there is always the problem that private demand is largely based on confidence. If confidence is high, this will benefit the construction industry. However by its very nature, confidence can reduce, or even disappear very quickly, and if this were to happen the impact on construction demand would be more destabilising than the fluctuating cycles of public sector demand. Similar ideas have been discussed previously, for example it was seen that a high level of confidence can lead to speculation in land (see Application B) and housing (see Application D).

Market structure in construction

The term market structure has been used previously to describe the extent of competition or monopoly in an industry. In Chapter 3 the methods of classifying market structures were introduced. In particular the concept of *degree of monopoly* which defines market power in terms of mark up on perfectly competitive price, was described. It was also shown that although an industry might evolve into a market structure where a high degree of monopoly exists, within this structure there may be polarisation between very large and very small firms, defined as core/periphery relationships. These ideas were further developed in Chapter 5.

Some discussion on market structure in the construction industry was undertaken in Chapters 3 and 5. It was shown that in the post-war period the structure of the industry evolved from being substantially comprised of large numbers of medium-size firms into an industry with a few very large firms and many small firms. The medium-size firms were usually general building contractors operating locally rather than nationally. They were capable of undertaking all but the largest building projects. The large firms were usually civil engineering contractors operating nationally. This structure changed, particularly in the 1960s and 1970s as the larger firms diversified into building, increasing their size quickly through mergers and takeovers rather than through internal growth. Firms from other industries also became involved, with the result that many large construction firms now form part of even larger diversified multi-divisional firms, or conglomerates. Alongside this emergence of a few very large firms, there has been a growth in the number of small firms. Many are of a specialist nature, and are often in a sub-contracting relationship with the large firms. Small firms are often labour-only sub-contractors employing operatives who would previously have been employed directly by the main contractor. The main contractor/sub-contractor relationship has implications for productivity which will be discussed in Application M relating to production methods.

The changes outlined above have resulted in the structure of the industry being characterised by a few very large firms (the core) with many small firms (the periphery). The middle ground is somewhat isolated, with the traditional, locally based, medium-size general builder left in a difficult situation. Whereas in the past such firms would probably have won most of the local building contracts including prestige projects, they now find themselves in competition with large national firms who seem to be awarded most of the substantial contracts. It is with increasing difficulty that the local, respected, possibly family controlled, building firm continues to exist. In some instances such firms have merged with similar firms; in other cases they have been taken over by larger firms. Occasionally medium-sized

257

firms, whilst not actually merging, have collaborated through joint ventures on larger projects. The strategy of the individual firm will be considered further in Application L.

In the future, the structure of the industry may be increasingly dominated by even larger firms. There is a move towards the industry becoming more international in character, a trend which is well established in many other industries. Overseas influence on UK practice has already been mentioned, for example in Application G when procurement methods were discussed. Two factors which may encourage the growth of even larger firms are:

1. The move towards the single European market projected to come into effect in 1992.
2. The tendency towards extremely large projects (sometimes called mega-projects). Examples include the Canary Wharf and Kings Cross developments in London, and the Channel Tunnel.

In the past, projects such as the Channel Tunnel have tended to be carried out by consortia, but because of the problems which arise with such arrangements, many people now advocate the formation of huge construction companies which can compete with the largest in the world. The implications of this could be more monopoly power in the construction industry. Further consideration will be given to this topic under market strategy of the firm in Application L.

Competition in the construction industry

When considering market structure the main interest centres on the extent of competition, or the degree of monopoly. The usual image of the construction industry is of many firms in keen competition with each other. However as shown earlier, the industry is increasingly dominated by large firms, which reduces competition. Even where there are a large number of firms apparently competing there are still problems of monopoly power. For example:

1. Although there are many firms, only a few may be capable of carrying out certain types of work, particularly the provision of large-scale infrastructure.
2. In certain localities a few firms may dominate the market although in theory firms from outside the area may be able to compete.

258

The market structure described earlier was characterised by a few large core firms with many small peripheral firms. The implication is that the many small firms are in a highly competitive situation, competing with each other to obtain sub-contract work from the large firm. The large firm (main contractor) has a high degree of monopoly and can drive a hard bargain with the small sub-contractors. If there is plenty of work available the main contractor can also drive a hard bargain with the client. However the situation can change very quickly for a variety of reasons.

1. If there is limited work available the main contractor would have to tender more tightly. This gives a competitive advantage to the client, although the main/sub-contractor balance might not be affected.
2. When work is plentiful, sub-contractors are often in short supply. In such circumstances they have the advantage and the main contractor is faced with rising costs.
3. In times of high demand there might also be shortages of materials. This places materials manufacturers and suppliers in a strong position to increase prices and their own profits.

These last two points highlight how resource shortages can affect the construction industry.

Construction resources

In common with other economic activities, the construction industry needs resources. It has already been seen that in the microeconomic process resources must be acquired by the firm before production can take place. Studies of resource price and availability tend to use microeconomic methods to examine the subject from the viewpoint of the firm. However there are some important aspects of resources which relate to the industry as a whole.

There are a large number of resources used in construction, the more commonly stated categories being:

1. land
2. labour
3. materials
4. plant.

The land resource has been discussed extensively previously, particularly in Application B. Plant represents the product of the manufacturing engineering industries. These industries have declined over the years as discussed in Part 2, particularly Chapters 5 and 7, and as a result many of these products are now imported.

The resources which will be considered separately are materials and labour.

Materials

The type of materials used in construction projects depends on the production methods used. Both production methods and materials have changed with time, a situation which will be studied more closely in Application M. There are two main categories of material.

1. Materials which are used in a relatively unprocessed condition. Examples include bricks, stone, aggregate, cement, timber and plaster. These materials are used in traditional construction and are made up on site to form elements of the building. A high degree of skill is usually required. Since these materials require extensive labour on site they have a low value/weight ratio, or a low value added.

2. Materials which have been processed into components off-site. Some components may be manufactured for use in specific building systems, while others may be used more generally. These materials require less work on site and therefore have a high value added. They also require a lower level of skill from the operative on site.

These types of material represent the two extremes. In reality the actual materials used will probably be processed to some extent. Changes in production methods have resulted in the increasing use of more sophisticated building materials and components.

There are a number of problems related to the supply of material resources in construction.

1. The industries which manufacture materials are more capital intensive than the construction industry itself. It has often proved difficult to vary materials production to meet demand, with the result that increases in building activity have led to shortages of materials very quickly.

260

These shortages have been reflected in increased costs and have made accurate tender prices difficult to assess.

2. Construction materials are usually manufactured on a large scale. Since there are few firms capable of producing on this scale a potential high degree of monopoly exists. The supply of materials such as common bricks, steel sections, cement and glass is dominated by a relatively small number of firms.

As mentioned earlier, there has been a substantial increase in the amount of materials imported in recent years, not only of manufactured components which have a high value added and high value/weight ratio, but also of traditional materials such as cement and bricks. The import of materials has both desirable and undesirable consequences. An undesirable effect is that imports worsen the balance of payments and may result in job losses in the UK. Conversely, materials can be imported to relieve shortages caused by an increase in demand. Furthermore, overseas competition can make it more difficult for UK materials producers to take advantage of their monopolistic position.

Labour

The general nature of the labour market was discussed in Chapter 4. The main functions of the labour market are to set wages for, and to allocate workers to, particular jobs in particular locations. As discussed in Part 2, there is some debate about whether the labour market adjusts smoothly when changes in demand occur.

A major problem of the labour market concerns the *immobility of labour*. It was shown in Chapter 3 that labour is often immobile in terms of location and skill. These factors have an impact on construction. Traditionally workers in the UK construction industry have been prepared to travel quite widely to find work. Despite this fact, shortages of labour still occur, particularly when much of the work available is concentrated in certain parts of the country. The inevitable consequence of a shortage of labour is higher wages and inflationary pressure on construction costs.

Labour shortages are more often the result of a lack of skilled workers rather than the unwillingness of workers to travel. Although the skill levels required are not as high as they once were, shortages seem to occur whenever there is an upturn in workload. The shortage of skilled workers appears to affect not only construction but much of British industry. A great deal of criticism has been levelled at the attitude to training in Britain. This criticism has been directed partly at governments for failing to devote sufficient resources to training, and partly at firms for not maintaining levels of training within their own organisations. The temptation to cut back on training programmes during periods of low demand in the industry leads to inevitable skill shortages when demand picks up.

In the construction industry, the training problem is exacerbated by the increase in labour-only sub-contracting. Such firms are paid on piecework and are therefore less likely to offer training to unskilled workers or young people (see Application M). The traditional apprenticeship system has almost disappeared in the main construction trades (except in the building departments of some local authorities) although it still exists in some services trades such as electrical contracting. Furthermore, the length of training periods has been greatly reduced over the years.

An additional problem which must be faced in the 1990s concerns demographic changes. There will be fewer school leavers available for training, and the construction industry will have to compete with other industries if it is to attract the workforce necessary for the future. This problem will affect both the managerial and operative levels of the workforce. The construction industry must therefore improve its image and make itself more attractive to young people.

Summary

In this application some of the issues which affect the industry as a whole have been highlighted. The construction industry makes a substantial contribution to the economy primarily as a supplier of investment goods. Construction is more labour intensive than, say, manufacturing and for this reason the industry is a large employer. The workload of the industry has changed significantly since the early 1980s with a public sector that has been much diminished. The result has been an increased dependence on the private sector. This is favoured by some who are pleased to see an end to the stop/go cycles in construction new orders. Others believe that the private sector demand is too dependent on confidence which could easily evaporate and make construction demand more volatile than in the days of a large public sector.

The construction industry has evolved from comprising mainly medium-sized general building contractors to having a more diverse structure with a few large national firms and many very small firms. This appears to have increased monopoly power in construction, although this is a fluid situation which might be influenced by more overseas competitors operating in the UK market.

The resources used by the construction industry are diverse. As land had been discussed previously, this application concentrated on materials and labour. Materials supply is problematical in that it is difficult to increase production quickly. In addition many construction materials are produced by firms with monopoly power. However overseas competition is affecting materials markets particularly for the supply of manufactured components. The major problem of labour supply concerns skills shortages, a problem faced by much of UK industry. This is often blamed on an insufficiently serious attitude to training from both firms and government. The problem will be exacerbated by a reduction in the number of young people available for training in the 1990s.

Having considered the industry as a whole subsequent applications will concentrate on further aspects of firms and construction projects. References will be made to the wider aspects of the industry where appropriate.

Tutorial questions

1. To what extent is the construction industry a cohesive entity?
2. What are the advantages of increasing government expenditure on construction?
3. Are there likely to be skills shortages in the construction industry in the 1990s?

Application K

Post-tender cost control

Introduction

Applications K, L and M are broadly concerned with the fourth stage of developing the built environment, that is the construction of buildings. While Applications L and M will concentrate on aspects of the construction firm's behaviour, this application is concerned with financial matters which affect both client and contractor.

It was shown earlier, for example in Applications H and I, that the control of costs is of great importance to the client. The sum allowed for building costs within the client's budget must be adhered to, otherwise it is unlikely that the client's objectives will be met. In an extreme case the project might not be feasible and may have to be abandoned. Cost control is therefore a continuing process which is designed to ensure that the client's objectives are being achieved. Application H explained how the sum allowed for building costs is calculated, whilst Application I showed how the design is formulated to meet the client's needs within the budget cost. This application will give consideration to the problems of staying within the budget cost after the completion of design.

On the assumption that other aspects of the budget are not exceeded, the client's objectives will be met providing actual building costs do not exceed budgeted building costs. The client's objectives, defined in Application F, are, in general terms, to achieve a net benefit (or profit) on the project. The majority of clients are either firms, or organisations which operate under similar criteria to firms. In Chapter 4 it was shown that whilst the major long term objective of the firm is to make a profit, in the short term the firm faces the financial problem of liquidity. If this concept is applied to a construction project, it will be seen that although the project might eventually yield a profit or net benefit, attention must be given to financial matters in the interim period. Liquidity was introduced in Application F during discussion of the problem of raising enough short term finance to stay liquid during the period before the project starts to yield a return. The construction industry is affected by liquidity problems at least as much as other industries, and this application will consider the issue from the points of view of both client and contractor during the construction phase of a project.

The stages of post-tender cost control

Cost control during design was considered in Application I. This covered approximate estimating, cost planning, cost checking and the preparation of contract documentation including working drawings, specifications and bills of quantities. When these documents have been finalised, the contractor is selected using one of the various methods described in Application G (although of course with some methods the contractor is selected before or during the design stage). In the traditional tendering system the contractor is selected when design is complete. The basis on which the contractor tenders will be considered in Application L. Once the tenders have been received, a further series of cost control measures must be undertaken to cover the period until the project has been completed and is ready for occupation. These measures are:

1.   tender reconciliation
2.   cost control during construction
3.   the final account
4.   cost analysis.

These will be described briefly.

Tender reconciliation

The tenders which are received from competing contractors are checked to ensure that the tender sums are within budgeted cost. The priced bills of quantities are also checked to ensure that they are reasonably compatible with the cost plans. Each contractor invited to tender is believed to be capable of carrying out the work satisfactorily, and the tendering process therefore becomes a pure price competition, as described in Application G, with the lowest tender figure being automatically accepted in most cases.

However it is important to check this figure to ensure that the contractor has not made any significant errors and that the tender price submitted is realistic.

If all the tender figures are higher than anticipated, it will be necessary to re-examine the budgeted cost and cost plan to ascertain whether these figures were realistic. If this re-examination reveals that the building costs will be greater than originally anticipated, the client has the same choices as outlined in the summary of Application I — allow for higher building costs; trim the project to fit budget cost; or abandon the project. Since costs are incurred at each stage as the project progresses, the decision to abandon the project becomes increasingly expensive.

Cost control during construction

It is hoped that once construction work is begun on site, the tender price will not be exceeded. However some variations to the contract can normally be expected. These can occur for various reasons.

1. The client has a change of mind on some detail of the accommodation required, or standard of finish.
2. The architect has a change of mind on some aspect of the design.
3. Some unforeseen difficulty, say in the groundworks, may arise which results in additional work being required.

Many, but not all, variations to the contract involve extra costs. While contingency sums are allowed for this, the variations may exceed this allowance. An agreement must be made between the client's representative (usually the quantity surveyor) and the contractor on the value of each variation from the contract. Where possible these values should be based on the rates for items of work in the bill of quantities. Where this is not possible a fair rate must be negotiated.

If faced with extra building costs the client must decide whether to bear them and perhaps save on other items in the budget, or whether to look for savings in other parts of the building costs element. It may be possible to reduce building costs by re-examining the cost plans and identifying the elements which might be modified. However, as stated in Application I, it becomes increasingly difficult to make savings at the later stages of design when more items are firm. If the same situation occurs

266

during the construction phase the problem becomes even more serious. Frequently variations to the contract will result in the client paying more.

The final account

This is the process by which the final sum due to the contractor is calculated. The figure is based on the contract sum, that is the tender price, with additions or subtractions made for a number of items. These include:

1. The value of any variations, as outlined above.
2. The re-measurement of work. In some instances it is not possible to measure work accurately at the time of preparing the bill of quantities. In such a situation the quantity of work actually carried out is re-measured retrospectively. The parts of the bill of quantities most commonly affected in this way are the substructure and drainage.
3. The replacement of prime cost and provisional sums allowed in the bill of quantities with the actual costs incurred. Prime cost sums cover the work of nominated sub-contractors, often for specialist work such as electrical and heating services. Provisional sums are an estimated figure for those parts of the work which could not be adequately measured *or* described at the time of preparing the bill of quantities.

Ideally the preparation of the final account should continue during the construction phase, and be completed within a few months of the completion of the contract. In practice the details of the final account often take some time to negotiate and finalise, a situation which adds to the liquidity or cash flow problem for the contractor, to be discussed later in this application.

Cost analysis

It was shown in Application I that approximate estimating and cost planning at design stage are usually based on data which has been collected from previous projects. The data is often in the form of a cost analysis which represents an elemental breakdown. At the completion of a project a cost analysis is carried out, based on the tender including the priced bill of quantities. The cost analysis can be used as a final check to identify where the final costs differed from the tendered costs. Lessons can be learnt and the data used for future projects.

Liquidity and the client

As discussed in Application F there are a wide range of clients and developers. A problem that all face concerns the time lag between paying for the land, building costs and other budget items, and receiving a return or benefit on the project. For example:

1. A housebuilder may have to wait until the houses are complete before sale can take place. Housebuilders have sought to overcome this problem and a solution will be discussed later.
2. A commercial developer must complete the project before tenants move in and pay rent.

Since the length of time taken to conceive, obtain approvals, design and build is considerable the client faces a number of uncertainties. These might include:

1. Changes in economic conditions. These could affect various aspects of the client's calculations. For example changes in interest rates will affect the cost of financing the project. Changes in demand will result in the income that the client receives being different from that predicted at feasibility stage. Although rising prices for housing and commercial property are regarded as normal, there have been instances where the market quickly became static or even fell. In such cases the projected increases in selling price or rental income have not occurred.
2. Problems with the building process could slow down completion and/or add to the cost. Problems could arise from a shortage of resources, unexpected technical difficulties on site, and so on.

To cover the interval between paying out and receiving back income, some form of *short term finance* is required. For the smaller client or housebuilder a bank overdraft represents the usual source of short term finance. Assuming the land is already owned, it can be offered as collateral. For the larger professional client it is likely that there will be a number of projects in progress simultaneously. Some projects will have already been completed and will be yielding an income which can be used to finance further projects. Where a large development is concerned the sums of money required are substantial and the active involvement of a financier is often necessary. This situation was mentioned earlier when considering the way in which the role of the client may be divided between several organisations (see Application F).

As previously mentioned, housebuilders have sought ways of alleviating their liquidity or cash flow problems. As seen in Application D the housing market is based largely on confidence, with the normal expectation being that values will increase. However the market can quickly stagnate, particularly if effective incomes are cut by, say, increases in the mortgage interest rate. Many small house-building firms cannot afford to retain stocks of houses ready for when the market might pick up. Although larger construction firms are now actively involved in, and possibly dominate, house-building, there are still major problems which can affect the market. If land is purchased during a boom the price paid will be high; if demand for housing then slows the eventual selling price might not be sufficient to justify the high price paid for the land.

In order to minimise the difference in time between payment and income and to improve liquidity or cash flow, many house-builders have introduced a deposit scheme. Under this system the houses are marketed immediately following the land acquisition and planning consent stages. Prospective buyers therefore make their decision based on the plans of houses. The price is fixed and a deposit of, say, ten percent is paid, even though the buyer will have to wait some considerable time before the house is ready for occupation. This system offers certain advantages to both housebuilders and buyers. The most obvious benefit to the house-builder is a cash injection at an early stage of the project. The firm's financial position is more secure, making it easier to raise whatever further finance is required. In addition, the house-builder is guaranteed a buyer at an early stage. The principal disadvantage of the system is that if the housing market were to rise rapidly between taking the deposit and completion, the final selling price could have been much higher. From the buyer's point of view there is the benefit of certainty on price, the guaranteed eventual occupation of the property, and the possibility of some choice of internal fittings and finishings. If the market rises strongly in the interim period the buyer will have a bargain. However the buyer loses the use of the deposit money and may lose out in the event of a downturn in the market.

In view of the precarious existence of many builders, anything which reduces the cash flow problem will be beneficial. Probably the major cause of bankruptcies among building firms is not the lack of profitability, but the lack of liquidity. Therefore it can be expected that housebuilders will try to use the deposit system described above. In a rising market, housebuilders will probably find buyers who are willing to pay a deposit relatively easily. However in a static or falling market, housebuilders may be less successful, as buyers may not be so eager to commit themselves in a 'buyers' market'.

Liquidity and the contractor

Much of this application has considered the client's interest, including the case where a construction firm may also be the client, as in housebuilding. However, traditionally, construction firms undertake work on a contract basis for clients. When firms act as contractors, another set of cash flow or liquidity problems must be confronted. A description of these is included in this application.

During a construction project there is potential for considerable imbalance in the contractor's cash flow.

Payments made

The contractor regularly pays out for labour, materials, plant hire, sub-contractors and so on. Some payments are made weekly (say for labour), and some are made monthly (say to merchants for materials). In some instances the contractor might delay payments to, say, builders' merchants and make use of trade credit. In other instances payments to sub-contractors might be delayed. This could be a strong possibility when many sub-contractors are competing for work. (This last situation is considered to be a problem throughout UK industry where large firms are often slow to pay smaller firms for goods and services.) If the contractor's cash outflow is plotted against time, a typical 'S' curve results as shown in Fig. K.1.

In Fig. K.1 a typical cash outflow pattern shows payments starting slowly and building up before levelling off at practical

270

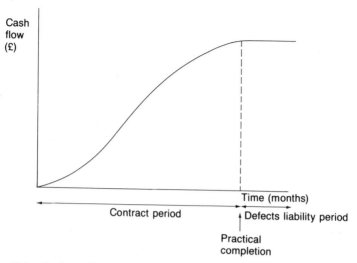

Fig. K.1   Cash outflow

completion. At the end of the contract there is a period of say six months, called the defects liability period, during which any problems can be resolved and the final account prepared.

Payments received

Since most construction contracts are lengthy, the contractor is not expected to wait until the work is finally complete before receiving payment. Normally the value of the work completed in the previous month is agreed between the client's quantity surveyor and the contractor. An interim payment is then made, less a retention sum which is held back until later. Half the retention is released at practical completion and half at the end of the defects liability period. In theory, work should be paid for within a month of its being carried out, however this will depend on the client paying promptly. Since the contractor receives a payment once a month, when cash inflow is plotted against time a stepped 'curve' results as shown in Fig. K.2.

In Fig. K.2 it can be seen that no payment is received in the first month, but following this there are regular payments until practical completion. By the end of the defects liability period the final account should have been prepared, and the final sum agreed and released together with the retention sum.

271

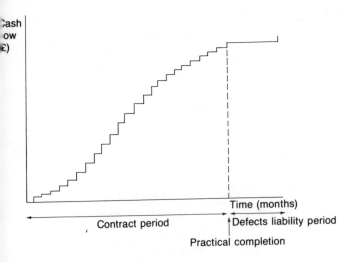

Fig. K.2　Cash inflow

The whole cash flow

The whole cash flow situation can be studied by plotting both outflows and inflows on the same axes, as shown in Fig. K.3. Figure K.3 shows a typical cash flow pattern. It can be seen that each month, before the interim payment is received, the contract is 'in the red'. This represents a deficit which has to be met by short term finance, the usual source being a bank overdraft.

Figure K.4 shows an expanded detail of part of the cash flow curves. It can be seen that the project is most in deficit each month just before the interim payment is received. The differences between the curves, shown as 'a' and 'b' represent the contractor's requirement for short term finance on the project in particular months. Larger contractors will no doubt undertake a number of different projects at the same time each of which will require a certain amount of short term finance in a given month. By advance planning the contractor should be able to calculate the short term financial requirements each month for all outstanding contracts and approach the bank for the necessary overdraft facilities.

Figure K.3 shows a fairly even cash flow pattern. The project requires a certain amount of finance each month. At practical completion the payment made should take the cash inflow curve above the outflow curve. At the end of the defects liability period

272

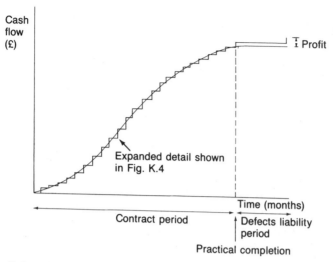

Fig. K.3   Whole project cash flow

the final payment is made, and the difference between the inflow and outflow curves represents the profit on the project.

The even pattern shown in Fig. K.3 could easily be upset by a number of events. As already mentioned, the promptness with which the client pays is important. Any delay has the effect of pushing the cash inflow curve to the right, and increasing the contractor's short term finance requirements. This could

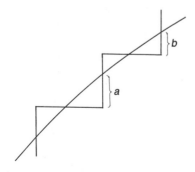

Fig. K.4   Expanded detail of whole project cash flow

significantly increase the interest charges incurred. In a competitive market, where the contractor had to tender keenly to win the contract, such a situation may put a considerable strain on the contractor's finances. This is a particular problem for contractors because traditionally profit margins on turnover are low, the expectation being that little of the firm's limited capital resources will be tied up in a particular project. In other words contractors have few assets and only limited capital, but expect to turn over their capital quickly, that is to use it many times without tying it up for long periods. (This contrasts with a manufacturer who would normally have a larger capital base and more assets.) Any delayed payment by the client would therefore put the contractor under pressure. While the contractor may try to offset this by delaying payments to merchants, plant hire companies and sub-contractors, this merely has the effect of transferring the problem to others. The vulnerability of contractors to cash flow difficulties and indeed bankruptcy has encouraged many construction firms to diversify into, say, development in order to build a more secure capital base. This will be considered in Application L.

The even cash flow pattern shown in Fig. K.3 may also be affected by the way in which the contractor prices the bill of quantities, and the effect this has on the timing and value of interim payments. The contract will be won on the basis of 'the bottom line', that is the tender figure. The final profit figure should therefore be the same regardless of how the total figure is distributed among the bill items. Some scope exists however for distributing the total figure so that more cash is received at the earlier stages of the contract. Such an arrangement has the effect of shifting the cash inflow curve shown in Fig. K.3 to the left. The short term finance requirements and interest charges for the project are thus reduced. This practice is usually referred to as 'front end loading' the bill. The rates applied to the early stages of the work, such as groundworks, are increased while rates in other, later, parts of the bill are trimmed, resulting in the same total tender figure as if the whole bill was priced accurately. This manipulation of rates should be limited since the client's quantity surveyor is unlikely to approve of the practice. The contractor may also find that there are dangers associated with it. As mentioned earlier the rates priced in the bill are used as the basis for valuing variations. If a bill item with a trimmed rate is later found to require a higher quantity of work, it will be priced at the trimmed rate and the contractor will be disadvantaged.

Summary

This application has considered aspects of financial control from the tender stage until the end of the construction period. The various stages of cost control undertaken on behalf of the client were outlined. These represent a continuation and updating of the cost control processes carried out at design stage, and involve ensuring that the tender figures are realistic; that costs stay within budget during the construction phase; agreeing the final sum to be paid, after taking into account all variations to the contract; and analysing the financial data generated by the project in order that it can be used to control costs on future projects.

A major problem faced by both client and contractor during construction concerns maintaining adequate cash flow or liquidity. Clients may have to wait until the project is complete before receiving any return or benefit. To assist with financial problems commercial developers may enter into partnership with a specialist financial institution. Housebuilders may seek to ease cash flow problems by agreeing prices with buyers and taking deposits before the houses are built. When the construction firm acts as a contractor a liquidity problem may arise because whereas payments to others are made continuously, payments from the client are only received once a month. Any delay in the monthly payment can put the contractor in severe financial difficulties. To help alleviate the problem, contractors may delay their payments to sub-contractors, or suppliers; or they may front load their priced bills of quantities to bring in more cash earlier in the contract. Alternatively construction firms may adopt a wider market strategy by expanding into housebuilding and/or commercial development, to build a stronger capital base and reduce their vulnerability to bankruptcy due to cash flow difficulties. The whole question of market strategy for construction firms will be considered in the next application.

Tutorial questions

1. Should the client automatically accept the lowest tender?
2. What effect is a slow down in the housing market likely to have on a house builder's financial situation?
3. Why is the bankruptcy rate among building contractors particularly high?

Application L

Market strategy of construction firms

Introduction

Applications L and M will consider important aspects of the firm's behaviour. Performance in market strategy and production largely determines the ability of the firm to meet its main objective of making a profit. This application will consider aspects of the market which are relevant to construction firms and should be read in conjunction with Chapters 3, 4 and 5.

Markets and the firm

The term **marketing** is often used in the management context. Many people think that marketing concerns only the advertising, promotion, and selling of the firm's products. In fact, marketing is much more than this because it involves deciding the kind of market in which the firm should operate. Important questions include:

1. which products should be produced?
2. in what quantities?
3. at what price?
4. to whom should the firm attempt to sell?
5. by which methods?

In short, marketing covers all aspects of the market in which the firm operates in pursuit of its objectives.

To understand the importance of markets to firms, reference should be made to concepts studied in Part 2, particularly:

1. the profit equation, that is, Profit = Revenue − Costs,
2. the microeconomic process, for example as depicted in Fig. 4.1,
3. the analysis of profit, shown in Fig. 4.2,

4. the diagrammatic representation of market forces, shown in Fig. 3.1.

The microeconomic process represents the firm's economic behaviour. It can be seen from Fig. 4.1 that the firm is involved in a market transaction both before and after the core activity of production:

1. Before production, the firm buys its resources through resources or factor markets.
2. After production, the firm sells its products through product markets.

The way in which the firm performs in its markets will clearly have a substantial influence on its ability to make a profit. Market performance influences both aspects of the profit equation — performance in resources markets influences *costs*; performance in product markets influences *revenues* (see Fig. 4.2). However studies of markets and marketing usually concentrate on the revenue side. This is because the purchase of resources, say through the labour market, is closely linked with the use of the resources in the production process which together determine the costs of production. As shown in Chapter 4 minimising the costs of production represents the first stage in the process of making profits, that is generating potential profits; maximising revenues represents the second stage in the process, that is realising potential profits.

The main objective of the firm's market strategy is to maximise revenues. Market strategy or marketing therefore concerns exercising control over revenue. The ability of the firm to maximise revenue depends on its market position, including how effectively it can sell its products and whether it can gain a larger share of the market. Ideally the firm seeks to sell its products at a high *price* and in large *quantities*, since

$$revenue = price \times quantity.$$

As shown in Chapter 3 a firm's market strength is largely determined by the extent of competition (or degree of monopoly). In market conditions of perfect competition the firm is passive with the price being determined by the market. In such circumstances the firm is only able to increase revenue by selling greater quantities, and the quest for higher profit is likely to concentrate on the cost side of the equation, that is by trying to become more efficient in production. However as the firm's market strength (or the degree of monopoly) increases there is more scope for price manipulation.

The construction firm and control over revenue

As already stated, market strategy is largely concerned with maximising revenue, consistent with the firm's ability to produce. The objective is to ensure that the price multiplied by quantity sold results in a figure which is as high as possible. However, because price and quantity are usually in an inverse relationship, the firm cannot simply increase price to increase revenue. The ability of the firm to mark up its price depends on the degree of monopoly which exists (see Chapter 3).

For the construction firm, control over revenue depends on the type of work the firm undertakes. In particular it is necessary to distinguish between work carried out as:

1. a contractor
2. a client or developer.

Work carried out as a contractor

In situations where the firm acts as a contractor, the client fully defines the quantity and type of work required, and the firm merely has control over the price. In the traditional tendering situation a pure price competition exists. The main aspect of marketing strategy therefore becomes deciding the highest price which it is possible to charge which is still compatible with winning the contract. Beyond this, market strategy will probably consist of endeavours to secure a place on the list of contractors who are invited to tender for certain clients. This may be a difficult task, best achieved by building up a reputation for carrying out similar work over a period of time. Regular clients such as public authorities may maintain their own lists, whilst more occasional clients are likely to seek the advice of their architect regarding which contractors should be invited to tender.

Some of the alternative procurement methods described in Application G might offer scope for a more active marketing approach, for example design and build or package deals might be offered. Firms seeking work might research the market by studying lists of planning applications made to local authorities,

278

so that a direct approach might be made to potential clients. Advertising in certain media may also be considered, since this can do much to raise the profile of the firm, even if it may not lead directly to new orders.

Work carried out as a client or developer

In this situation the firm has more control over its ability to raise revenue since both price and quantity can be controlled to some extent. The housebuilder is in a situation which is similar to a manufacturer, in that decisions can be made on the market to be targeted. For example, a housebuilder may decide that revenue from a plot of land can be maximised by building either:

1. a small number of high priced houses, or
2. a larger number of lower priced houses.

Depending on the kind of consumer that the builder wishes to attract, land in certain locations may be purchased, and a particular image promoted. Since housebuilding involves selling to consumers, various kinds of advertising or promotion commonly found in other industries may be used.

In the case of housebuilding it is probably true to say that the building process is relatively straightforward, and that the secret of success (that is, profit) lies in market strategy — purchasing land at the right price in the right location; pricing the houses correctly, and so on.

For the firm seeking to enter commercial development the marketing problems are different. The sites will often be more valuable; the market research more difficult, the purchasers (that is, those who lease space) more professional and better advised. In such cases construction firms are quite likely to form partnerships or joint ventures with others in the commercial development field, such as financial institutions.

When construction firms take on the role of developer, one effect is to increase their capital base. For example they may own land, and buildings under construction or completed. Some of the problems of cash flow difficulties discussed in Application K should therefore be alleviated.

Pricing

As already discussed, the main objective of market strategy is to control revenue. Whether the firm is involved in contracting or speculative (that is, self-initiated) work, the price of the firm's product or service is of central importance. The price which the firm can charge is determined by its market strength which, in turn, is determined by the extent of competition that the firm faces, or, put another way, the degree of monopoly which the firm has. Chapter 3 explained the various market conditions which a firm might face.

In conditions of perfect competition, the firm is passive to the market. All firms in the market have to accept the market price because none of them can influence it. In such a situation the firm can only increase its profits by becoming more efficient and reducing costs. In a perfectly competitive situation the price which firms charge is equivalent to the basic cost, defined in Chapter 3 as being high enough to cover costs and allow the firm to make enough profit to replace its assets as they wear out. A price below this level would threaten the firm's survival. Any departure from perfect competition is measured by the degree of monopoly, that is the mark up of price over and above basic cost (that is, the perfectly competitive price). The degree of monopoly, or mark up, is determined by the number of firms; the extent of collusion; and the strength of demand as measured by elasticity.

In the construction context, the firm needs to be aware of its market strength when pricing a job. Where the firm tenders to win a contract two stages are necessary, commonly referred to as:

1. estimating
2. tendering.

Estimating

This process calculates the cost of carrying out the proposed work. The direct cost of the site work must be included together with a proportion of the firm's overheads, or fixed costs, which are allocated against the project. The estimator therefore calculates the minimum price for which the firm could afford to undertake the contract without having its survival threatened. In other words, a notional perfectly competitive price is calculated. Methods of estimating were briefly described in Application I. In this case the first principles method is usually applied to each bill of quantities item and the estimated total cost is calculated. This estimating function is regarded as a technical process.

Tendering

This process transforms the estimate into the tender price which the contractor submits to the client. It is sometimes called the adjudication of the tender, and is regarded as a managerial function since it involves assessing the market and the firm's strength within it. As a result of this assessment the firm's management decide how much mark up there should be on the estimated cost. This figure will be as high as possible consistent with the firm winning the contract. If the firm operated under conditions of perfect competition then by definition the mark up would be zero and the tender price would be equivalent to estimated cost. However in practice some degree of monopoly will exist, and the mark up of tender price over cost will reflect this. The extent of degree of monopoly and hence the mark up depends on the extent of the three determinants, that is number of firms, extent of collusion, and strength of demand. A further decision which has to be taken in the process of tender adjudication is whether to front load the contract to alleviate cash flow problems, as described in Application K.

On occasions a contractor might submit a tender price below estimated costs. This could occur when:

1. Work is restricted in supply and below cost work is taken to keep the firm 'ticking over' until work becomes more plentiful. The direct costs of construction would normally still have to be covered although the overheads may not be fully recouped. This situation cannot continue for long as it threatens the survival of the firm.
2. The contractor seeks to gain a foothold in a particular market and offers a low price as a loss leader, in the hope that subsequent work will follow at a more profitable price.

The firm which acts as a developer has to carry out a similar process of assessing the market before fixing the selling price (in the case of a housebuilder), or rental (in the case of a commercial developer).

The consequences of a wrong assessment of the market are:

1. If the price is too low, the firm, whether contractor or developer, will make a loss on the project. If this happens regularly the firm's survival will be threatened.
2. If the price is too high, the contractor will fail to win the contract and the developer will be unable to sell the houses or let the space. Again, regular poor assessment of the market will threaten the firm's survival.

Protecting and improving market position

Even when a firm is in a strong market position it cannot afford complacency. There is always the risk of new competition entering and gaining market share. There are a number of ways in which a construction firm may protect its present market position, and/or improve its position for the future. A number of possible strategies will be discussed:

1. Maintaining *barriers to entry* to deter competitors.
2. Adopting a *growth strategy* over time, for example by a merger, takeover and diversification policy.
3. *Image-building* exercises to secure a larger share of the market and/or enter new markets.

Barriers to entry

Barriers to entry were described generally in Chapter 3. In some instances it may be possible for construction firms to protect their markets by deterring competitors. For example:

1. With very large projects, particularly of a civil engineering nature, there may be only a few firms with the resources or expertise to carry out the work. Thus there is a *technological* barrier to entry. Although barriers to entry are usually considered undesirable from the public policy point of view, situations may exist where a very large firm would be beneficial, as mentioned in Application J. For example, a very large firm could compete effectively in international markets, and could undertake massive projects such as the Channel Tunnel without the need to form consortia.
2. A cost advantage for large firms is possible through *economies of scale*. The cost per unit of building, say, a large number of houses on a site may be lower than building a few.

3. There is an increasing amount of advertising, particularly associated with housebuilding. This raises the possibility of *artificially created high costs*, since builders spend considerable sums on creating an image. New firms may find difficulty in competing without incurring the same high costs.
4. There may be scope for *limit pricing* and/or the maintaining of *excess capacity*. For example, selling price or rentals may be trimmed temporarily below cost to discourage new competitors. Stocks of finished houses could be left unsold, and completed office space could be left unlet as a deterrent to potential competitors.

The above examples should be regarded as possibilities, since there is no clear evidence that these barriers are actually used extensively.

Growth strategy

The owners of many firms may wish that the firm remains a manageable size. For example they may fear that too much expansion would result in a loss of control. Medium size family firms have a long tradition in the construction industry. However as discussed in Application J, the middle ground has become somewhat untenable, with the result that many medium-size firms have had to reconsider their attitude to growth.

The traditional route to growth for the construction firm has been through *internal growth*. This slow steady process involves the ploughing back of profits into the business and the acquisition of capital through loans or sales of shares. Many of the most well known firms in the construction industry have grown this way, with the founding family often still retaining a major interest.

Internal growth is one of several methods of expansion described in Chapter 5. Since the 1960s all of these methods have become more widely used. In particular there has been a growth in the number of *mergers and takeovers*, with some firms growing very rapidly indeed. In addition there has been a great deal of *diversification* with firms whose interests were outside the industry buying construction firms, and construction firms diversifying into related activities.

Many large construction firms renowned for large scale contracting have diversified into other areas of activity. In particular every major firm now has a housebuilding division, an area which previously would have held little interest for them.

Firms have become housebuilders because it makes commercial sense. Housebuilding usually makes a major contribution to profits, and contributes to a stronger capital base as previously described. In addition successful housebuilding will depend as much on successful marketing as on building. This emphasises the importance of market strategy to the construction firm.

A further growth strategy has been the formation of *consortia*. As previously stated consortia have sometimes been formed to undertake major projects, where no single firm would have sufficient resources or expertise. In such cases the consortia have been necessary to produce more efficiently and save costs. However at least one consortium has also been formed for the purpose of large scale housebuilding. Proposals have been put forward to build new, privately funded, country towns with their own facilities and infrastructure, to house up to 20,000 people. It is argued that a limited number of developments of this type would be a better solution to the housing shortage problem in the South East of England than a plethora of piecemeal developments. Whilst a consortium of this kind may offer efficiency and cost advantages, the growth of potential monopoly power is a danger. If what is in effect one firm builds a large number of houses in an area, other firms will probably find it extremely difficult to compete. This problem could become widespread if planners advise local authorities that new housing provision should be made in this way. It is clear that proposals of this nature will meet with a great deal of opposition.

The problems of medium-size firms have already been examined when first considering growth strategy. Many medium-size firms have disappeared; some have been taken over by large firms; some have merged with firms of a similar size to form a larger unit. In addition some firms have entered into collaborative agreements, short of actual merger, with other firms. Consortia or joint ventures have been formed to compete for larger contracts which the individual firm would be unlikely to win. However since joint ventures can be problematical, collaborative efforts could lead to merger.

Image building

As already mentioned, the objective of successful marketing is to improve the position of the building contractor with the client. A contractor may be able to break into new markets by offering to carry out a job at low cost. It has also been seen that many housebuilders have directed advertising campaigns at consumers in order to sell more effectively.

A further strategy also exists which is particularly related to the inner city problem discussed in Application C. Many construction firms have set up divisions which are specifically concerned with urban renewal or urban regeneration. In most cases the objective is to work with the relevant local authority in the ways previously described. For example the local authority will help with land assembly and infrastructure provision, and the firm will carry out development which is both profitable and in the interest of the local community. The objective of the firm is, of course, to make a profit, but many firms have also proclaimed their desire to contribute to the creation and rebuilding of communities, through co-operation with the public sector. Consideration was given in Chapter 4 to the ability or otherwise of firms to pursue objectives other than profit maximisation. It could therefore be argued that public limited companies would be unable to assist in the rebuilding of communities unless such projects are highly profitable. It may also be possible that some firms might promote a caring image in order to improve their standing and reap rewards elsewhere.

Summary

This application has considered an important aspect of the firm's behaviour, that is the way in which it responds to, and influences its market position. A fuller understanding will be gained if reference is made to Chapters 3, 4 and 5. When considering the general question of how markets affect firms, an important point to emerge is that control over revenue generation is central to market strategy. A construction firm which acts as a contractor has less control over revenue because the quantity is determined by the client, leaving the contractor to tender in a pure price competition. By contrast the firm which initiates its own work, as a housebuilder or commercial developer, has more control over revenue since it can influence quantity as well as price. In pricing a project, the firm must take account of its market position. This will affect the amount of mark up over the estimated cost that the firm will be able to charge. The estimated cost includes direct costs and overheads and represents the minimum price for which the firm can afford to undertake the project without threatening its survival. This figure therefore represents the price the firm would charge if it were operating under conditions of perfect competition.

Market strategy has a long term element in that complacency could result in the firm losing its share of the market. Firms therefore seek to protect and improve their market position. A variety of methods may be used by the construction firm, including attempting to maintain barriers to entry; aiming for growth through mergers, takeovers, diversification and forming consortia; and improving its image through advertising and the active promotion of a caring image.

As individual firms pursue the market strategies which best suit their objectives, this will have an impact on the construction industry as a whole. As shown in Application J the structure of the industry has polarised with a few very large firms and many small firms. The middle ground position of medium-size general building contractors has become increasingly difficult to maintain. Many such firms have gone out of business; others have been taken over by larger firms; others have come to collaborative arrangements or merged with similar firms in order to maintain their market position.

Tutorial questions

1. What are the features of the demand curve facing the individual housebuilder?
2. Does it ever make sense for a contractor to take on a project at below cost?
3. Is the urban regeneration market likely to be profitable to construction firms?

Application M

Production methods in construction

Introduction

The importance of production has frequently been highlighted, for example in Chapters 1 and 2 and particularly in Chapter 4. The main concepts discussed previously will be re-examined and applied to production in the construction industry. Production is the term used to describe the process whereby resources are combined to create a product. This process forms the core of economic activity. In production the value of output exceeds the sum of the resource inputs. The production process is therefore said to **add value** to the resources.

One important point to emerge from the various issues discussed in Chapters 1, 2 and 4, is that the production process is influenced by a range of factors which can be categorised as either **technological** or **social**. It will be necessary to bear this distinction in mind throughout this application. Firstly, consideration will be given to production methods generally, including the importance of various management approaches to the organisation of production. This initial study, whilst being particularly relevant to manufacturing industry, will form the basis for consideration of production methods in construction. A study will be undertaken of the way in which production methods have evolved — technologically and socially, in absolute terms and in comparison with manufacturing. The possible implications of these changes in production methods on certain aspects of construction such as safety and training will also be considered.

Throughout this application it is important that the reader refers to earlier material concerning production, particularly in Chapter 4.

Production methods

Production methods are of great importance because they determine productivity. The costs of production are, in turn, determined by productivity and the price of the resources used. It will be remembered that the main objective of the firm is to make a profit, and that the costs of production represent one of the main elements which determine this (see Figs. 4.1 and 4.2).

It is important to emphasise the relationship between the price of resources and productivity. A firm may be able to reduce its costs of production by either paying less for its resources and/or increasing productivity. These two alternatives may be in a trade off position in that lower priced resources (such as lower wages or cheaper materials) may be offset by lower levels of productivity or higher wastage. Whilst a firm may prefer to improve productivity through more efficient production methods, these might be more difficult to implement than cuts in resource prices. For example, the introduction of new technology and changes in working conditions are often met with resistance.

As discussed in Chapter 4 the performance of labour is the key to production with labour being variable in both quantity and quality. For example, it was shown that the quantity of labour can be varied when advantage is taken of the division of labour, that is the splitting up of tasks in order to achieve greater productivity. Over a longer period choices can be made on whether to adopt production methods which are labour intensive or capital intensive. Labour is also variable in quality due to differences in education, training and attitude. Since labour is variable and unpredictable the production methods chosen are partly determined by what is technologically possible and partly determined by what is socially or organisationally possible. The choice of production methods is therefore a complex matter for management.

Management approaches to production

It was shown in Chapter 4 that, in general, management will have a variety of attitudes on matters such as whether people work willingly or need to be coerced; the role of trade unions and so on. These attitudes will shape the production methods chosen. It was also shown that it is common for many firms to regard part of their workforce as core, and part as peripheral, with peripheral workers often employed on a casual or sub-contract basis. However, for much of the industrial era the dominant approach to production methods in manufacturing has been mechanisation, a process which has also come to be known as **de-skilling**. This will be considered before returning to the core/periphery issue.

Since the industrial revolution in the late eighteenth and nineteenth centuries, production has been characterised by a number of features.

1. **The division of labour**, whereby total production is divided into a number of separate tasks, each undertaken by a different individual, as opposed to one person producing an entire product. Initially, the division of labour leads to specialisation with each person acquiring a particular trade or skill. However division of labour can be taken further to become more detailed as each trade is split into a series of less skilled tasks.

2. **Mechanisation**, whereby the simpler tasks which have resulted from the division of labour can be taken over or assisted by machine. The pace of work is thus determined by machine rather than by the craft worker or supervisor.

3. **Factorisation**, whereby production takes place in a factory, that is in a closely supervised setting. Whilst factory production is usually associated with mechanisation, it is possible for production to take place without machinery. For example the large increase in manufacturing production which occurred during the industrial revolution, may owe as much to people working systematically in a factory (rather than more informally at home), as to advances in technological possibilities.

In the twentieth century the three factors mentioned above were reinforced through the ideas of scientific management, which sought to put into practice the conventional economic assumption that labour is homogeneous. By taking the division of labour and mechanisation as far as possible, a substantially technological solution could be applied to production problems. A variety of techniques including work study were developed to improve productivity. The social aspects of production were not considered problematical as they were limited to the need to pay monetary incentives as a means of motivating people to work.

The scientific view has been regarded as a universal managerial approach to production. From time to time this view has been adjusted particularly during times of economic boom. Such periods are usually accompanied by low unemployment and a shortage of labour. This has necessitated alternative management styles which take account of the social aspects of production. Various schools of management thought advocate good working conditions, the fostering of social groups at work, motivating workers through more interesting and fulfilling work and so on. Attitudes to these alternative management approaches vary. There are those who argue that these tactics are forced on management at a time of labour shortage and that scientific management will be resumed as soon as practicable. Others argue that alternative approaches represent genuine differences in management strategy, and that many managers believe that the way to achieve high productivity and profits is through assuming that workers can be motivated to perform better and do not need to be coerced. In other words they stress the positive rather than the negative qualities of labour as described in Chapter 4.

Another difference in views concerns the role of trade unions and collective bargaining. Advocates of the scientific management school tend to see a very limited role for trade unions as they believe wages should be fixed by market forces and working practices are the prerogative of management. However some management thinking is more likely to see collective bargaining as a positive way of creating good industrial relations.

In contemporary industry, mechanisation and the division of labour are well established. However it would appear that the concept of homogeneous labour is not universally accepted as variations in the quality of labour are evident. As mentioned in Chapter 4 firms may regard some of their workers as *core* and some as *peripheral*. The core workers will generally have better wages, conditions and security and be 'motivated' to work. In contrast, peripheral workers will be insecure, and probably have inferior wages and conditions. In situations where market forces determine that more needs to be paid to obtain workers, wages might be better in some cases. Core and periphery strategies might be implemented by management in the following two ways:

1. **Sub-contracting.** In this case core/peripheral strategies are implemented *outside* the firm. Those people who

work directly for the firm would have good conditions, but the bulk of the work would be sub-contracted out to smaller firms where conditions are inferior. In more recent times this situation has been characteristic of manufacturing industry in Japan, where the major firms assemble components manufactured by sub-contractors. This management approach has had a strong influence in the UK, both through Japanese firms who have set up factories in Britain and through UK firms who have copied the approach. Where sub-contracting is used, the firm maintains control over costs by driving a hard bargain with the sub-contractors, and through payments-by-results systems which link pay directly to productivity.

2. **Flexibility.** In this case core/peripheral strategies are implemented *within* the firm. The firm's main objective is to ensure that its employment and use of labour is completely flexible. For example, there might be *flexibility of task* whereby workers undertake a variety of tasks rather than specialise in one. This strategy is linked to the division of labour which by de-skilling the work has enabled workers to perform a variety of tasks. There might be *flexibility of time* through the employment of part time workers or the working of variable shifts. Sometimes a worker's terms of engagement might stipulate annual rather than weekly hours so that the firm can use more workers at peak times without incurring extra labour costs. There might be *flexibility of numbers* through the use of sub-contracting, self-employment and temporary workers. There might be *flexibility of earnings* through relating pay to profits or to productivity.

The foregoing has outlined some of the trends in production methods which have occurred in industry generally, particularly in manufacturing. In some respects developments in the production methods used in the construction industry have followed a similar pattern. These similarities, together with the differences, will now be considered.

Approaches to production in construction

As with any other industry, the production process in the construction industry is the key to high productivity, lower costs and hence high profits. It is therefore reasonable to assume that the changes which have occurred in production methods have been motivated by the need for lower costs, particularly through higher productivity. As previously mentioned, the production process is influenced by both *technological* and *social* factors. Technological factors include the technology, degree of mechanisation and skills required. Social factors include the organisational aspects and the conditions (including contractual) under which labour is employed. Over time there have been continual changes in both technological and social influences. Some, though not all, of these changes have occurred in the construction industry at the same time as similar changes in manufacturing production methods. For ease of study the development of production methods in construction will be divided into four phases.

1. traditional construction (until approximately the late 1950s)
2. the first industrialised phase (until approximately the late 1960s)
3. the sub-contracting phase (until approximately the late 1970s)
4. the second industrial phase (continuing).

These four phases should not be regarded as separate entities, but rather as an indication of important developments which occurred in the 1960s, 1970s and since the 1980s.

Traditional construction

From the technological point of view, traditional production methods are characterised by the practice of craft work in various trades. Typically materials are in a relatively unprocessed state and are shaped on site to form whatever is required. The workforce consists of highly skilled craft workers, assisted by labourers. By its nature craft work leaves a great deal of autonomy with the worker who can plan and execute the work as required. The ability of management to ensure that the craft worker conforms to an overall plan may be limited, particularly where workers are employed directly by the firm under a normal contract of employment. Such a contract can specify the number of hours to be worked but cannot easily specify the actual amount of work required. The link between pay and productivity is therefore not very strong.

The practice of traditional craft work with its low level of mechanisation persisted in the construction industry for considerably longer than in manufacturing industry. Attempts to change this method of production were introduced in the 1950s.

The first industrialised phase

Industrialised building techniques were introduced in the 1950s. Sections of the building were prefabricated as far as possible in factories and then transported to the site for assembly. In many instances complete building systems were prefabricated, with the individual components being specifically designed to fit together. Many of these systems were used in the construction of high rise residential blocks.

The use of industrialised building techniques sought to follow the mechanisation and de-skilling pattern established in manufacturing industry, by dispensing with a labour intensive, low productivity, craft based process and replacing it with a mechanised, high productivity process. Initially, many clients were eager to make use of these techniques particularly local authorities who were looking for fast construction of housing units. In addition, contractors believed the techniques would result in increased productivity and higher profits. However this first attempt at extensive industrialisation was unsuccessful for a number of reasons:

1. Local authority clients became disillusioned with the buildings produced as they proved unsuitable for meeting the needs of those people who most needed housing, that is families with young children. In addition, production difficulties led to various problems including damp penetration which generally made the blocks undesirable places in which to live. In addition the structural stability of high rise residential blocks constructed using these industrialised building techniques was brought into question when one block (Ronan Point) partly collapsed following a gas leak explosion.
2. The production difficulties encountered on site were very great. Whilst many of the technological factors influencing production had changed, the social factors had not. The main problem was that industrialised building systems required semi-skilled workers who could accurately assemble the various sections and waterproof the joints. As the workforce was still craft orientated,

such workers were not readily available. Most craft workers were unused to performing tasks of this kind, and the level of skill required was greater than that usually possessed by labourers. Closer supervision was therefore required, and in many cases work on site did not proceed as quickly as expected. As a result, the anticipated productivity gains and cost savings were not widely achieved.

The market for industrialised building systems eventually became unstable. For the reasons mentioned above, demand fell until it became impossible to produce the prefabricated units in large enough quantitities to gain the economies of scale necessary for the economic production of the units.

The first attempt to mechanise production extensively in the construction industry was therefore unsuccessful.

The sub-contracting phase

As already stated, one of the main reasons why industrialised building was initially unsuccessful concerned the unsuitability of the workforce. Although further technological changes occurred in the 1970s, the principal change occurred in social factors. In particular, for many people there was a change in their conditions of employment. Direct employment fell whilst at the same time there was a growth in labour-only sub-contracting and self-employment. This was popularly known as 'the lump' because rather than being paid hourly or weekly, workers were paid a lump sum for completing a particular job, say a rate per square metre of brickwork. Such workers were no longer subject to a contract of employment but were instead engaged to perform a service. The main effect of this change was that pay was related to productivity much more closely.

Whilst sub-contracting had always existed in the construction industry, it had previously been mainly of a specialist, or supply and fix type. The growth of labour-only sub-contracting was a relatively new innovation, which had gained momentum towards the end of the 1960s. By 1972 sub-contracting had become such a major issue that it culminated in only the second national building workers' strike this century. The strike was unsuccessful from the unions' point of view. Sub-contracting became more widespread until by the end of the 1970s the majority of workers were either engaged through labour-only sub-contractors or self employed (which is in effect a one man sub-contractor). This trend continued throughout the 1980s. The use of sub-contracting and self-employment in the construction industry has largely preceded this practice in manufacturing industry where, as discussed earlier, sub-contracting and the flexible use of labour have been increasingly used.

Although changes in social factors were most significant in the 1970s, technological changes also occurred. These were mainly possible because the changes in methods of employment which had led to an increase in sub-contracting and self-employment had also reduced the emphasis on craft skills. In fact the demarcation lines between crafts had been largely eroded. Although the end of the first industrialised phase witnessed a return to more traditional construction methods, some technological changes continued to occur. Building design became simpler and more rationalised. Certain traditional materials were replaced with alternatives which required lower levels of skill. For example, plasterboard was more widely used instead of plaster; plastic pipes were increasingly used in plumbing.

To summarise production methods in the 1970s, it can be said that the introduction of a payment system (payments by results, or the lump) which encouraged faster and often lower quality work, together with the erosion of the divisions between crafts through the replacement of traditional materials, led to the emergence of a different kind of workforce. The typical building worker was becoming more flexible and able to carry out a variety of semi-skilled jobs. The main contractor had greater flexibility in the employment of labour and was able to relate pay more closely to productivity. The longer term effects of this will be considered later.

The second industrialised phase

The changes which occurred in the nature of the workforce in the 1970s removed one of the main obstacles to mechanisation, in that craft divisions had been greatly diminished. The workforce was less highly skilled but more flexible. This trend continued in the 1980s with the number of workers directly employed by the main contractor very much in a minority. The new form of industrialisation has not been as ambitious as that introduced in the 1960s. In fact it has largely been an extension of the technological changes of the 1970s, when traditional materials were replaced by materials which required less skill. The trend continued in the 1980s with the increased and widespread use of factory made components in the production of buildings. Components commonly used include roof trusses, doors and windows ready-hung in frames, sheet finishings, cladding panels and so on. The use of these components has made much of the on-site craft work previously required unnecessary. In addition the components can be used in a wide range of applications, and are not restricted to specific building systems, as were many of the components manufactured in the 1960s.

Components are very extensively used for houses, particularly those of timber frame construction. In commercial developments, 'fast track' building techniques often use quickly erected steel frames and 'pan' floors. Building services have been streamlined through the use of materials which are quicker and easier to handle. It is even possible to supply units containing complete bathroom and toilet facilities which fit into their allocated place in the building and which then require only simple connections to water supplies and waste outlets.

As previously mentioned, the trend towards sub-contracting and self-employment continued throughout the 1980s. There is a great need for skilled labour, although the level of skill required is generally lower than that associated with the traditional crafts. Building workers are potentially multi-skilled, although for reasons of maximum productivity they may specialise in only one skill, for example the fixing of copper pipework.

The final part of this application will consider some of the impacts that changes in production methods have made on the construction industry in the last thirty years.

Impact of changes in production methods

Probably the most significant change that has occurred is in the nature of the construction site. The traditional construction site was a labour intensive place where craft workers used their skill and relatively unprocessed materials to create a building. In the past thirty years mechanisation has grown due to the changing nature of the workforce, and through the increased use of factory made components. The construction site has become a place where production largely takes place through the assembly of components by flexible and multi-skilled 'fitters' rather than through skilled craft workers. Alongside these technological changes, the social conditions have changed. In particular most operatives are no longer directly employed by main contractors. Most are self-employed and/or employed through labour-only sub-contractors, and paid on a payment-by-results system. This has been a long term trend which therefore has long as well as short term implications and effects.

A number of consequences of these changes have been suggested including possible effects on:

1. education and training
2. health and safety
3. industrial relations
4. market structures.

These effects, some of which were discussed earlier in Application J, will be briefly outlined.

Education and training

The traditional craft apprenticeship system has almost disappeared in the main building trades, although the system operates to some extent in trades such as electrical services. Some training courses are run by technical colleges, skill centres and the like, but since they are shorter the levels of skill reached are lower than before, a situation which often causes concern to the craftsmen who teach on the courses. Of equal importance is the problem of possibly inadequate on-the-job training. The payments-by-results system does not encourage skilled workers to take the time to teach apprentices, and on-the-job training appears to survive only in some public sector building organisations, such as local authority direct labour organisations. Whilst it is true that the technology of modern production methods no longer requires a very high level of skill, it is still the case that when an upturn in construction activity occurs, there is very often a shortage of adequately skilled labour.

Health and safety

The construction industry has always had an unsatisfactory safety record. Undoubtedly many firms have a very strong safety policy

297

which they enforce among their sub-contractors. However, it has been suggested that payments-by-results systems and emphasis on productivity encourages faster work, and possible neglect of safety measures. In addition the construction industry has its disreputable side and firms who disregard many of the legal obligations connected with running a business. In this 'unofficial economy' cost cutting predominates and safety measures are often ignored.

Industrial relations

Employers' associations and trade unions negotiate on pay and conditions through the official collective bargaining machinery which exists in the construction industry. However the agreements reached are not always implemented, and actual wages usually reflect local labour market conditions. In situations where self-employment is the norm, union membership is low and agreed conditions of employment are not adopted. Where trade union membership is higher, safety issues and the qualifications of operatives often receive more attention. Traditionally the unions have sought to discourage labour-only sub-contracting and self-employment, although more recently some union leaders have advocated the recruitment of self-employed building operatives into union membership.

Market structures

As previously discussed the structure of the industry has tended to polarise into a few very large firms and many small firms. This structure is one consequence of the sub-contracting system. The majority of contracts are awarded to large firms who then sub-contract the work to a great number of smaller competing firms. The small firms are often in a highly competitive and financially precarious position. For this reason, a further possible consequence of these changes in production methods is the high number of bankruptcies among construction firms. This situation seems to confirm the theory of competitive markets (see Chapter 3) which implies that resources can be transferred from one activity to another in line with demand, and that inefficient firms who cannot offer competitive prices will go out of business. The composition of the construction industry's small firm (sub-contractor) sector is therefore liable to continual change.

Summary

This application has considered the production methods which have been used in the construction industry. The general importance of production in the economic process was discussed, with reference made to Chapters 1, 2 and particularly 4. It was seen that there are various management approaches to the production process. The developments which have taken place in manufacturing industry such as de-skilling, sub-contracting and flexibility were discussed, and used as a basis for considering changes in production methods in construction. It was shown that production methods have become more mechanised as ways have been sought to increase productivity, reduce costs and increase profits. The first attempt was unsuccessful, partly because the social factors which influence production had not changed although changes had occurred in the technological factors. As a result, the method of employment evolved from being direct under a contract of employment, to being self-employed or sub-contract with payment in accordance with work carried out. At the same time mechanisation continued to take place as traditional materials were replaced by those which required less skill to fix, and by components which were largely manufactured off-site for assembly on-site. The construction site is now characterised as a place where components are assembled by flexible and multi-skilled operatives, rather than craft workers using relatively unprocessed materials to create buildings.

It seems likely that the technological changes which have occurred will continue in the future and the construction site will become increasingly mechanised with more off-site production of components. However, there are a number of problems associated with self-employment, labour-only sub-contracting, and payments by results. In particular concern has been expressed regarding quality of work, labour shortages, training and safety. If the workload in the industry remains stable and high, there may be a possibility that some firms will seek to alleviate these problems by a return to more directly employed labour.

Tutorial questions

1. Why are the industrialised systems of the 1950s and 1960s regarded as unsuccessful?
2. What are the advantages and disadvantages to the worker of being self-employed?

3. Is it likely that construction firms will be more inclined to use directly employed labour in the future?

Application N

The life of buildings

Introduction

The fifth and longest stage of developing the built environment concerns the lifetime of the building. This stage, introduced in Part 1, was described as the occupation and use of buildings. The main point of interest to the client who sells the building on completion will be the selling price. However if the client retains ownership, questions arise concerning long term finance and managing the building so that it continues to meet the objectives. In fact there are a number of aspects related to the life of any building which have to be taken into account by either the owner, occupier or society at large.

This application will consider some aspects of economic decision making which arise during the life of a building. The first aspect which will be considered concerns long term finance, followed by aspects of management such as ensuring the building meets the objectives of owner and/or occupier, and ensuring the building is maintained without exceeding the sum allowed for such costs in the budget. Finally consideration will be given to replacing the building — when this should be carried out, and the methods that should be used. This returns to the beginning of the process of developing the built environment — what kind and quantity of buildings are required?

Long term finance

As mentioned, the question of long term finance will not concern the client or developer if the building is sold on completion. If however complete ownership or an interest in the building is retained by the client or developer, arrangements will need to be made for long term finance. Since buildings represent long term investment assets, their ownership entails a financing cost, either the rate of interest (that is, the cost of borrowing) or, if the purchasers use their own money, the amount of interest that is forgone. Whilst costs are inevitably incurred in owning an investment asset, the owner expects to receive a return, either in the form of a stream of income or as an appreciating capital value. For the houseowner the expected return is an increase in the value of the property when it is eventually sold, as well as consumption benefits in the meantime; for the manufacturer the return is increased productivity; for the commercial developer or investor the return is a stream of income, together with a probable rise in the value of the land on which the building is constructed.

For the householder, long term finance is usually obtained through a mortgage which is repaid over twenty or twenty-five years. During this time the lender, usually a building society or bank, retains the deeds of the property. For the manufacturer, the building of, say, a new factory will form part of the capital expenditure programme of the firm. The long term finance required for such a programme is usually raised through share issues or loans. For the commercial developer, there are a number of ways of arranging finance.

1. The developer may retain ownership of the building and use it as security against which to borrow the funds necessary for its purchase. This situation is similar to that of a householder taking out a *mortgage.*

2. The developer may sell the building to a financier, such as an insurance company or pension fund. However the developer takes out a long lease on the property to manage, maintain and use it to the best advantage. This method of finance is called *sale and leaseback.*

3. A *joint company* may be formed with the developer and financier holding shares in the property in agreed proportions. The developer's funds may be obtained through loans or share issues.

4. An extension of the above method of finance which is increasingly used for major developments, is to form a separate company to finance the project. The shares of the company are offered for sale to individual investors who buy as many or as few shares as they wish. This method of finance is particularly useful when very large sums have to be raised, as on major projects even the largest financier may be reluctant to carry the risk alone.

302

Management of buildings

As already stated, buildings represent long lived investment assets. During the course of its life, a building must continue to meet the objectives of the occupier and/or owner. It can be seen from Application F that a building may fulfil a variety of functional purposes — consumption, factor of production, or social. In addition, if the owner is not the occupier, the building will have to generate a direct financial gain. Proper management of the building ensures that the functional purposes are fulfilled and/or that revenue is generated. It also ensures that the costs of operating the building are as low as possible, consistent with achieving its purposes. It can therefore be seen that a great similarity exists between managing a building and managing a firm. The latter entails maximising the difference between revenue and costs. The former entails maximising the difference between the benefits of the building (that is, functional purposes or revenue) and the costs of operating it. Consideration will now be given to the generating of benefits.

A client who wishes to sell a building on completion must ensure that it is fit for its intended purpose. Any building which does not meet the necessary requirements will be difficult, or even impossible to sell without incurring the costs of rectifying the faults. Similarly if a client wishes to let space, the building must be fit for the purpose, otherwise tenants will be difficult to find and the client will own an investment asset which does not generate adequate revenue.

As stated, the functional purposes of buildings are:

1. consumption
2. factor of production
3. social.

Consumption

The primary purpose of housing is to satisfy consumption needs, that is to provide shelter, comfort and enjoyment. In addition, many people regard their home as an investment. A housebuilder who wishes to sell effectively over a period of time must ensure that the houses meet these requirements. In the rented housing sector, a landlord must also ensure that the functional purposes of housing are met if satisfactory levels of rent are to be achieved. Certain aspects of the functional purposes of housing are governed by a legislative framework, for example the Building

Regulations stipulate minimum room heights, standards of thermal insulation and so on.

Factor of production

Many buildings are factors of production. These include factories, offices and shops. Their essential function is to improve productivity in the manufacture of goods and provision of services. A firm will buy or rent space in such buildings if it believes it will increase productivity, reduce costs and increase profits. When a firm constructs its own factory or office space, the building can be designed to meet the firm's specification. However such space is increasingly provided by developers and leased to firms as occupiers. Since one occupier may not lease the space for the entire lifetime of the building, the space provided should be flexible enough to attract and satisfy the needs of a variety of occupiers. Typically a serviced shell is provided which can be fitted out to meet the precise needs of the individual occupier.

To perform well the building must be adequately serviced and laid out internally so that machinery, plant and equipment can be positioned for maximum efficiency. It is equally important that the environment created by the building is pleasant particularly in shops where layout and attractiveness will influence the amount of revenue that can be generated. A good environment in factories and offices will add generally to the comfort and productivity of the people who work in them. Concern has frequently been expressed regarding the health and productivity problems which arise from dirty, noisy production lines in factories. More recently there has been growing concern regarding modern office blocks which often have sealed, air conditioned environments. In such an environment air changes may be reduced and illnesses can result. The problem is known as building related illnesses or 'sick building syndrome'. To date the causes and cures have not been clearly identified. Apart from the social considerations of ill health, sick building syndrome can have a detrimental effect on productivity through lower quality of work, increased absenteeism and high turnover of staff. Whilst relatively simple solutions may be found through better maintenance, or the unblocking of air vents, the owner of such a building may find that solving the problem will incur considerable additional expense.

Social

Some buildings fulfil social purposes — leisure and cultural, as well as the creation and maintenance of human capital in schools and hospitals. In addition, construction projects such as the provision of infrastructure generate social benefits. Buildings which are constructed to meet social criteria may also have to fulfil the consumption and/or factor of production purposes described above, the difference being that they are likely to be provided through non-market rather than market means. A building which does not fulfil the purpose adequately, either because of its design, or the way in which it is built or subsequently maintained, may not be utilised fully or may quickly deteriorate and require repair. There are many examples of social construction projects which have not fulfilled their purpose — high rise residential blocks have proved unsuitable for housing families; the motorway network is often unable to cope with the increased volume of traffic.

Management of buildings constructed for direct financial gain

This is of relevance to clients or developers who provide space which others occupy and use. As with any marketing exercise, the developer must provide a product which satisfies the customer's requirements — in this case a building which fulfils the functional purposes outlined above. If the building does not fulfil the purpose, the developer may be unable to lease the space at the anticipated level of rent, if at all.

Other aspects of marketing which must be considered include deciding the price that the market will bear (this will largely depend on the degree of monopoly which exists), and the promotion and selling of the product. The property developer must assess the level of rents which can be achieved from the building. Since buildings have a long life, an essential aspect of management relates to the periodic renegotiation of tenants' leases to take into account anticipated inflation and changes in market conditions.

Cost control during the life of a building

As previously described, the effective management of a building entails maximising the net benefits, that is the difference between

305

the revenues or benefits generated by the building, and the costs of owning and/or occupying the building. Consideration will now be given to the various costs which arise.

Costs are of two main types:

1. **Operating costs** which are usually of a regular, continuing nature
2. **Refurbishment costs** which cover major programmes of upgrading and improvement and which are periodically necessary throughout the life of the building.

Operating costs

These regularly incurred costs include energy, cleaning, security, management costs, and routine building maintenance. The level of some of these costs will depend on the design of the building. For example a building with good thermal insulation will require less energy to heat; higher quality components will require less maintenance, and so on. Most operating costs are self-explanatory, although the category maintenance requires more consideration. Maintenance involves sustaining the building and its contents in its present state of repair. It includes carrying out work which prevents damage from occurring later, and the rectification of problems which have already occurred. As it is generally believed that prevention is better than cure, a programme of regular maintenance is usually considered more sensible than simply responding to damage once it has occurred.

Refurbishment

In some instances the difference between maintenance and refurbishment may be difficult to discern. If the existing layout and content of the building require continual repairs and small alterations, it may be decided that the building is no longer meeting its functional purposes and a more thorough refurbishment may be necessary. Periodic refurbishments are also required to take account of new technology in factories and offices. In shops, restaurants and places of entertainment, refurbishment may be necessary to reflect changing attitudes to selling and the promotion of goods and services. Refurbishment costs are usually regarded as capital expenditure, whereas operating costs are regarded as current expenditure. However it will be remembered that *all* costs must be taken into account at feasibility stage (see Application H) in order that an accurate assessment can be made of whether the building will meet the client's objectives.

Replacement of buildings

The life of a building, although long, is not infinite. In Part 1 a distinction was drawn between the *economic* and the *physical* life of a building. The projected economic life of the building needs to be known so that it can form part of the calculations undertaken at the feasibility stage before the decision to proceed with the project is taken (see Application H). For example it might be anticipated that an office block will yield a rent for fifty years. The expected economic life of the building will be one factor which influences the standard of construction and hence the physical life of the building. In general, the likely physical life will be considerably greater than the economic life, although there are instances of the reverse situation. This may occur when a building which is in poor physical shape is kept in operation because a private sector client does not find it profitable to replace it; or because a public sector client does not have the necessary funds available.

In recent years a number of factors have changed the basis on which replacement occurs. These include:

1. rising land values
2. the debate on planning and architecture in the built environment.

Rising land values

The importance of land has frequently been discussed, especially in Application B. The speculative value of land has become a crucial factor in determining the replacement of buildings and the redevelopment of land. In many cases, particularly land for commercial development in city centres, the value of land has risen dramatically. This situation could not have been easily foreseen at feasibility stage when a life of, say, fifty years may have been projected for the building. If the site value has risen greatly in the meantime, the existing building may not be making the most profitable use of the site. Therefore it may be replaced by a new building which can generate more revenue. There are

307

examples of office blocks in central London which are less than thirty years old but which are being replaced. This tendency has been aided by the development of modern 'fast track' construction techniques (see Application M), which ensure that the replacement of an existing building with a new one is carried out as quickly as possible to minimise the lenth of time that the site does not generate revenue.

The planning and architecture debate

Increasing interest has been shown in the way that the built environment is planned and in the visual quality of the buildings which result. This interest has applied to both new developments on green-field sites and to the replacement of existing buildings through redevelopment. The debate has covered both residential and commercial developments. Many people argue that much of the built environment created in the 1950s and 1960s was of a poor standard. Particular criticism has been levelled at high-rise residential blocks, and at many skyscraper office blocks in central London which some feel are inferior to the modern skyscrapers of American cities. The widespread dislike of these buildings has contributed to decisions on replacement in a time scale which could not have been foreseen. High-rise blocks have been demolished and commercial redevelopments have taken place. Tall buildings are becoming generally less popular. However it should be emphasised that there are various reasons why clients build (see Application F), and in most cases there is a commercial motivation. There may be a conflict between commercial necessity and what many people regard as good planning and architecture. The point is that decisions to replace buildings can be influenced by architectural factors, particularly if a new development is designed to be more attractive to occupiers and therefore potentially more profitable.

Summary

This application has considered some of the economic issues which arise during the lifetime of a building. Since buildings are long-lived, ownership entails some long term financing cost, either the cost of borrowing, or the interest forgone by using one's own money. The various methods of financing were considered, ranging from the developer retaining ownership by taking a long term loan, to the formation of a company in which an investor can purchase a large or small number of shares in the project. Buildings have to be managed to ensure that the owner and/or occupier receives the expected benefit. This might be the meeting of functional purposes such as consumption, factor of production or social. Or it might be the achievement of a direct financial gain. In addition to managing the building to ensure maximum revenue or benefit, it is also important to control the costs of ownership and/or occupation. These include the continuing operating costs such as energy, cleaning and maintenance, together with periodic refurbishment costs. Finally, the cost of replacement of the building has to be taken into account. Usually the economic life of the building is projected at feasibility stage. However it should be remembered that whilst all buildings may have a long life physically, they are products of their times. A number of factors may occur during the life of a building which can change the length of its economic life. At the current time such factors include rising land values and views on planning and architecture in the built environment. At a particular point in time it may therefore be appropriate to replace an existing building by redeveloping the site, or to build on a previously undeveloped site. This returns to the very beginning of the process of economic decision making in developing the built environment — what kind and quantity of buildings are required; how should the available land be used; should development be carried out by market forces or public intervention; and who should benefit from development?

Tutorial questions

1. What is the relationship between building design and operating costs?
2. To what extent can buildings contribute to industrial and commercial productivity?
3. Is there a conflict between good architecture and the need to meet the client's needs?

Index

advertising 70, 73, 89, 283
announcements policy 141
architect 22–3, 249
assets 109, 237, 274
  human 109
  intangible 109
  investment 233, 301
  physical 109

balance of payments 139, 143, 152–4, 261
balance sheet 15, 87
barriers to entry 65, 69–71, 282–3
behavioural theories 90
betterment 191
bill of quantities 19, 221, 225, 244, 266, 274
borrowing 149–50
budget deficits 142–3
builder 221
  as client or developer 18
building costs 15, 16
building design 17–19, 295
building societies 196, 202
buildings
  construction of 19
  economic life of 22, 307
  maintenance of 20
  management of 21
  physical life of 22, 37
  replacement of 22

capital 30, 52, 214, 234
  gain 218
  goods 107, 118, 139
cash flow 82, 267

centrally-planned system 47
circular flow of income 119, 123, 125, 145
client's brief 243
collective bargaining 42, 89, 91, 131, 156, 160, 290, 298
commercial activities 9
commodities 103
commuters 8, 9, 200, 204
compensation/betterment 183
competition 20, 88, 222
components 254, 296
compulsory purchase 8
congestion 79, 169
consortia 110, 258, 284
construction clients 13, 14, 18, 21, 168
consumer 48, 66, 105
  goods 107, 118, 139
  sovereignty 49, 60
consumption 15, 125, 149, 213, 303
contractor 221–3
core/periphery relationships 77, 100, 110, 160, 257, 290
corporate planning 97
cost benefit analysis 237–8
cost indices 245
cost limit 18, 241, 248
costs 19, 66, 84–6, 111, 151, 240
  operating 306
  private 172
  social 172
credit availability 150

defects liability period 271–2

de-industrialisation 107
demand 32, 48, 57, 61, 195, 256
  aggregate 124, 125, 132, 139
  derived 179
  elasticity of 63–4, 76, 86
demand management 132, 135, 139–46
demography 255, 262
depreciation 124, 181
design and build 227, 278
design period 223
design team 221
de-skilling 101, 289
developer 174, 211, 215, 268, 279, 302
discounted cash flow 236
distribution 13, 22, 171
diversification 110, 283

economic actors 49
economic rent 180
economic systems 46–8
ecomomies of scale 69, 111
education and training 297
efficiency 13
elements of a building 247–9
employment 9, 124, 254
energy 34, 104
enterprise zones 190
equilibrium 60–1, 126, 199
estimating 243–50, 280–1
  approximate 243, 267
European market 104, 255, 258
exchange processes 52
exchange rate 140
exports 122, 125, 139, 152, 254
externalities 35, 171–2, 206, 237

factors of production 30, 36, 50, 178, 213, 304
fast track building 296, 308
feasibility 13, 307
feudal system 46
finance for development 212, 301
financial gains 15

firm 19, 48, 66, 81–102, 120, 253
fiscal policy 139
full employment 138, 148

green-field sites 9, 12, 72, 188, 199
gross development value 239
growth 118, 139, 153, 155, 160
growth of firms 283

health and safety 297–8
historical data 245
homogeneous products 66, 73
horizontal integration 109
housebuilders 13, 18, 20, 182, 216, 268, 279, 284
households 120
housing 8, 169
  new 10
housing market 149, 269
human capital 31, 237, 305

imports 139, 152
income 132, 195, 217
  distribution of 38, 117, 138, 156
  permanent 135
incomes policy 140
industrial activities 9
industrial structure 106
industry 103–6, 187–8
inflation 116–17, 137, 140, 144, 224
infrastructure 3, 8, 11, 20, 111, 174, 190, 200, 214, 237, 305
inner city areas 8, 22
inner city regeneration 9
interest rate 34, 73, 129, 132, 134, 148, 153, 195, 234, 253, 268, 302
intermediate goods 53, 124
internal capital markets 97, 111
international economy 103
international trade 119, 122
investment 14, 34, 119, 125, 132, 151, 153, 160, 217–19

Keynesianism 43, 67, 128, 131–4, 137

labour 30, 35, 50, 261, 288
  craft 292, 295
  division of 37, 99, 288–9
  flexibility of 291, 295
land 11, 30, 168, 240
  as a speculative commodity 180, 189, 234, 256
  assembly 176, 190, 212, 285
  inelastic supply of 77, 169, 178, 182, 199
  public ownership of 184
  publicly created values 11, 179, 183
  taxation 183–4, 191
  values 11, 179, 194, 269, 307
liquidity 82, 218, 264–5, 267
local authority 8, 10, 174
location 179

macroeconomics 39–40, 115
maintenance of buildings 306
management 52, 100, 276
management contracting 17, 228
management of buildings 212, 305
manufacturing 106–7, 143, 222, 254, 291
market
  capital 121, 159
  factor 50, 85
  goods 120, 129, 157–9
  labour 38, 89, 92, 120, 130, 156–7, 202, 261, 298
  money 120, 129, 197
  product 52, 85
  stock 94–5
market conditions 19
market forces 4, 10, 29, 32, 59, 104, 154, 161, 168, 186, 226
market imperfections 67, 170, 189
market model 59, 93
market structures 74–7, 108–113, 298

market system 46–7, 56–80, 137
marketing 212, 276, 305
materials 260, 292, 296
measurement of building work 244
mechanisation 289
mergers of 89, 109, 257, 283
microeconomics 39–40, 45, 115
middle managers 83, 90
mixed economy 41, 68, 146
mobility of labour 202
Monetarism 43, 49, 67, 107, 128, 134, 137, 148
monetary policy 140, 147, 154
monopoly 20, 68, 159
  degree of 75, 89, 108, 256, 278, 280
mortgage interest relief 198
multi-national companies 104, 107, 161
multiplier 133, 135, 139, 187, 190, 254

national economy 103, 115–36
national income accounting 123–4
negotiated contract 226
neo-classical 74, 108, 128–31
net present value 236
normative economics 42

oligopoly 69, 75
opportunity cost 33
output of construction work 253

package details 17, 227, 278
partnerships 175
payback 235
peak loading 205
perfect competition 60, 65–7, 95, 147, 169, 280
positive economics 42
post-war consensus 42
price 19, 33, 57, 61, 66, 76, 194, 222, 278
  escalating 193, 199
private interest 3, 170

312

private sector 8, 22, 121
privatisation 60, 158
procurement 220
product differentiation 73, 89
production 36−7, 45, 51, 85,
     97−101, 287
  social influences on 37, 52,
     288, 292
  technological influences on
     36, 51, 288, 292
  workers 90, 91−2
productivity 16, 37, 51, 85,
     91, 98−9, 148, 157, 288,
     304
profit 10, 19, 66, 82, 84−6,
     124, 274, 277
  maximisation 83, 90, 96
profit and loss account 87
profitability 82−3, 111, 160
  constraints on 88−102
project management 229
project team 220, 225
public expenditure 125, 134,
     151−2, 253, 256
public interest 3, 7, 12, 170
public intervention 10, 32,
     107, 125, 137−62, 168
public policy 13, 20, 101−2,
     112, 137, 255
public sector 22, 122, 134, 194
public utilities 69, 158, 205

quantities 247−8

Radical/Marxist school of
     thought 43, 68
raw materials 104
redevelopment 9, 12
refurbishment 306
regional problems 186
rents 15, 124, 178
residual 240
resources 6, 30−1, 50, 116,
     155
  allocation of 6, 29, 31−2,
     71, 139, 168
  immobility of 71−2
revenue 84−6, 112, 277, 307
risk 176, 218
road pricing 207

savings 122, 132, 149
schools of thought in
     economics 42, 125
scientific management 289
self-employment 124, 294
separate contracts 228
shareholders 83, 90, 109
sick building syndrome 304
skills shortages 261
social benefits 10, 16, 22, 237,
     305
social capital 214
social sciences 41
speculation 178, 203
Standard Industrial Classification
     106
structure of firms
  m-form 95−7, 104, 111
  traditional 95
sub-contractors 158, 257, 270,
     290, 294−5
  labour only 51, 98, 294−5
supply 32, 48, 57, 61, 156,
     195
  elasticity of 64
systems building 293

takeovers 89, 109, 283
tastes 195
tender reconciliation 265−6
tendering 19, 220−30, 246,
     265, 281−2
time value of money 233
town planning 10, 11, 18, 47,
     174
trade unions 94, 290, 298
training 262
transport provision 4, 5

uncertainties in investment
     233−4, 239
unemployment 39, 89, 93,
     116, 131, 134, 141−2
  relationship to inflation 144
urban area 3, 4, 5, 9, 11, 133,
     186, 204
urban development corporations
     190−1
urban renewal 177, 186, 285
urban sprawl 8, 10, 199

value added   105, 124, 260, 287
variations to contract   224, 267
vertical integration   109

wages   93, 130, 133, 157
wealth   6, 29, 32
  distribution of   6, 29, 37–8, 52

measurement of   33–6
negative   33
work packages   229
working capital   82
working practices   92

zoning of land   174